Edible Flowers

Edible Flowers

FROM GARDEN TO PALATE

CATHY WILKINSON BARASH

FULCRUM PUBLISHING
GOLDEN, COLORADO

Library of Congress Cataloging-in-Publication Data

Barash, Cathy Wilkinson
    Edible flowers from garden to palate / Cathy Wilkinson Barash.
        p.   cm.
    Includes bibliographical references and index.
    ISBN 1-55591-164-1 (cloth)
    ISBN 1-55591-246-1 (paperback)
    1. Cookery (Flowers) 2. Flower gardening. 3. Herb gardening.
    I. Title.
    TX814.5.F5837   1993
    641.6—dc20   93-22379
                                                            CIP

Printed in Korea by Sung In Printing, Inc.

0 9 8 7 6 5   4 3

Fulcrum Publishing
350 Indiana Street, Suite 350
Golden, Colorado 80401-5093

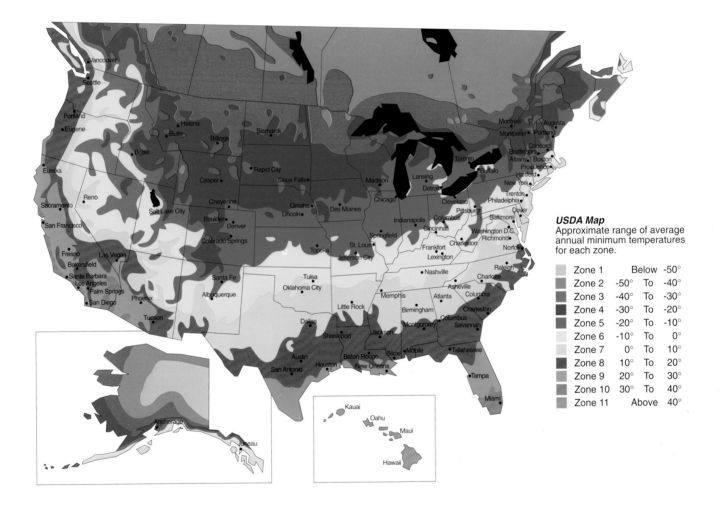

USDA Map
Approximate range of average annual minimum temperatures for each zone.

Zone 1		Below	-50°
Zone 2	-50°	To	-40°
Zone 3	-40°	To	-30°
Zone 4	-30°	To	-20°
Zone 5	-20°	To	-10°
Zone 6	-10°	To	0°
Zone 7	0°	To	10°
Zone 8	10°	To	20°
Zone 9	20°	To	30°
Zone 10	30°	To	40°
Zone 11		Above	40°

CONTENTS

ƒOREWORD

As long as I have known her, Cathy Wilkinson Barash has been an edible flower maven. She has served me flower petal confetti salads, introduced me to deep-fried sage blossoms and convinced me that daylilies are exciting fare. As much as we've shared over the years, as I read through the pages of this book I found myself continually saying "I didn't know that" or caught up in her enthusiasm saying "I can't wait to try that!" This is a book filled with new information.

My own interest in edible flowers spans over a decade. Working on a book that included many edible flowers I found myself frustrated; it was very difficult to get reliable information. The number of books on the subject are few, and many that have been considered classics in the field use common names only with no reference to botanical names. I consider these interesting for historical notes, but not definitive by any means, much less safe. As few of us grew up with these foods, as with mushrooms, it is critical to identify them by their botanical, not common, names. We are surrounded by poisonous flowers every day, it is critical to know which is which.

This book, with its clear descriptions and photographs identifying each of the flowers, helps to sort out much of the confusion about which flowers are edible and which are not—and none too soon. Over the last decade, I have seen numerous chances taken with the public safety. Incorrect lists have been published, common names have been used incorrectly, and well-meaning people have failed to identify their flowers properly. Food professionals, with no horticultural background, have sometimes unknowingly recommended the wrong plants. I've seen poisonous lily of the valley suggested for ice cream, been served toxic delphiniums on my cheesecake, and seen the cover of a food magazine feature throat-irritating calla lilies stuffed with sorbet. There is a crying need for a thorough and definitive book on edible flowers. Fortunately for us, Cathy has spent much time sorting out fact from dangerous fiction. She has reviewed the available material on edible flowers with ethnobotanists, horticulturists and food experts and searched through poison plant literature, eliminating as many questionable plants as possible. Cathy and I believe strongly that if a plant cannot be documented as edible it should not be eaten. The result of all her research is an in-depth and reliable book on edible flowers.

There is a real joy of feasting with edible flowers! I see cooking with edible flowers as the new culinary frontier, continuing on where cooking with fresh herbs leaves off. Cathy has assembled a grand array of recipes from appetizers to desserts, showing the vast possibilities for this new cuisine. Many of the recipes are her own; the others represent some of the best creativity America's chefs have to offer. There's a recipe for every palate, every cook. The range of options is exhilarating. This book will become a classic and a major step toward making edible flowers a permanent and exciting part of America's new cuisine.

—*Rosalind Creasy*

PREFACE

The reintroduction of flowers into cuisine began, as have many innovative ideas, on the West Coast. I say reintroduction because flowers have been used in cooking for millennia. Chinese recipes commonly call for daylily flowers, although they are often used in the dried form. The ancient Romans introduced many herbs into their kitchens. They also added cultivated flowers, including mallows, roses and violets into their repertoire. Many European and Asian cuisines use flowers with regularity. Squash blossoms are commonly used in Italian cooking. Indian and Middle Eastern cooking, especially desserts, make use of flowers. Through the ages edible flowers continued to flourish. In Victorian England, rose petals were included in sweet and savory dishes. It seems to be in this century, and perhaps only in this country, that we have forgotten about using flowers to enhance food.

Today there is a resurgence of interest in edible flowers. They started showing up on plates in trendy restaurants more than a decade ago. Magazines have carried articles on the phenomenon. Several books have touched on the subject. In large cities, upscale green grocers now regularly stock types of edible flowers. Several years ago I was pleasantly surprised to find nasturtiums, pansies and pinks in the produce section at a local supermarket (but appalled at the price). A fine kitchenware catalog featured an edible flower salad on the cover. Some seed companies now have a separate listing for edible flowers. Even some of the more mainstream companies mention that some of the herb flowers are edible.

There is an increasing awareness and interest in edible flowers by people in general. I lecture on a wide variety of horticultural and culinary topics. Of all my lectures, the one on edible flowers is most popular and in greatest demand. Despite a growing awareness of edible flowers, most people are ignorant of which flowers can be eaten and enjoyed. Where does one draw the line between flowers that are edible and flowers that are used for garnish? This is one of the purposes of this book, to define clearly for consumer, gardener, cook and restaurateur the rules of edibility. Otherwise, it is just a matter of time before someone eats a nonedible flower placed purely for ornamentaion and becomes ill. There needs to be a clear delineation. If a flower is in a vase, in water or decorating the table in any way, it is not to be eaten. On the other hand, if a flower is on a dish with food, it should be considered safe to eat. In British Columbia, by law, any flower that is put on a plate with food must be edible. This book sets the standard for areas without such laws. Use it to learn which flowers may safely accent and flavor different foods.

For everyone else, cooks and gardeners alike, this book opens up new realms of culinary possibilities, often using plants already in the garden.

It is hard to classify flowers in a culinary manner. The beauty and range of tastes flowers can bring are like no other component of a dish. Neither spice nor herb—although many herbs have edible flowers—they fit into a category of their own. Edible flowers range in flavor from bland to spicy, sweet to piquant. Many can be eaten raw, while others need to be cooked. Regardless of the variety of flavors they may impart to food, flowers differ from all other ingredients in the impact they can make, even when used simply as a garnish. Flowers add a totally new dimension to cooking, that of *color*.

This book is designed to give as much information about the flowers that are safe to eat in as clear a manner as possible. The ten most popular and versatile flowers are grouped together in the section called *The Big Ten*. All other edible flowers are included in the next section. Each flower is presented with an individual photograph for identification purposes. The accompa-nying text includes the botanic name as well as common names, information on the historical use of the flower, specific cultural information for growing the plant, its best use in a garden scheme, harvesting and/or storage tips unique to that particular plant and original recipes. For the past several years I have been hard at work in my kitchen creating recipes for this book. Over the course of nine months, I visited chefs and gardens in various areas of the United States and Canada who have generously created recipes using flowers for inclusion in this book. The recipes vary from simple to complex.

The possibilities for using edible flowers in cuisine are limited only by your imagination and flavor preferences. The inclusion of edible flowers in a garden is evidence of their dual purpose. They are truly flowers for beauty and taste, adding beauty to both garden and food, while reflecting the good taste of the gardener who plants them and the cook who uses them in the kitchen.

I will offer, however, one warning: Only the flowers featured in this book are edible.

ACKNOWLEDGMENTS

So many people were helpful in creating this book. I could never have done it without all their generous help and support. My heartfelt thanks go to:

The Inspiration

All those who have been involved in this project from its inception, saw its potential, and whose enthusiasm kept me and this book going—Mary Moss, Toodie Walt, Anne Raver, Rue Judd, Dave Dobbins, Margaret Hayes, Lynne Shaner, Sam Barash, Barbara Wilkinson, and my agent Kit Ward.

The Plant People—Green Thumbs Up

The people who are on the cutting edge with edible flowers, those who grew gardens for me, and the friends who let me run amok in their gardens, pillaging and photographing—Ros Creasy; Sinclair Philip and Byron Cook at Sooke Harbour House; Carole Saville; Kate Frye, John Ash, and George Rose at Fetzer Vineyards; Joe Queriolo at Mudd's Restaurant; Katarina Eriksson at the Parkway Grill; Eileen and Fred Mendyka at Good Thyme Farm; Marsha Hyll and Richard McCarty of Spongeware Farm; Elisa Robinson, Tom Pattison, and Tom Gaines at Panfield Nurseries; Liz Ball; Toodie Walt; Happy Post; Franny Elder; Jim Peters; Georgene McKim; Craig Zaffee and Tricia Sweeney; Susan and Jay Kuhlman.

The Food People

All the chefs, cooks, and gardeners whose creative recipes grace these pages. Food tasters—Dency Kane, Bill Barash, David Corrody, Rizz and Tucker Dean, Janine Adams, Dean Celesia, "Annie Hyssop" Arthur.

The Technical Support

Ethnobotanists—Dr. James Duke and Dr. Nancy Turner for their expertise in checking the flowers for edibility, safety, and especially for keeping cautious. Computer help—Jeff Ball, Richie Machtay, Steve Beyers, and the folks at Xyquest. Photographic technology—Joe and Mike at Village Camera; the guys at Slide Tech. Proofreaders—Meyer Barash, Brendan Earls, Anne Breitstein, Jay Mallin. General assistance—David Corrody. Moral support and sharing her abundant knowledge—Ros Creasy.

The Other Helpful Folks

Carol Hetherington, Mary Hoffman, Verne Nelson, Sally Ferguson of Netherlands FlowerBulb Information Center; Robin and Jill Hughes of Manor Farm Inn; Georgene McKim, Felder Rushing, John and Lynne Walt (what a wedding cake I made for them!).

The Home Front

Those who kept things going while I was on the road photographing and gathering recipes, and while I was home—my landlady and dear friend Rizz Arthur Dean, who let me grow edible flowers throughout the property; my husband Bill; and especially my cat Sebastian.

The Ten Rules of Edible Flowers

1. Eat flowers only when you are positive they are edible.

2. Just because it is served with food does not mean a flower is edible (see Rule 1).

3. Eat only flowers that have been grown organically.

4. Do not eat flowers from florists, nurseries or garden centers (see Rule 3).

5. If you have hay fever, asthma or allergies, do not eat flowers.

6. Do not eat flowers picked from the side of the road. They are contaminated from car emissions (see Rule 3).

7. Remove pistils and stamens from flowers before eating. Eat only the petals.

8. Not all flowers are edible. Some are poisonous.

9. There are many varieties of any one flower. Flowers taste different when grown in different locations.

10. Introduce flowers into your diet the way you would new foods to a baby—one at a time in small quantities.

INTRODUCTION

Have you ever eaten a flower? Think before you answer. You may have enjoyed edible flowers without realizing it. Do you like artichokes? They are immature flowers. What about broccoli? Ditto—if you've ever grown broccoli you've probably seen the green flower buds elongate and open into yellow flowers. You may argue that technically speaking, you haven't eaten flowers, only buds.

When was the last time you had Chinese hot and sour soup? Dried daylily petals are a key ingredients. Have you had a cup of refreshing herbal tea lately? Look at the box on your kitchen shelf. The ingredients may include rose petals, hibiscus, mint, chamomile or other familiar flowers.

As much as I enjoy edible flowers, I rarely graze through a flower border. Take a moment before you rush outside to your own garden to consider how to get the most out of your edible flower experience.

evaporated. Choose flowers that are at their peak. Flowers that are not fully open, those that are past their prime, and flowers that are starting to wilt should be passed. Think of flowers as fruit. Unripe fruit or flowers do not have the superb flavor of those at the height of ripeness, while those that are overripe also pall by comparison with those at peak development.

After picking, put those with long stems into water. Keep them cool, flowers are perishable and will wilt in a warm place. Pick short-stemmed blossoms, such as borage and orange blossoms, within three or four hours of using and put them between layers of damp paper toweling or in a plastic bag in the refrigerator. Immediately before using, gently wash the flowers, checking carefully for bugs and dirt. Before washing all the flowers, do a test on one flower. Some are fragile and water will discolor them. Such flowers need an extra careful insect inspection.

FLOWERS FOR THE PALATE— FRESH AND PRESERVED

It is more important to collect flowers for eating at the optimum time than those going into an arrangement. Pick flowers in the cool of the day, preferably in early morning after the dew has

THE PROOF IS IN THE TASTING

Always sample a flower before using it for cooking. Obviously, if a recipe calls for a cup of lavender flowers, don't taste each flower. Taste one as representative. If you are picking lavender from two different areas in the garden or

from two different varieties, sample one of each. Do the tasting before beginning picking. In that way, if for some reason the flower tastes terrible, no time or energy is wasted on picking flowers that won't be used.

When tasting a flower, especially for the first time (even if it is something growing in the garden for years, do it at least once a season), I use a technique somewhat similar to wine-tasting that I am happy to share with you. Choose a flower at its peak of perfection. Examine it, looking for lurking insects which might badly affect

the taste test. Remove the pistils and stamen. If at any point during this process you find that the flower is disagreeable or objectionable in any way—spit it out (discretely, of course). There is nothing that says that you have to like every flower. Soil and growing conditions can effect the flavor. Some flowers have so many different hybrids or cultivated varieties (cultivars) that there are bound to be one or two that don't suit your taste.

Smell the flower. If it smells good, continue. Take a tiny bite of the flower. Relax and close your eyes so that all your attention is focused on the sensations you are getting from the flower. Chew it carefully with your front teeth. Breathe in through your mouth to get the essence of the flower. After chewing the flower, slowly roll it over your tongue, allowing the taste buds to sense the different components that make up a flavor—bitter, sweet, sour, salty. Finally swallow the flower.

WHAT PART OF THE FLOWER TO EAT

Remove the stamens and styles from flowers before eating. The pollen can detract from the flavor of the flower. In addition, the pollen may cause an allergic reaction in susceptible individuals. Remove the sepals of all flowers except violas, Johnny-jump-ups and pansies.

Only the petals of some flowers such as rose, calendula, tulip, chrysanthemum, yucca and lavender are edible. When using just the petals, separate them from the rest of the flower just prior to use to keep wilting to a minimum. Others, including Johnny-jump-up, violet, runner bean, honeysuckle and clover can be eaten in their entirety.

Roses, dianthus, English daisies, marigolds and chrysanthemums have a bitter white portion at the base of the petal where it was attached to the flower. Break or cut off the bitter part off the petal before using.

PRESERVING FLOWERS

In the scheme of things, plants are trying to reproduce themselves. The flower is the first step in that process. In simplistic terms, after the flower is fertilized, a seed is set and the plant can die happy, knowing it has furthered its species. If, however, the flower is picked (or even better all the flowers are picked), the process is disrupted and the plant has to start all over again, by putting out additional flowers. Thus with many, but alas not all, plants you can extend the bloom period by harvesting flowers before they set seed.

For me the edible flowers go by in my garden too quickly. It is nice to be able to extend the enjoyment of the flowers past the weeks or months they are available fresh from the garden. There are several ways to preserve

INTRODUCTION

flowers for days, weeks or months. Each has it advantages and disadvantages and may not work for all flowers. Freezing, which is the best way of preserving vegetables, unfortunately, does not work for most flowers (daylilies are an exception); they are too fragile. However, flowers or petals can be successfully frozen in ice cubes to enliven a drink any time of year. Drying works well for some, yet flavor is somewhat altered. Candying is time-consuming, but will preserve sweet flowers and petals for a long time. Flowers can also be preserved by making flower butter, sugar, oil, vinegar, syrup, etc. Flower butter changes the flavor the least.

DRYING

Gather flowers early in the day before the sun shines on them. Hang by the stems in a warm, dark area with good air circulation.

Individual flowers can be dried differently. Place the clean flowers in a single layer on fine mesh. Let them dry in a warm, dark, dust-free area.

Once flowers are dry, store them whole, crumbled or pulverized (sieved) in airtight glass containers in a cool, dark place. In recipes calling for fresh flowers, substitute half the amount if using dried.

CANDIED FLOWERS

1 egg white
100-proof vodka
superfine granulated sugar
thin artist's paintbrush
violets (or other flower to be candied—pansy, Johnny-jump-
   up, rose petals, lilac, borage, pea, pinks, scented geranium)
wire cake rack
baking parchment

In small bowl, beat the egg whites to a light froth. Add 1 or 2 drops of vodka and mix. This helps the flower to dry quicker. Pour sugar into a shallow bowl. Have the paintbrush at hand and some freshly picked violets. I find it best to pick no more than 4 or 5 at a time, candy them and then pick more. Even with putting them in water, they wilt quickly, making the process more difficult. Cover a wire cake rack with baking parchment. Now you are ready to start.

Grasp the top of the stem of a violet between thumb and forefinger. Dip the paintbrush in the beaten egg white. Gently paint all surfaces of the petals of the flower with the egg white. Make sure to get between all petals. Gently sprinkle the

sugar on the flower, making sure to cover all surfaces and between the petals. Place the flower, face up on the parchment. Repeat process with another flower.

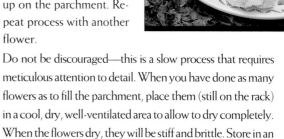

Do not be discouraged—this is a slow process that requires meticulous attention to detail. When you have done as many flowers as to fill the parchment, place them (still on the rack) in a cool, dry, well-ventilated area to allow to dry completely. When the flowers dry, they will be stiff and brittle. Store in an airtight container.

If you live in a very humid area, it can complicate matters. You may dry the flowers in a room with a dehumidifier. Once dry, gently place them in a heavy duty plastic freezer container, layered no more than 3 deep, separated by a sheet of parchment. Keep them in the freezer up to a year. If you store them at room temperature, the humidity creeps in and they can turn into green mush after a couple of months.

EDIBLE FLOWERS

FLOWER BUTTER

—

1/2 cup flowers
1/2 pound sweet (unsalted) butter

Finely chop flower petals and mix into softened butter.
Put in a glass bowl and cover with plastic wrap.
Let the mix sit at room temperature for several hours,
then refrigerate for several days to bring out the flavor.

Flower butter may be kept refrigerated for 2 weeks or
frozen for up to 6 months.

Almost all edible flowers may be mixed in with butter.
Of course the flavors will vary with the flowers.

Spread butter or bread or make your favorite sugar
cookie or pound cake, substituting flower butter for
regular butter.

FLOWER HONEY

—

1/2 to 1 cup chopped fresh flower petals or crushed dried petals
1 pound honey

Add flowers to a jar of honey. Cover the jar loosely and
place in a pan half full of gently boiling water. Remove
from heat and let sit in the hot water for 10 minutes.

Remove the jar from the water and allow to cool to
room temperature. Tighten the cover. Let it sit for at
least 1 week. If desired, strain before eating.

To preserve the flavor of good quality, never heat it to
more than 140°F.

Makes about 2 cups honey.

FLOWER SUGAR

—

2 cups granulated sugar
1/2 to 1 cup minced flower petals (a sweet flavor is preferable)

Pound sugar and minced flower petals in a mortar, or
process them well in a food processor. Put into a clean
glass jar, cover, and let stand 1 week. Sift, if desired, and

store in an airtight container. Flower sugar is an elegant
topping, lightly sprinkled over a fruit sorbet.

Makes about 2-1/2 cups sugar.

INTRODUCTION

FLOWER SYRUP

———

1 cup water
3 cups granulated sugar
1/2 to 1 cup flower petals, whole or chopped

Boil all ingredients for 10 minutes, or until thickened into a syrup. Strain through cheesecloth into a clean glass jar. Seal and store in the refrigerator for up to 2 weeks.

Use as a base for making sorbet or pudding. Pour over fruit. Delicious on pancakes.

Makes about 2 to 3 cups syrup.

FLOWER JELLY

———

from Libby Goldstein, Philadelphia, Pennsylvania

1 cup solidly packed flowers (1 or more types according to taste)
1-1/4 cups water
1/2 cup herb or flower vinegar
3-1/2 cups granulated sugar
1 pouch liquid pectin

Steep the flowers in the water in a covered glass or ceramic container for 1 to 2 days or until the liquid smells and tastes of the flowers.

Strain the infusion into a 6-quart nonreactive Dutch oven or preserving pan. Add the vinegar and the sugar. Stir once and let sit until the sugar has dissolved. Then put the pot over a high heat and, stirring all the while, bring to a full rolling boil. Add the pectin. Return to boil for 1 minute or as long as package directions suggest. Remove from heat and skim off any foam. Ladle jelly into 3 or 4 hot, sterilized half-pint jars, leaving 1/8-inch head space. Wipe the jar rims with a hot damp cloth, screw on canning lids that have been prepared according to manufacturer's directions and tighten. Process for 5 minutes in a boiling water bath, or turn upside down for 5 minutes to make sure the lids seal.

An alternative is to boil the water and pour it over the flowers in a glass or stoneware container. Let steep, covered for 10 to 15 minutes. The cold water method usually results in a clearer jelly.

These jellies make excellent glazes for roast or broiled poultry and pork. Some are good on fish, carrots or sweet potatoes.

Makes 3 to 4-1/2 pints.

EDIBLE FLOWERS

FLOWER OIL

1/4 cup to 1/2 cup chopped fresh flower petals, or crushed dried petals
1 quart vegetable oil

Add flowers to a bottle of vegetable oil. Cover loosely and place in gently boiling water. Simmer for 30 minutes. Remove from water and let cool. Tighten cover. Let sit at least 1 week before using.

Strain before using, if you wish.

Use in sautéing for extra flavor. Keep a range of different flower oils to use for simple salad dressings.

Makes about 1 quart oil.

FLOWER VODKA

2 cups good quality vodka
1/4 to 1/2 cup flower petals

Add flowers to the vodka. Let sit at least 48 hours at room temperature. Strain the vodka. Pour into attractive bottles and store in the freezer. Serve in small thimble-sized glasses.

The best flowers to add to vodka are tuberous begonias (what a great color it turns!), clove pinks, orange, lemon and rose, but experiment with other flowers as well. Drink this straight for best enjoyment.

Makes about 2 cups vodka.

FLOWER VINEGAR

2 cups white wine vinegar
1/4 to 1/2 cup flower petals

In a stainless steel or glass saucepan (not aluminum) bring vinegar to a boil. Place petals in an attractive bottle. Pour hot vinegar to within 1/2 inch of the top. Allow infusion to cool to room temperature. Cover and allow it to sit at room temperature for several weeks. If desired, strain and discard petals. Add a fresh flower or sprig of greens, if desired.

The colors of the different vinegars are beautiful: pale lavender—chive, deep pink—red rose, bright pink—dianthus (pinks), yellow-orange—nasturtium, fluorescent pink or orange—tuberous begonia. The most obvious use is in salad dressings, either with plain oil or a flower oil. Try mixing and matching, using different oils with other flower vinegars.

Makes about 2 cups vinegar.

INTRODUCTION

UNCOOKED VINEGAR

———

2 cups white wine vinegar
1/4 to 1/2 cup flower petals

Place petals in a clear bottle. Fill the jar with vinegar. Stopper with a cork. Place in a cool, shady place for several weeks. If desired, strain and discard petals and replace with fresh.

Use same as cooked vinegars. Also excellent for deglazing a pan after sautéing meat or vegetables. It helps create a uniquely flavored sauce.

Makes about 2-1/2 cups vinegar.

FRITTER BATTER

———

1 cup whole wheat flour
1/8 teaspoon salt
1 egg, separated
1 tablespoon olive oil
8 ounces beer
1 cup flower petals
1 tablespoon peanut oil (or more if needed)

Mix the flour and salt. In a separate bowl, beat the egg yolk with the olive oil. Slowly add the flour to the egg yolk mixture. Once that is mixed, gradually beat in the beer. Allow to stand for at least 30 minutes. Beat the egg white until stiff. Fold it into the batter just before cooking. Gently fold in flower petals.

Heat a skillet. Add enough peanut oil to lightly coat the bottom. Drop the batter by rounded tablespoonful into the hot skillet and fry to a golden brown. When bubbles on top of fritters break, turn fritters over and brown second side. Serve immediately. These are best fresh, but frozen fritters keep well up to 3 months.

Serves 4.

EDIBLE FLOWERS

A CONFETTI OF PETALS—MIXTURES OF FLOWERS

When I began to cook with flowers, I experimented with them one at a time. It was not long before I started mixing them in recipes. I use flowers much like I use herbs, blending flavors that complement one another.

Now I tailor the flower mixtures to the dish—sweet flowers for desserts, savory flowers with meats and a great mixture on salads and in cheeses for dips and spreads. Sometimes I try to coordinate colors. That is the fun of using edible flowers.

Here are a few recipes using a mixture of flowers. Even something as simple as a salad is interpreted in different ways by different chefs.

FLOWER DIP

1 cup cottage cheese
1/2 cup plain yogurt
3/4 cup assorted flower petals, coarsely chopped

Process cottage cheese in a food processor until smooth. Transfer it to a nonmetallic bowl. Stir in yogurt and flowers. Cover and refrigerate overnight for best flavor.

This will quickly replace the standard sour cream and onion soup dip used as a standby for years in many kitchens. Use a wide range of flower colors to give the dish a festive look.

Great for dipping larger flower petals as well as the traditional crudités—raw vegetables.

Makes about 2 cups dip.

SAVORY FLOWER SPREAD

8 ounces whipped cream cheese
1 tablespoon chive florets, coarsely chopped
1 tablespoon garlic chive florets, coarsely chopped
1 tablespoon oregano flowers, coarsely chopped
1 tablespoon thyme flowers, coarsely chopped
1 teaspoon winter savory flowers, coarsely chopped
1 teaspoon basil flowers, coarsely chopped
1 tablespoon 'Tangerine Gem' marigold petals, coarsely chopped
1 tablespoon calendula petals, coarsely chopped

In a nonmetallic bowl, fold all ingredients together. Cover and refrigerate for at least 24 hours.

This makes a great stuffing for nasturtium blossoms or celery sticks. Even a plain cracker turns into a gourmet presentation when covered with this delicious spread. It is a colorful, flavorful, inexpensive alternative to ready-made herbal cheese. Use within 1 week, or freeze up to 3 months.

Makes about 1-1/2 cups spread.

INTRODUCTION

WVALDO'S GARDEN CITRUS BLOSSOM BUTTER

from Wvaldo Zuniga, sous-chef, Mudd's Restaurant, San Ramon, California

1-1/2 pounds butter, softened
juice and zest of 1 lemon
juice and zest of 1 orange
1 cup mixed edible flower petals
pinch of salt

Soften butter (do not melt) to the consistency where it will whip easily. Add juices and zests to butter, blending well. Gently fold in the flowers. Roll butter into a log shape in waxed paper and chill.

Use slices on grilled fish.

MESCLUN SALAD MIX WITH FRESH HERBS AND FLOWERS

from James O'Shea, chef, West Street Grill, Litchfield, Connecticut

6 cups mesclun
1 cup green leaf herbs
1/2 cup edible flower petals

Mesclun is a mix of baby lettuces and other immature greens with a range of flavors. Choose organically grown mesclun, or grow your own mix. Suggested greens include: Red Oak Leaf lettuce, mizuna, tat soi, radicchio, Lolla Rossa lettuce, mâche, cress, Lolla Biando lettuce, arugula and frisee.

Toss greens with a nice mixture of green leaf herbs such as basil, tarragon, Italian flat-leaf parsley, chervil, etc.

Toss in your choice of one or a mixture of flavorful and colorful edible flowers.

Vinaigrette
Use a 6 to 1 ratio of extra virgin olive oil to nasturtium vinegar or balsamic vinegar. Shake well to mix. Season to taste with salt and pepper. For extra zip, add a little minced shallots.

Serves 6 to 8.

MEXICAN COCOA CREPES STUFFED WITH LOBSTER, SERVED WITH LOBSTER SAUCE AND FLOWER CONFETTI

from Hugo Molina, executive chef, Parkway Grill, Pasadena, California

Crepes:

1 bar of Mexican chocolate, chopped fine

24 ounces milk

2 large eggs

3 tablespoons black pasilla chile powder

1 teaspoon garlic powder

1/2 teaspoon cayenne pepper

pinch of salt and pepper

6 to 8 ounces all-purpose flour

1/2 cup mixed edible flowers, julienned, for garnish

Blend all ingredients except flour and flowers. When mixture is completely smooth, add flour and blend for a few more minutes, until very smooth.

Heat a crepe pan or nonstick skillet. Rub with butter and pour about 2 ounces of batter on center of skillet and swirl around to make a thin crepe. Cook for about 1 minute, flip and cook an additional 15 seconds. Remove from pan and keep in warm place. Repeat until all of the batter is used.

Yields about 18 crepes.

Lobster bisque sauce:

3 1 to 1-1/2 pound lobsters

2 ounces olive oil

1 tablespoon garlic, chopped

1 white onion, chopped medium

3 ounces brandy

1 carrot, chopped medium

1 celery stalk, chopped medium

1 tablespoon fresh thyme, chopped

2 bay leaves

6 black peppercorns

1 quart chicken stock

6 ounces heavy cream

2 ounces sun-dried tomatoes

salt and pepper to taste

Separate lobster tails from heads. Cook tails in boiling water for about 7 minutes. Set aside. Cut lobster heads in half. Pour oil in saucepan. Add onions, garlic and lobster heads. Cook for about 5 minutes, stirring constantly. Add brandy (be careful, it will flame up). Add the rest of the ingredients except the cream and tomatoes. Simmer for about 7 minutes. Add the cream and cook for 5 more minutes at medium heat. Remove from heat and strain. Pour liquid in blender, adding sun dried tomatoes. Blend to a smooth consistency.

(continued on next page)

Stuffing for crepes:

4 ounces leeks, white part only, cleaned and julienned

1 ounce butter

8 ounces lobster meat (from tail), chopped medium

4 ounces heavy cream

4 ounces Monterey Jack cheese, shredded

Sauté leeks in butter in a skillet for about 1 minute. Add lobster and cook for an additional minute. Add cream and Monterey Jack cheese. Cook until it is quite thick.

To assemble:

Pour sauce on bottom of plate. Place stuffing on half of each crepe and fold. Place two crepes per plate. Decorate with julienned edible flowers.

This is an absolute knock-your-socks-off dish. Of all the dishes I sampled in creating this book, this is my favorite entree.

Serves 8.

EDIBLE FLOWERS

GARDEN SALAD WITH EDIBLE FLOWER PETALS

from Ron Ottobre, chef, Mudd's Restaurant, San Ramon, California

6 cups mixed greens, washed and broken into bite-sized pieces
Mudd's Honey Mustard Vinaigrette
4 tablespoons mixed edible flower petals
6 fresh button mushrooms, sliced
4 teaspoons grated Parmesan cheese

Toss mixed greens with Vinaigrette. Put greens on individual plates. Garnish each with flower petals, mushroom slices and Parmesan cheese.

Mudd's Honey Mustard Vinaigrette

1/2 cup honey
1/8 cup Dijon mustard
1/8 cup whole grain mustard
1/2 cup sherry vinegar
juice of 1 lemon
1 egg yolk
1 tablespoon thyme, chopped
1-1/2 cups safflower oil
1 cup olive oil

Combine first seven ingredients in a blender or food processor. Gradually add oils. Season with salt and pepper to taste.

Serves 6.

GOOD THYME SALAD

from Eileen Mendyka, Good Thyme Farm, Bethlehem, Connecticut

6 cups mixed greens—lettuces,
baby spinach, chicory, arugula, etc.
3 tablespoons calendula petals
2 tablespoons garlic chive florets
24 nasturtium flowers
12 anise hyssop flower stalks
24 borage flowers

Toss greens together in a large bowl. Place flowers and petals on top of greens in an artistic arrangement.

Serves 6 to 8.

tHE BIG TEN

This section is the beginning of a delicious journey into the edible flower garden and on into the kitchen. If a flower has never crossed your lips, start here. If you have only tried one or two flowers, use this chapter as a guide. Even if you are a long-time flower eater, browse through this chapter first. No doubt you will get new ideas of how to prepare some of your favorite flowers.

To gain membership in The Big Ten, edible flowers have to meet some rigorous standards. The first and most important is that they taste good. Among the ten flowers there is a wide range of flavors: spicy (nasturtium), oniony (chives), vegetal (squash, daylily), bitter (calendula), minty (mint, pansy), herbal (sage, marigold) and floral (rose). To say that these are the best-tasting of all the flowers might be a bit presumptuous on my part. Taste is, after all, very subjective.

The second standard is that they are versatile. Each of the ten flowers chosen can be used in a range of foods from appetizers to desserts, as you can see from the sumptuous recipes the chefs and I have created. These flowers, not individually but as a group, cover the color spectrum, adding to the beauty of these dishes and any you may create.

Finally, these flowers are commonly and easily grown in gardens throughout the country. Even if you do not consider yourself a gardener, you may have several of these flowers growing in your yard already. If you are a gardener, you probably have more of them in your garden. If you don't have a house with any garden space, miniature roses, chives, mint and pansies can be grown indoors.

CALENDULA

The word calendula is derived from the Latin *calens* meaning the first day of each month. Christians called it "marygold" and "marybud" because it bloomed at all the festivals celebrating the Virgin Mary.

I have already stated the importance of knowing a plant by its botanic name. This is even more important than the common name, as the common name can be variable in different regions, countries, and certainly in different languages. The botanic name is the same throughout the world. Calendula is an excellent case in point. It often is referred to

CALENDULA
(Pot Marigold)
Calendula officinalis
Composite family
 Asteraceae (Compositae)
Slightly bitter flavor
Annual
Rich loam
Cool weather

as pot marigold. In some older books the name was shortened to marigold, leaving the reader in confusion as to whether the plant referred to was *Calendula officinalis,* or one of the many *Tagetes* (marigolds).

The culinary use of calendula dates back to ancient Rome. The use of saffron (the powdered stigmas of the exotic saffron flower) was a sign of wealth and power. The common

people couldn't afford to buy saffron, and they discovered that powdered calendula petals were an excellent substitute.

Calendula is native to Asia and southern Europe and was brought to America by the early settlers. It was introduced to Britain by the Romans.

Calendula is a flowering annual that grows to a height of twelve to eighteen inches. The stem is slightly fuzzy, and the leaves are soft, growing to six inches long. Flowers may be yellow or orange. The flowers are about one and one-half inches in diameter, consisting of concentric rows of ray florets surrounding the smaller ones making up the center disc. 'Kablouna', a recent hybrid, has long-lasting, vibrant orange flowers. For all their beauty, calendula flowers have no fragrance.

The petals can be dried and kept in a tightly sealed container in a cool, dry place for use out of season. To dry flowers, place them on a piece of canvas or cheesecloth stretched over a screen in a warm, dry, shady place. Do not let the flowers touch one another. Once the flowers are completely dried, pick the petals off by hand and put them in a container and seal it tightly. Before adding dried petals to a recipe, pulverize them.

The flavor of calendula is slightly bitter. The petals are more often used for the color they impart than for their flavor. Calendula has been called "poor man's saffron," as the petals can be used in place of saffron in recipes. Petals must be well bruised to give off any color. The easiest way to do this is to chop the fresh petals finely.

THE BIG TEN

CULTURE

Calendulas grow in a wide range of soils, but prefer a rich loam. Direct seed calendulas in the garden once the last chance of frost has past. A second planting can be made at the beginning of July to ensure a fall harvest. Thin plants to twelve inches apart.

Calendulas do not like very hot weather. They will put on a big show of color in late spring and early summer. If the summer is not too hot, they may bloom intermittently. If you deadhead the plant religiously in spring and summer, it may give another burst of color as the weather turns cooler.

CHEESE BALL

1 pound cream cheese, softened to room temperature
1 cup extra sharp cheddar cheese, finely grated
1/4 cup green bell pepper, finely chopped
1/4 cup sweet red pepper, finely chopped
1/4 cup carrot, finely chopped
1/2 cup calendula petals, chopped
2 tablespoons scallion, finely chopped
1 teaspoon garlic, crushed
1/4 teaspoon tamari
freshly ground black pepper

Mix all ingredients together in a bowl. Refrigerate for at least 1 hour. Form into a ball.

For an elegant touch, press the stems of whole calendula or nasturtium flowers into the ball. Serve on nasturtium leaves as an alternative to a dip for crudités, or with crackers.

Serves 15 to 20 as hors d'oeuvres.

CALENDULA RICE

from Pat Lanza, Shandelee Herb Garden,
Livingston Manor, New York

4 cups water
1/8 teaspoon salt
1/2 cup onion, finely chopped
2 chicken bouillon cubes
1/2 cup calendula petals, finely chopped
2 cups long-grain rice

In a medium saucepan bring water to a boil. Add salt, onion, bouillon cubes, calendula petals and rice. Stir. Reduce heat, cover and simmer for 18 minutes.

Serves 8.

CARROT SOUP

4 tablespoons butter

1 cup sweet Vidalia onion, coarsely chopped

4 cloves garlic, crushed

1 cup tart (Granny Smith) apple, coarsely chopped

1/2 cup peanuts, chopped

1/4 teaspoon cinnamon

1/2 teaspoon freshly ground nutmeg

1/4 teaspoon cumin

2 pounds carrots, coarsely chopped

4 cups vegetable stock or chicken stock

1/2 cup milk

1 cup calendula petals

In a large stock pot, melt butter over a medium low heat. Add onion and garlic, sauté until they turn translucent. Add apple, peanuts, cinnamon, nutmeg and cumin. Continue to cook for 3 minutes. Add carrots and cook for 5 minutes over a low heat, stirring intermittently. Pour in stock, cover and allow to simmer for 20 to 25 minutes. Remove from heat and allow to cool slightly before pouring into a blender or food processor. Puree until smooth. Return to pot and stir in milk. Cook over a medium-low heat for 5 minutes. Do not let it come to a boil. Stir in petals just before serving.

Serves 4 to 6.

CALENDULA POTATOES

from José Gutierrez, executive chef, Chez Philippe, Peabody Hotel,
Memphis, Tennessee

4 medium potatoes, peeled and shaped into oblongs

petals from 8 to 10 calendula flowers

1 tablespoon butter

Boil potatoes in water with half of the calendula petals until potatoes are just tender. Drain potatoes. Melt butter, then roll potatoes in butter to coat completely. Roll in remaining petals to coat with flowers.

This dish is a show-stopper when served with Johnny-Jump-Up Veal Chops (see page 142).

Serves 4.

THE BIG TEN

CALENDULA BISCUITS

adapted from Diana Clare, Malahat Farm, Sooke, British Columbia, Canada

2 cups all-purpose flour
4 teaspoons baking powder
1/2 teaspoon salt
1/4 cup margarine
2 tablespoons calendula petals, finely chopped
3/4 cup milk
2 tablespoons margarine

Preheat oven to 450°F. Mix dry ingredients together in a bowl. Cut in margarine and calendula petals with a pastry knife until the mixture is mealy in texture. Quickly stir in the milk.

Turn out onto a floured board. Shape and knead (as little as possible) into an oblong shape about 1-1/2 inches thick. Place on a heavy cookie sheet (or use one cookie sheet atop another). With a sharp knife, cut dough into 2-inch squares. Dot well with margarine. Bake for 10 to 12 minutes or until lightly browned.

Serves 6 to 8 (or 3 very hungry hikers).

SOOKE HARBOUR HOUSE CALENDULA RICE

from Frank von Zuben, co-chef, Sooke Harbour House,
Sooke, British Columbia, Canada

1/4 cup brown rice miso (or substitute chicken broth or water
  with 1 teaspoon salt for miso and water)
1-3/4 cups water
1-1/4 cups calendula petals, divided
2 tablespoons sunflower seed oil
1 medium Walla Walla onion, diced
1 cup brown rice

Add miso and water to a blender. Blend at high speed. Add 1 cup of calendula petals and blend until liquefied. In a heavy saucepan, heat the oil. Sauté the onions until soft and translucent. Add rice and stir. Make sure all of the grains of rice are coated with oil.

Add the calendula liquid. Bring the entire mixture to a boil. Reduce heat to low. Cover and simmer until all liquid is absorbed, about 35 to 45 minutes. Remove from the heat and stir in the remaining calendula petals.

This can be placed in a Japanese rice mold. The cooked rice holds it shape when pushed out of the mold onto the plate.

Serves 6 to 8.

EDIBLE FLOWERS

ZUNI RICE

from Robert Werst, chef/owner, y.e. coyote, Hicksville, New York

1/4 cup oil

1/4 cup calendula petals, finely chopped

1 cup rice

2 cups water

2 tablespoons chili powder

1/4 cup frozen peas, thawed

1/4 cup sweet red pepper, diced

2 tablespoons tuberous begonia petals, coarsely chopped
  (optional)

Preheat oven to 375°F.

Heat oil in an oven-safe saucepan. Add calendula petals and rice. Sauté for several minutes, stirring frequently. Add water and chili powder. Bring to a boil and cover with aluminum foil.

Remove from heat and place in the oven. Bake for 45 minutes to 1 hour, or until all liquid is absorbed. Remove from oven. Stir in peas and red pepper. For added zest, garnish with tuberous begonias.

Serves 6 to 8.

MOROCCAN CHICKEN

from Applewood Seed Company, Golden, Colorado

1 cup long-grain rice

1/4 cup butter

2 pounds chicken, cut in eighths

1 large onion, coarsely chopped

1/3 cup dried apricots, coarsely chopped

1/2 cup raisins

1/2 cup pistachio nuts, chopped

1/2 cup pine nuts

3 tablespoons ground cinnamon

4 cups chicken broth, boiling

2 tablespoons rose water

1/4 cup rose petals, preferably red

1 tablespoon calendula petals

Wash and drain rice. In a large skillet, melt butter. Add chicken and brown over a medium heat, turning to brown all sides. Remove chicken to a shallow casserole and set aside. Add onion to skillet and sauté for 2 minutes. Add rice and stir. Add apricots, raisins, nuts, cinnamon and mix. Sauté for 1 to 2 minutes. Add broth and bring mixture to a boil. Add mixture to chicken in casserole. Cover and bake at 350°F for 1 hour and 15 minutes. Remove from oven and transfer to a serving bowl. Sprinkle with rose water and toss gently. Decorate with rose and calendula petals and serve.

Serves 4.

ORANGE CAKE

———

Cake batter:

5 eggs

1/2 cup butter, softened to room temperature

1-1/2 cups granulated sugar

rind of 2 lemons, grated

rind of 1 orange, grated

1 cup sour cream

1/2 cup plain yogurt

3 cups all-purpose flour

2 teaspoons baking soda

1/2 cup calendula petals, chopped

Preheat oven to 350°F. Separate eggs. Beat whites until they form stiff peaks. Set aside.

Cream butter and sugar together. Blend in egg yolks, lemon rind, orange rind, sour cream and yogurt. Beat until smooth.

Sift dry ingredients together. Slowly add dry ingredients to wet, mixing well. Gently fold in beaten egg whites and calendula petals.

Butter and flour a Bundt cake or angel food cake pan. Pour in cake batter and bake for 60 minutes. Remove from oven and let cool in pan 10 minutes, then remove to a cooling rack and allow to cool completely.

Syrup topping:

1/2 cup orange juice

1/4 cup lemon juice

1/4 cup Grand Marnier

1/4 cup granulated sugar

Combine all ingredients in a saucepan over a low heat. Bring to a boil, then simmer for 3 minutes. Pour hot syrup over cooled cake and garnish with calendula petals.

CHIVES

CHIVES
Allium schoeonoprasum
Amaryllis family
Amaryllidaceae
Onion flavor
Perennial
Slightly moist, well-drained soil
Partial shade to full to sun

Chives and their other allium relatives have been honored as herbs for millennia. They were noted in Chinese herbals over five thousand years ago for their ability to stimulate the appetite and ease a cough. The botanic name for chives is derived from the Greek *schoinos*—rush, and *prason*—leek. Rush-leek was the common name during the Middle Ages.

Chives are native to northern Europe and can be easily grown throughout America.

Chives are perennial herbs (although they technically come from bulbs) with hollow grasslike leaves growing in clumps ten to eighteen inches tall. Chives are attractive in the garden, not only for their foliage, but for their flowers as well. In mid-spring they send up lavender-pink pom-pom–like flowers. Upon close examination, the flowers are comprised of smaller florets.

Do not be deceived by the delicate beauty of the flowers, they are quite flavorful—oniony but not overpoweringly so. For best flavor, harvest the flowers when they just open. Keep picking the flowers and the plant will continue to bloom until frost, not profusely, but sufficiently for culinary use.

Chives are among the most versatile of all the edible flowers.

CULTURE

Chives can be grown successfully indoors in pots as herbs. Often the plant is only kept for one season indoors, so flowering does not occur. Chives can easily be grown from seed on a sunny windowsill, providing plenty of leaves for cutting throughout the winter. Transplanting the chives into a larger pot or directly into the garden in the spring will encourage new growth and eventually flowering.

Outdoors, chive prefer slightly moist, well-drained soil in partial shade, although they will grow in full sun. A perennial herb, chives will die back during the winter in cold areas and will regrow each spring.

Chives can easily be propagated in mid-spring by dividing a clump. Simply dig the clump up and gently tear it into two or more sections, separating from the leaves down through the soil and roots. Replant the smaller clumps and they will flourish.

WARNING

As tempting as it may be to pop a whole chive flower into your mouth, refrain from doing so, as the pungency in that quantity can be overwhelming. For garnish and in cooking, always break the flower into individual florets.

THE BIG TEN

GAZPACHO

2 ears of fresh corn

6 large ripe tomatoes, coarsely chopped

1 small zucchini, coarsely chopped

1 sweet pepper, coarsely chopped

1 sprig parsley, minced

1 sprig cilantro, minced

6 chive flowers, broken into florets

Cut kernels of corn off the cob, and place in a large bowl. Reserve a small amount for garnish. Coarsely chop all ingredients, except flowers, and add to corn.

For a smooth soup, puree entire mixture in a food processor or blender. For a chunky soup, puree four of the tomatoes, then add the other chopped vegetables. Add chive flowers (reserve some for garnish), mix well. Garnish with corn and chive florets. Can be served immediately or up to 2 days later.

This low-calorie version of the classic is a great hot-weather meal.

Serves 4.

STIR-FRY CHICKEN AND WALNUTS

2 tablespoons peanut oil

6 chive flowers, broken into florets

1 tablespoon grated ginger

2 boneless chicken breasts, cut into 1-inch cubes

1 sweet red pepper, cut into 1-inch pieces

1 sweet yellow pepper, cut into 1-inch pieces

1 green bell pepper, cut into 1-inch pieces

2 cups broccoli, cut into 1-1/2–inch pieces, steamed until bright green

1/4 cup sherry

2 tablespoons tamari or soy sauce

3 tablespoons rice wine vinegar

1 tablespoon water

1 teaspoon sesame oil

1 tablespoon cornstarch

1 cup walnut halves, toasted in a nonstick frying pan

2 cups cooked rice

Heat a wok or large frying pan over high heat. Pour in peanut oil and swirl to coat pan. Add chive florets and ginger. Stir and allow to sizzle for 1 minute. Add chicken pieces, stirring frequently so they cook quickly and evenly. Cook for 3 or 4 minutes, then add peppers. Continue to cook and stir for an additional 1 to 2 minutes. Toss in broccoli.

Mix sherry, tamari, vinegar, water and sesame oil together in a cup with the cornstarch. Add the liquid to the wok and stir; after several minutes it will thicken and turn clear while coating the chicken and vegetables. Toss in walnuts. Garnish with chive florets. Serve immediately with rice.

Serves 4.

EDIBLE FLOWERS

PARSLEY-CHIVE NEW POTATOES

from Bob Holmes, Creation Gardens, New Albany, Indiana

15 to 20 small, new red potatoes
2 tablespoons parsley, chopped
2 tablespoons chives, chopped
2 tablespoons butter
salt to taste
2 tablespoons chive florets

Place potatoes, parsley and chives in a saucepan with about 1/2 to 1 inch of water. Cook until potatoes are fork tender. When done, do not pour off cooking water. Add butter and stir. Salt to taste. Serve the potatoes and broth sprinkled with chive florets.

Serves 4.

FAVA BEANS WITH BACON AND CHIVES

1 pound fava beans, shelled
6 strips bacon
6 chive blossoms, broken into florets

Boil fava beans until tender, about 10 to 15 minutes. Drain. Fry bacon until crisp. Remove from frying pan and drain. Reserve 1 tablespoon of bacon fat, discard the rest from the pan. Return the reserved bacon fat to the pan over a low heat. When the fat is hot, add the chive florets and allow to sizzle for 1 minute. Add the fava beans and stir well. Remove from heat and cover. Let stand 5 minutes. Garnish with crumbled bacon and chive florets.

A colorful variation on a classic Italian dish.

Serves 4.

THE BIG TEN

CORN CAKES WITH SMOKED SALMON, CREME FRAICHE AND CHIVES

from James O'Shea, chef, West Street Grill, Litchfield, Connecticut

Crème fraiche:

2 cups heavy cream

1/4 cup sour cream

Mix together, cover and let stand in a warm place for 24 to 48 hours until thickened. Refrigerate and keep for up to 2 weeks.

Fresh corn relish:

2 cups corn kernels, cut from cob

2 tablespoons red onion, finely diced

2 tablespoons red bell pepper, finely diced

2 tablespoons celery, finely diced

3 tablespoons cider vinegar

2 tablespoons vegetable oil

salt and pepper to taste

Mix all ingredients and let sit for 4 hours.

Corn cakes:

3 cups corn kernels

1 cup milk

4 eggs

4 egg yolks

1 cup all-purpose flour

1 cup cornmeal

1/2 cup chive blossoms, broken into florets

1/4 pound butter, melted

1/4 teaspoon baking powder

salt and pepper to taste

vegetable oil

Puree corn, milk and eggs, stopping while mixture is still chunky. In a large bowl, combine corn mixture with remaining ingredients. Refrigerate 1 hour before proceeding.

Heat a frying pan and add just enough oil to lightly coat the bottom. Pour dollar-size cakes into the pan. Cook over a medium heat until golden, about 2 minutes on each side.

To assemble:

1/4 pound smoked salmon, sliced very thin

chive florets

3 chives, cut in 1/2-inch pieces

Place 3 corn cakes around the center of each plate. Add 3 small bundles of smoked salmon around the corn cakes. Sprinkle corn relish over the rest of the plate. Put a dollop of crème fraiche on top of each corn cake. Garnish with chive florets and snipped chives.

Serves 6 to 8.

EDIBLE FLOWERS

GRILLED CHIVED CHICKEN SALAD

Marinade:

5 chive blossoms, broken into florets

1/2 cup balsamic vinegar

1/4 cup tamari

1/2 cup lime juice

1/4 cup sesame oil

2 tablespoons grated ginger

4 boned and skinned chicken breasts, cut into 1-1/2–inch strips
  arugula

red leaf lettuce

Romaine lettuce

3 tablespoons fresh dill

3 chive blossoms

1 sweet red pepper, sliced in strips (raw or grilled)

Mix all marinade ingredients together. Pour into a glass bowl or baking pan and add chicken strips. Cover and refrigerate at least 2 hours or up to 24 hours.

Grill or broil chicken strips, being sure to place some of the chive florets from marinade on each piece.

Toss together washed and dried salad greens, dill and florets from 2 chive blossoms. Divide greens and place on 4 plates or large, shallow bowls. Top with grilled chicken and red pepper.

Serves 4.

COLE SLAW

1 small red cabbage, grated

1 small green or Savoy cabbage, grated

3 carrots, scrubbed and grated

3 medium-sized green tomatoes, cut into small wedges

6 chive flowers, broken into florets

3 sprigs thyme flowers, broken into florets

4 tablespoons mayonnaise

1 tablespoon balsamic or flower vinegar

1 tablespoon dill weed

1 tablespoon celery seed

In a large nonmetallic bowl, toss vegetables together. Mix mayonnaise, vinegar, herbs and flowers together. Add mayonnaise mixture to vegetables. Toss well. Refrigerate at least 6 hours prior to serving to let the flavors meld. This slaw gets better the longer it sits.

Serves 6 to 8.

AYLILY

The daylily is not a true lily, but it is related and in the same family. Both its botanic and common names describe the flower perfectly. Each flower lasts for only one day. On one daylily plant there may be several flower spikes, each with the potential of a dozen or more successive buds, ensuring that flowering occurs over a period of time. The botanic name comes from the Greek *hemera* for day, and *kallos* for beauty. In the Victorian language of flowers, the daylily was a symbol of coquetry.

The earliest written Chinese records (although they are believed have been used even earlier) cite the daylily for its use as a food plant. The buds were found to be not only tasty and digestible, but nutritious as well. The root and crown of the plant were used medicinally as an analgesic. The brightly colored flowers were used to lift the spirits of those in grief.

Today there are tens of thousands of hybrid daylilies, with hundreds of new cultivars introduced each year. The range size of the plant—from grassy leafed miniatures growing only six to ten inches high to sturdy, broader-leafed plants growing three feet tall—is great. The flowers, formed from three outer sepals and three inner petals also range in size, form and color. Flowers vary from flat to trumpet-shaped, star-shaped to round, recurved to ruffled petals and even varieties that are double, with more than twelve segments.

DAYLILY
Hemerocallis spp.
Lily family
Liliaceae
Vegetal, sweet flavor
Perennial
Slightly acid, rich loam
Full sun to partial shade

In nature daylilies are limited to shades of yellow, orange and fulvous (a blend of orange, yellow and red as seen in the species daylilies that grow along roadsides, *Hemerocallis fulva*). Many years of hybridizing created daylilies of nearly every color of the rainbow, with only true blue and true white as yet to be achieved. From solid colors to contrasting tipping of the petal edges, bicolors with sepals and petals of different colors to a colored midrib, the variations of colors and hues are almost limitless. The size of the flowers vary as well—from miniatures (classified if under three inches in diameter) to large flowers (classified if over four and one-half inches in diameter) that can get to seven inches, on branching flower stems (scapes) also ranging from under twelve inches (dwarf) to over thirty-six inches (tall). Indeed there are daylilies to match or contrast with any garden scheme.

Daylilies are fibrous rooted (not a bulb, tuber or rhizome), hardy herbaceous perennials. Emerging in early spring, the long narrow, heavily ribbed leaves form a fan shape. When planning the garden, choose varieties to extend the period of bloom. The first flowers can appear in March in the deep South and California, but not until May or June in more northern zones. Flowering continues later in the North, until fall, but usually ends by late summer in warmer areas.

You may have eaten daylilies and not have been aware of it. Dried daylily petals (known to the Chinese as golden needles) are an ingredient in Chinese hot and sour soup. The Chinese have as many variations on that recipe as we do for apple pie. Two are included here. At the mature bud stage (the day before the bud opens into a flower), the flavor of a daylily has been compared to green beans and eggplant. Picked as an open flower, the flavor is milder. As there are so many hybrids, it is impossible to give a definitive flavor for daylilies. In general, however, the darkest colors tend towards bitterness while the pale yellows and oranges are sweeter. Taste each variety before you use it as the flavor can vary greatly.

CULTURE

Daylilies are easy to grow. They are readily available from numerous sources—mail-order plant catalogs, local nurseries and garden centers and from specialty breeders. The easiest and most inexpensive way to obtain plants is from people who are already growing daylilies. A single daylily plant can multiply, and, if growing in ideal soil and conditions, it may be left for ten to fifteen years. Eventually, however, the plant needs to be divided to rejuvenate the plant. See what your friends, neighbors and relatives are growing. People are usually more than happy to share their plant material, especially if you offer to help them divide their plants.

Daylilies prefer at least six hours of sun a day. The paler colors especially benefit from full sun, while darker colors can tolerate partial shade. Although daylilies will grow in almost any type of soil, a slightly acid, rich loam with good drainage is ideal.

Daylilies can be planted almost any time from spring through fall, however, planting them in extreme heat (over ninety degrees Fahrenheit) may increase their chance of rotting. Mail order plants need to be soaked for several hours in tepid water before planting. Inspect the plants and cut off any damaged roots. Space daylilies eighteen to twenty-four inches apart. Dig a hole twice the size of the root area. Incorporate organic material into the soil. Make a mound in the center of the hole and place the plant on top of the mound, spreading the roots out around it. Add soil, working it around the roots as you go. Usually you can see the planting depth—the band of white at the base of the leaves was originally underground. The crown (the area where the roots and leaves join) should be no more than one inch below the soil. Firm the soil and water it well. Once the plants are established, fertilize once in early spring and again in fall after blooming with a general-purpose organic fertilizer.

FREEZING DAYLILIES

Daylilies open in hot water, so if you wish to freeze buds, pick them a day earlier than usual.

Blanch flowers or buds for three minutes in boiling water. Immediately plunge into ice water. Once completely cooled, pat dry and pack into freezer bags.

Daylilies can be kept up to eight months in the freezer, allowing you to enjoy them almost year-round.

WARNING

Since the time of the Sung Dynasty (about 1059 A.D.), daylilies (especially the tubers) have been recognized for their diuretic properties. They may also act as a laxative, so it is best to eat them in moderation.

HOT AND SOUR SOUP

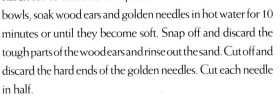

from Yun Liu Frowine, White Flower Farm, Litchfield, Connecticut

4 ounces chicken breast, shredded

4 ounces lean pork, shredded

2 teaspoons soy sauce

1 tablespoon dry sherry

4 tablespoons cornstarch, divided

12 dried wood ear mushrooms (opional)

24 golden needles (dried daylilies, available in Oriental markets)

4 cups chicken broth

1/4 pound medium firm bean curd (tofu), drained and cut into shreds

1/3 cup water

1 egg, beaten

3 tablespoons Chinese rice vinegar

1/2 teaspoon white pepper

2 tablespoons soy sauce

1 teaspoon sesame oil

1 green onion, minced

hot pepper oil to taste

Marinate shredded chicken and pork with 2 teaspoons soy sauce, dry sherry and 1 tablespoon cornstarch for 15 minutes. In separate bowls, soak wood ears and golden needles in hot water for 10 minutes or until they become soft. Snap off and discard the tough parts of the wood ears and rinse out the sand. Cut off and discard the hard ends of the golden needles. Cut each needle in half.

Pour chicken broth into a 2-quart saucepan and bring to a boil over medium-high heat. Add the marinated pork, chicken, wood ears and golden needles. Stir and cook for 2 minutes. Add the bean curd as soon as the soup reaches a boil. Cook for 1 minute. Mix 3 tablespoons cornstarch with 1/3 cup water. Stir mixture into soup, stirring until soup thickens. Pour in beaten egg, stir and remove from heat. Add vinegar and 2 tablespoons soy sauce. Garnish with white pepper, sesame seed oil and green onion. Add hot pepper oil if desired.

Serves 6.

EDIBLE FLOWERS

There are innumerable variations on hot and sour soup; here is another one from the West Coast.

HOT AND SOUR SOUP

from Yujean Kang, chef/owner, Yujean Kang's, Pasadena, California

2 ounces soft tofu, julienned

2 ounces dried daylily flowers

2 ounces black tree fungus (tree ears)

2 ounces chicken breast, julienned, then blanched

3 cups chicken stock

3 tablespoons dark soy sauce

2 tablespoons white pepper, freshly ground

2 tablespoons white vinegar

pinch of salt

1/4 teaspoon sesame oil

1 tablespoon cornstarch blended with 1/2 tablespoon water

1 egg, beaten to a froth

cilantro for garnish

In a deep pot, mix all ingredients except egg and cilantro. Bring to a boil, stirring frequently. As soon as the soup thickens, drizzle the scrambled egg with a circular motion (do not stir with a spoon). As soon as egg congeals, ladle soup into serving bowls. Garnish, if desired, with cilantro sprigs.

Serves 2.

DAYLILY BLUEBERRY PANCAKES

4 eggs

1 cup cottage cheese

1/8 teaspoon salt

2 tablespoons oil

1/2 cup sifted all-purpose flour

1 tablespoon granulated sugar

1/2 teaspoon vanilla

petals from 10 daylilies, coarsely chopped

1 cup blueberries

Mix first 7 ingredients in a blender or food processor. Blend until smooth. Pour into a bowl. Gently stir in daylily petals and blueberries. Let sit for 10 minutes. Drop by the 1/4 cupful onto a hot, lightly greased griddle or skillet over medium heat. Cook until bubbles on top of pancakes break. Turn over and brown other side.

May be served with syrup (floral or maple), butter or plain. A delicious dish for a Sunday brunch.

Serves 4.

THE BIG TEN

SAUTEED DAYLILIES

12 daylily flowers
2 chive flowers broken into florets
1/2 teaspoon salt

Put all ingredients into a frying pan. Cover and simmer until just tender and all moisture is cooked away. Do not overcook. Serve hot as a cooked vegetable. For added richness, toss with butter just before serving.

Serves 2 to 4.

FRIED GOLDEN NEEDLES

12 daylily flowers
1 egg beaten with 1 teaspoon water
1 cup all-purpose flour
vegetable oil

Dip each flower in the beaten egg. Roll it in flour. Sauté the coated flowers in hot oil until crispy.

This recipe works just as well with frozen daylilies as with fresh. A real treat to have in mid-winter.

Serves 2 to 4.

ORIENTAL DAYLILY BUDS

2 cups daylily buds
1 tablespoon peanut oil
1/4 cup almond slivers
1 teaspoon freshly grated ginger
1 tablespoon rice wine vinegar
1 tablespoon tamari or soy sauce
1 tablespoon water
2 cups cooked brown rice

Steam daylily buds for 10 to 15 minutes, until tender. In a wok or heavy skillet, heat the oil over a high heat until very hot. Add the almond slivers, sauté until browned. Quickly remove the almonds from the pan, set aside. Turn heat down to medium. Add grated ginger and let it cook for 1 to 2 minutes. Add vinegar, tamari and water. Stir to mix. Toss in daylily buds. Serve over hot rice, topped with sautéed almonds.

Serves 4.

STIR-FRY DAYLILY SHRIMP

peanut oil

1 tablespoon freshly grated ginger

1 clove garlic, finely minced

1/2 cup onion, chopped

4 daylily buds

petals from 4 daylily flowers

8 ounces mushrooms, sliced

1 cup Chinese cabbage, coarsely chopped

1/2 cup red bell pepper, chopped

1 pound medium shrimp, cleaned, peeled and deveined

Sauce:

1 teaspoon sesame oil

1 tablespoon tamari

1 teaspoon granulated sugar

1 tablespoon rice wine vinegar

2 tablespoons cornstarch dissolved in 2 tablespoons water

Heat a wok over a high heat. When the wok is hot, swirl in peanut oil to lightly coat wok. Add ginger and garlic, stirring constantly. Add onion and cook for 1 minute. Add daylily buds and petals, mushrooms, cabbage and pepper a bit at a time so wok does not cool down. Cook for 1 minute, stirring frequently. Add shrimp and cook until they just turn pink. Mix sauce ingredients together in a bowl. Pour into wok, stirring until sauce turns transparent and glossy. Serve immediately.

Serves 4.

DAYLILY SLICED PORK

3 shoulder pork chops, meat cut into small pieces

1 teaspoon salt

1/4 teaspoon granulated sugar

1 clove garlic, crushed

1 onion, chopped

1 tablespoon tamari

1 teaspoon fresh ginger, chopped

1 tablespoon cornstarch

3 tablespoons peanut oil

1 onion, sliced

1 tablespoon sherry

3 cups daylily flowers

1/4 cup water

Mix the meat, salt, sugar, garlic, chopped onion, tamari, ginger and cornstarch together in a bowl. Allow to sit for 5 minutes. In a large frying pan, heat the oil over a medium-high heat. Add onion slices and sauté until browned. Add the meat mixture and sherry and cook for 3 to 4 minutes, stirring frequently. Add daylilies, sliced onion and water. Cook an additional 3 to 4 minutes. Serve immediately.

Serves 4.

THE BIG TEN

BUCKSNORT TROUT WITH MIXED FLOWER BUTTER AND GRILLED DAYLILIES

from José Gutierrez, executive chef, Chez Philippe, Peabody Hotel, Memphis, Tennessee

1 12-ounce trout, cleaned, filleted and skinned
10 daylily buds
1 tablespoon olive oil
salt and pepper
2 pats of mixed edible flower butter

Rub fish and daylily buds with olive oil, salt and pepper. Grill over a very hot fire—trout for 1 to 2 minutes, daylily buds for 1 minute per side.

Serve trout accompanied by daylily buds. Place a pat of butter on the trout. The butter will begin to melt slightly as the dish is being served. For a special presentation, serve the fish on a bed of frisee, fennel and Lollo Rosso lettuce.

Serves 2.

DAYLILY CHICKEN STIR FRY

1 tablespoon fresh ginger, finely chopped
1 tablespoon tamari or soy sauce
1 tablespoon sherry
1 tablespoon rice wine vinegar
2 tablespoons corn starch
2 chicken breasts, cut paper thin
1 small onion, chopped
3 tablespoons peanut oil
1 medium onion, sliced and cut in half
3 cups daylily flowers
1/3 cup water

Mix the ginger, tamari, sherry, vinegar and cornstarch together in a bowl. Add the chicken pieces and chopped onion, mix to coat each piece evenly. Heat a wok or heavy frying pan on high. When wok is hot, add 2 tablespoons of peanut oil, swirling to coat the pan. Quickly add the chicken mixture and cook for about 2 minutes, stirring to cook evenly and avoid burning. Remove chicken from wok, set aside. Wipe out wok. Heat wok over a medium heat and add 1 tablespoon oil. Add onion slices and cook slowly until browned. Add daylily, water and cooked chicken. Cook for 3 minutes. Serve immediately.

Serves 4.

MINT

MINT
Mentha spp.
Mint family
Lamiaceae (Labiatae)
Minty flavor
Perennial
Rich, well-drained soil, but will grow anywhere
Prefer partial shade

The exact origins of mints have been lost, with some sources suggesting that they are native to Europe, others the Mediterranean, still others the Near East, and another Hindustan. Today mints are grown around the world. There are more than twenty-five species of mint, hundreds of cultivars and unknown numbers of garden hybrids. In North America, both spearmint and peppermint have naturalized and can be found growing wild in damp places from Nova Scotia to Minnesota and south to Utah, Tennessee and Florida.

Mint is mentioned in the Bible used in lieu of money as a tithe. According to the Victorian language of flowers, mint symbolizes virtue, peppermint is warm feeling and spearmint is warmth of sentiment. Medicinally, mint has been written about since the first century A.D. Even today mint's role as a stomach palliative is evidenced by the number of after dinner drinks and candies aimed to soothe the overstuffed stomach. For centuries mint was used as a strewing herb to dispel foul odors. Today, mint is used in mouthwashes and toothpastes. The culinary uses are broader in the Middle East than in North America. Yet with our increasing interest in international cooking, dishes like tabbouleh are not totally unknown in mainstream America.

In general, mints are hardy perennials, growing from one and one-half to three feet tall. Mints are distinguished by their square stems, which often have a reddish hue.

There are many different mints, each different in appearance as well as flavor. Try some suggested here or experiment with others you run across.

American Apple Mint (Golden Apple Mint)
Mentha Gentilis Variegata

This culinary herb has smooth, grayish-green leaves variegated with yellow. It has a tendency to sprawl in the garden. In midsummer light purple flowers are borne in whorls along the stems. The flowers have a delicate, fruity, spearmint flavor.

Curly Mint *Mentha* (*Spicata* Var.) *Crispa*

Curly mint has wide, crinkled, dull leaves. It spreads quickly in the garden. It grows to two feet in height, but tends to sprawl by midsummer when it blooms. The violet flowers are borne on slender spikes. It has the flavor of spearmint.

Orange Mint (Bergamot Mint)
Mentha Citrata

Orange mint's smooth, broad, dark-green leaves are lightly edged with a touch of purple. Purple flowers appear at the tips of short spikes in midsummer. At that point, the plant often sprawls. However, this is one of the least aggressive mints, an admirable quality.

Peppermint (Lamb mint, Lammint)
Mentha Piperita
English Black Peppermint
Mentha Piperita Vulgaris
White Peppermint
Mentha Piperita Officinalis

Peppermint is highly cultivated for its essential oil. Traditionally mint sauce is served with lamb, perhaps that is the origin of its other names.

Two distinct peppermints are commonly grown: black peppermint (with dark green leaves tinged purple, purple stems and purple flowers tinged with red at the tips of long spikes) and white peppermint (with light green leaves and purple flowers at the tips of slender, long spikes). Black peppermint is taller than white. According to some experts, the oil distilled from the white peppermint is the best. Peppermint will die out if grown in the same spot in the garden for several years. Often it is a self-solving problem—the mint will run off and start growing in a new area all by itself. The flavor of the flowers is peppermint.

Spearmint *Mentha Spicata*

This is the most common mint, the mint of julep fame. It is found garnishing glasses of iced tea and lemonade throughout the summer. Spearmint grows to three feet tall with medium-green stalkless leaves with strongly toothed edges on green stems. The plant has a more compact habit than peppermint. The flowers, in whorls on slender spikes at the ends of stems and branches, are off-white to lavender and appear in midsummer. The flower flavor is spearmint.

CULTURE

Mints grow best in rich, moist, well-drained soil. Although they prefer partial shade, a sunny location will do. I remember mint in numerous gardens in the small beach front community of my childhood. Very sandy soil, full sun, dry, but well drained—the mints thrived. I have yet to see a growing condition that deters mint.

Mint is usually not grown from seed, but is easily propagated from roots or runners. This is very simple to do. Pull up a stem of mint and you will pull up some roots. Lay the stem in a furrow four inches deep in a shady location. I like to gently bend the top six inches so they extend above the soil. Cover the stem with soil and tamp it down. Space furrows three feet apart. In warm areas of the country, this can be done in early March, in other areas wait until after any danger of frost is past and the ground has warmed up.

Young plants are available at nurseries, garden centers and through mail-order companies. Wait until the weather and soil warm up before planting. Allow at least twelve to eighteen inches between plants. If mint starts crowding the garden, simply pull up stems—you can always replant them elsewhere, but be aware that the stem is usually attached to an underground runner, so it will continue to flourish.

Mints are very aggressive in the garden, spreading by underground runners. Once established in a garden they can be difficult to keep within bounds. One way to control them is to grow them in containers rather than in the ground. Be careful where you place the container. After several years, a container of mint on my patio had rooted down between the flagstones and

suddenly I found mint popping up all around. Another method is to grow mints as annuals, planting them in a container and then planting the container in the garden. After the patio incident, I have resorted to growing mint in a relatively large (for the size of the plant) pot without drainage holes. I then sink the pot into the garden, leaving about an inch of the rim above ground. At the end of the growing season, I take no chances and dig up the pot. Other growers suggest surrounding a planting of mint with strips of metal sunk eighteen inches into the ground.

TABBOULEH

3/4 cup no. 2 (fine) bulgur
2 bunches parsley, finely chopped
1-1/2 cups mint flowers, chopped
4 scallions, finely chopped
2 medium tomatoes, finely chopped
1/8 teaspoon cinnamon
1/2 cup freshly squeezed lemon juice
1/2 cup olive oil
Romaine lettuce

Put bulgur in a bowl with enough water to cover. Soak for 1 hour. Drain excess water. Mix in parsley, mint flowers, scallions and tomatoes. In a separate bowl, mix

together cinnamon and lemon juice. Stir into bulgur mixture. Toss with olive oil just before serving. Arrange smaller leaves of Romaine lettuce on each plate and top with the tabbouleh.

For a change serve with the tabbouleh in the center of a plate surrounded by small lettuce leaves, which are used to scoop up the tabbouleh and eat it without using utensils. The mint flowers are milder than traditional mint leaves.

Serves 4 at a meal or 8 for hors d'oeuvres.

THE BIG TEN

CHAMPAGNE FRUIT TERRINE

———

from José Gutierrez, executive chef, Chez Philippe, Peabody Hotel, Memphis, Tennessee

6 oranges
4 grapefruit
1 cup raspberries
1 cup blueberries
2 packets plain gelatin
1 cup orange juice, strained
1 cup champagne
1/2 cup granulated sugar
10 sprigs mint flowers

Cut top and bottom off oranges and grapefruit. Cut off skin, removing any white pith, preserving the round shape. Cut the sections from the oranges and grapefruit. Place in a sieve to allow excess juice to collect in a bowl beneath. Reserve drained juice.

Layer a terrine (or a loaf pan), starting with grapefruit, then oranges, raspberries and blueberries. Repeat layers to within 1/2 inch of the top of the pan, finishing with a citrus layer.

Dissolve gelatin in 1/2 cup of orange juice over a low heat. Beat sugar into remaining orange juice and champagne. Gently rub the flowers of the mint over a plate to release the florets. Some of the green sepals will release as well—that is all right. Add flowers and dissolved gelatin. Pour over fruit. Chill in refrigerator at least 2 hours.

This elegant dish can be served as an appetizer or a dessert. It can easily be made a day or two ahead of a party. Unmold just before serving. Serve alone or with Champagne Mint Sauce (see below) on the side.

Serves 8 to 12.

CHAMPAGNE MINT SAUCE

———

from José Gutierrez, executive chef, Chez Philippe, Peabody Hotel, Memphis, Tennessee

1 cup granulated sugar
2 cups champagne
4 pears, peeled, cored and cut into small pieces
3 tablespoons water
1/3 cup mint flowers

Boil sugar and champagne together until sugar is dissolved. Add pears and simmer over a medium heat until pears are cooked, becoming almost transparent. Add water. Blend until smooth. Add mint flowers and puree until completely smooth.

This sauce was created as an accompaniment to the Champagne Fruit Terrine. It is also delicious served with roast lamb—lighter and more delicate than mint jelly—or with vanilla ice cream.

EDIBLE FLOWERS

MINT CHOCOLATE CAKE

2 cups granulated sugar

1-3/4 cups cake flour, sifted

3/4 cup cocoa

1-1/2 teaspoons baking soda

1 teaspoon salt

2 eggs

1 cup milk

1/2 cup vegetable oil

2 teaspoons vanilla extract

1 cup boiling water

1/3 to 1/2 cup mint flowers, coarsely chopped

butter and flour for greasing pans

confectioners' sugar

mint flowers for garnish

Preheat oven to 350°F. Mix dry ingredients together in a large bowl. In a separate bowl, mix wet ingredients.

Pour wet mixture into dry, beating for 2 minutes. Add mint flowers.

Butter and flour baking pans: use a Bundt pan, 2 9- or 10-inch round baking pans or a 13-by-9-inch baking pan. Pour batter into prepared pans. Bake 30 to 35 minutes or until a toothpick inserted in the center comes out clean. Cool on wire rack 10 minutes; remove cake from pan and cool completely on wire rack.

Just before serving, dust top of cake with confectioners' sugar. Garnish with mint flowers.

Makes 2 9- or 10-inch round cakes, 1 Bundt cake, or 1 13-by-9-inch cake.

Serves 12.

CHOCOLATE MINT ICE CREAM

1/2 cup mint flowers, coarsely chopped

1/4 cup granulated sugar

1/2 cup water

juice of 1/2 lemon

3 egg yolks

3 cups half-and-half

3 ounces chocolate chips

Put the mint flowers, sugar and water into a heavy saucepan over a low heat. Stir until sugar dissolves. Bring to a boil and simmer for 5 minutes. Remove from the heat and strain the syrup. Add lemon juice to the strained liquid. Beat the egg yolks until light and

frothy. Slowly pour in the syrup, beating constantly. Continue to beat until the mixture thickens.

Place the half-and-half and chocolate chips in a saucepan over a low heat. Stir until the chocolate melts. Heat until the mixture is almost to the boiling point, then remove from the heat and cool the saucepan in a large bowl filled with ice cubes. Whisk the chocolate and egg mixtures together. Pour into an ice cream maker. Freeze according to manufacturer's instructions.

For a devilishly decadent presentation, serve with crème de menthe drizzled over the ice cream.

Serves 6 to 8.

NASTURTIUM

The nasturtium gets its common name from the Latin *nasus*, nose, and *torquere*, to twist, or nose twisters. Whether this is because of the fragrance of the plant or its peppery quality that can twitch the nose is uncertain.

Nasturtiums have been appreciated by political notables. Louis XIV of France had nasturtiums growing in his royal gardens. Of all the herbs he grew at Monticello, nasturtiums were Thomas Jefferson's favorite. In the Victorian language of flowers, nasturtium signifies patriotism.

In Peru, where nasturtium is native, it is a perennial. In most parts of North America, it is grown as an annual, although in areas with mild winters it can survive to a second year.

Nasturtiums grow from six inches to about twelve inches tall. The trailing varieties spread outward horizontally and can be trained upward on a trellis six to eight feet high. The leaves are smooth and round, ranging from one-half to three inches in diameter. Pale green veins radiate outward from the center of the leaf. The underside is a lighter green than the top of the leaf. The leafstalk is fleshy and easily curls around anything it touches. This enables the taller varieties to climb up to ten feet. Five sepals join at their base, with three elongating to form a spur at the back of the five-petaled flower. The flowers average two and one-half inches in diameter.

There are many hybrid cultivars of nasturtium,

NASTURTIUM
Tropaeolum majus
Nasturtium family
Tropaeolaceae
Spicy, peppery flavor
Annual
Full sun
Well-drained soil

giving a choice of color including orange, yellow and scarlet. 'Whirlybird' has no spur, making it easier to clean—no place for insects to hide. It comes in seven different colors: cream, tangerine, soft salmon, bright gold, deep mahogany, bright scarlet and cherry-rose. 'Alaska' has variegated leaves, off-white against a light green background, giving it additional visual interest in the garden. 'Empress of India' has deep crimson flowers contrasting with deep blue-green foliage. 'Gleam' is an old-fashioned trailing variety, excellent for climbing up a trellis or winding its way down a hillside.

Nasturtiums have a great spicy-peppery flavor. Both the brightly colored flowers and leaves are edible—the leaves have a cresslike taste. Nasturtiums are a flavorful accompaniment to salads, vegetables, pasta, meat dishes and even sorbets.

EDIBLE FLOWERS

CULTURE

Nasturtiums prefer full sun, but in hot climates they do better in light shade. They grow happily in poor soil, as long as it is well-drained. Rich soil or fertilization results in luxuriant leaf growth but little or no flower production. Nasturtiums are easily grown from seed.

Plant the seeds outdoors in the garden two weeks before the last frost. Cover with one-half inch of soil and water well. Although it is hard to imagine at first, nasturtiums, depending on the variety, can grow into large mounds, spreading twelve to twenty-four inches, so allow enough space between each plant.

Nasturtiums are susceptible to mealybugs and especially susceptible to aphids. Examine the stems every few days. The first signs of an aphid infestation are tiny black, brown or green bugs on the stems or base of the flowers. Often a forceful spray with a water hose will dislodge (and drown) the aphids. If that does not work, spray, according to package instructions, the infested areas well with insecticidal soap. Keep spraying at four-day intervals. I do not harvest flowers until a day after I have sprayed, even though the manufacturer may say it is safe to eat the same day. Be sure to wash the flowers well after spraying. Occasionally if there are only one or two stems infested, it is easier to simply cut them off and destroy them.

CITRUS AND NASTURTIUM BEURRE BLANC

from John Ash, culinary director, Fetzer Vineyards, Hopland, California

3 tablespoons shallots or scallions, chopped

1/3 cup mushrooms, sliced

1/4 pound sweet (unsalted) butter at room temperature

2 cups flavorful fish or lobster stock

3/4 cup chardonnay

1 tablespoon fresh lemon juice

3 tablespoons frozen orange juice concentrate

outer peel of one orange, roughly chopped

1/2 cup nasturtium flowers and leaves, roughly chopped

large pinch dried calendula petals (or saffron threads)
  (optional)

3/4 cup heavy cream

sea salt and freshly ground white pepper

Sauté shallots and mushrooms in a heavy 8-cup saucepan with 1 tablespoon butter until lightly golden brown. Add stock, wine, lemon juice, orange juice concentrate, rind, nasturtiums and calendula. Reduce over a moderately high heat to approximately 1 cup. Add cream and reduce again by approximately one-half or until a light sauce consistency is achieved. Remove from heat. Add remaining butter in bits, whisking continually. Correct seasoning and strain.

Sauce will hold for an hour or more on a warm spot near the stove (not over 100°F) or in a thermos.

Use on grilled fish or poultry.

THE BIG TEN

NASTURTIUM VINEGAR

——

2 cups nasturtium flowers

4 cloves

8 peppercorns

3 cloves garlic, peeled and cut in half

1 pint malt vinegar

1 pint white vinegar

Put all ingredients except vinegars into a large bottle or small crock. In an enamel or stainless steel saucepan (do not use aluminum for vinegar), heat vinegars to a boil, then pour into the bottle. Seal and set aside to steep for several weeks.

After at least two weeks (up to 6 weeks), strain the vinegar and discard the solids. Using an enamel or stainless steel saucepan, boil the vinegar for 5 minutes. Remove from heat and allow to cool to room temperature. Pour into a clean bottle, add several whole nasturtium flowers. Seal.

For a milder flavor, use white vinegar instead of malt vinegar.

Makes 1 quart.

NASTURTIUM VINAIGRETTE

——

from Dale Englehorn, Sebastopol, California

1 cup olive oil

2 teaspoons Dijon mustard

1/2 cup Nasturtium Vinegar (see above)

1 egg yolk

salt and pepper to taste

Whisk ingredients together. Do not store any unused dressing as it contains raw egg yolk.

Makes 1-1/2 cups dressing.

LEMON-PEPPER VINAIGRETTE

——

from Kevin Ckoud, chef, Misto Caffe & Bakery, Torrance, California

15 black peppercorns

1/4 cup buttermilk

zest of one lemon

juice of one lemon

clove garlic, finely minced

1/2 cup olive oil

Toast peppercorns in a small frying pan. Allow to cool. Place peppercorns between two pieces of waxed paper and hit them with a rolling pin to crack them. Pour buttermilk into a bowl. Whisk in peppercorns, buttermilk, lemon zest, lemon juice and garlic. Gradually add olive oil, whisking continuously to emulsify.

Makes approximately 1 cup.

EDIBLE FLOWERS

SOOKE HARBOUR HOUSE RED AND GREEN NASTURTIUM OILS

from Edward Tuson and Peter Zambri, co-chefs, Sooke Harbour House, Sooke, British Columbia, Canada

Red Nasturtium Flower Oil

2 cups nasturtium flowers or petals
1 cup safflower oil
1 clove garlic, skinned (optional)

Pour all the ingredients into a blender. Blend at high speed until smooth and colorful, approximately 3 minutes.

Pour the mixture into a jar and let sit for 2 days in a cool, dark place. The petals will settle. Use the clean oil, or stir and use with the sediment.

Green Nasturtium Leaf Oil

Use 2 cups nasturtium leaves instead of the flowers or petals. Makes 1-1/4 cups oil.

EDIBLE MANDALA

adapted from Renee Shepherd, Shepherd's Seeds, Felton, California

15 to 20 nasturtium leaves and flowers
1 medium red onion, thinly sliced
3 ripe tomatoes, thinly sliced
3 stalks celery, finely chopped
1 sweet yellow pepper, coarsely chopped
2 carrots, thinly sliced
1 to 2 cups alfalfa sprouts

Arrange the nasturtium leaves around the outside of a large, flat, round plate. Place flowers on the leaves. Arrange the other vegetables in concentric circles, working toward the center of the plate, with the alfalfa sprouts at the center. Serve with Nasturtium Vinaigrette (see page 39).

Serves 4 to 6.

RADIATORE WITH NASTURTIUMS AND SNOW PEAS

8 ounces radiatore, cooked al dente and drained
1 cup snow peas (edible podded peas), lightly blanched
6 tablespoons creamy ranch dressing
3 tablespoons basil leaves, finely chopped (purple basil is especially attractive)
1/2 cup nasturtium flowers
1/3 cup nasturtium leaves
ruby leaf lettuce, coarsely chopped

Mix pasta with peas, dressing and basil leaves. Toss well. Add petals from half of the nasturtiums and nasturtium leaves and gently toss. Serve on a bed of ruby leaf lettuce, garnished with remaining flowers.

Serves 4 to 6.

THE BIG TEN

TOMATOES, MOZZARELLA AND NASTURTIUMS

——

from Anoosh Shariat, executive chef, Remington's, Louisville, Kentucky

16 large nasturtium leaves

4 medium beefsteak tomatoes, sliced

12 ounces fresh mozzarella cheese, sliced thin (12 slices)

16 nasturtium flowers

Arrange 4 nasturtium leaves on each plate. Add 4 slices of tomato and 3 slices of mozzarella cheese. Arrange in an attractive manner. Garnish with 4 nasturtium flowers (whole or broken into petals). Serve with Nasturtium Dressing .

Serves 4.

Nasturtium Dressing

2 tablespoons shallots, finely chopped

1 tablespoon Dijon mustard

1 tablespoon chives, chopped

2 tablespoons nasturtium stems, chopped

1-1/4 cup salad oil

1/4 cup white wine vinegar

salt and fresh black pepper

In a mixing bowl combine shallots, mustard, chives and chopped flower stems. Stir in vinegar. Slowly add the oil, whisking continually. Season with salt and black pepper to taste.

Makes 1-3/4 cups dressing.

NASTURTIUM FETTUCINE

——

1 pound fettucine

6 tablespoons olive oil

4 cloves garlic, crushed

20 black olives (preferably Greek style), pitted and cut in half

3/4 cup parsley, finely chopped

1/4 cup thyme blossoms, chopped

2 tablespoons chives, finely chopped

4 chive blossoms, broken into florets

24 nasturtium flowers, chopped (reserve 4 whole for garnish)

Cook pasta al dente. While pasta is cooking, heat oil and garlic in a small, heavy frying pan over a very low heat. You do not want to cook the garlic much, just warm it to release the essential oils. Drain the pasta and put it in a very large bowl. Toss with warm garlic and oil, olives, parsley, chives and chopped flowers. Garnish with whole nasturtium flowers.

Serves 4.

SALMON NASTURTIUM PIZZA

from José Gutierrez, executive chef, Chez Philippe, Peabody Hotel, Memphis, Tennessee

pizza dough for a 10- to 12-inch pie *

1 cup peas, pureed

1/8 cup olive oil

1/4 cup Parmesan cheese, grated

salt and pepper to taste

1 cup frisee or chicory—small leaves

6 slices smoked salmon

1/4 cup red onion, thinly sliced

15 nasturtium flowers

Preheat oven to 450° F. Shape pizza dough and bake for 2 to 3 minutes—do not allow it to brown. Remove from oven and allow to cool. Puree peas with olive oil and Parmesan cheese. Salt and pepper to taste. Spread on pizza dough and bake for 5 minutes. Remove from oven and arrange salmon, onion and flowers on top.

Serves 2 as appetizer or 1 for main meal.

SALMON WITH NASTURTIUM BUTTER

from Kevin Cloud, chef, Misto Caffe & Bakery, Torrance, California

1 Alaskan salmon steak

1 cup mixed greens

1/4 cup red onion, thinly sliced

1/4 cup sweet red bell pepper, thinly sliced

Nasturtium Butter

Grill salmon steak. In a bowl mix greens with onion and pepper. Toss with Lemon-Pepper Vinaigrette (see page 39). Arrange dressed salad on a plate and top with grilled salmon. Place a dollop of Nasturtium Butter on the warm salmon and serve immediately.

Serves 1.

Nasturtium Butter

1 pound sweet (unsalted) butter, softened to room temperature

1 quart nasturtium blossoms

juice of 1 lemon

In a food processor, blend butter, flower petals and lemon juice until completely mixed.

This is a very colorful, strongly flavored flower butter.

Makes 2 cups.

*You can buy ready-made focaccia and use that as a time-saver, or see pizza dough on page 75 (Anise Hyssop Mushroom Pizza).

GRILLED SALMON WITH NASTURTIUM VINAIGRETTE

―

from Jimmy Schmidt, chef/owner, The Rattlesnake Club, Detroit, Michigan

1/4 cup red wine vinegar

1/4 cup shallots, finely diced, placed in a clean linen towel and
  rinsed under cold running water, excess moisture squeezed out

3/4 cup extra virgin olive oil

salt to taste

freshly ground black pepper

3/4 cup snipped nasturtium flowers

1/4 cup snipped fresh chives

8 escalopes salmon, 3 ounces each

4 sprigs of chives or parsley for garnish

Preheat the grill or broiler. In a small bowl combine the vinegar, shallots and all but 2 tablespoons of the olive oil. Whisk until combined. Season with salt and pepper to taste. Add the nasturtiums and chives.

Rub the salmon with the remaining olive oil. Season the salmon with salt and pepper. Place on the grill, allowing to sear, about 3 minutes. Turn the escalopes over and cook until done, approximately 3 minutes, depending on thickness. Test by inserting a skewer for firmness and warmth.

Place two escalopes of salmon on each serving plate, slightly overlapping each other. Whisk the vinaigrette and spoon over the salmon. Garnish the plate with sprigs of herbs and serve.

Serves 4.

STEAK AND POTATOES, CALIFORNIA STYLE

―

from Kevin Cloud, chef, Misto Caffe & Bakery, Torrance, California

1 T-bone steak

red wine

1 potato, swirl cut with a Chinese cutter to form a single, thin
strip of potato

oil for deep frying

Nasturtium Butter (see page 42)

squash blossoms for garnish

nasturtium flowers for garnish

Marinate steak in red wine for several hours. Shape potato to form a flat circle, 1 inch larger than the steak. Heat oil in a deep skillet and deep fry potato. Drain and set aside. Grill steak to desired doneness. Place potato on a large plate, lay steak on bed of potato. Top with a dollop of Nasturtium Butter and garnish with squash blossoms and nasturtium flowers.

Serves 1.

PANSY

PANSY
Viola x Wittrockiana
Violet family
Violaceae
Vegetal flavor
Annual
Moist, rich loamy soil
Cool weather

The name pansy comes from the French *pensée* for thought or thinking of you. The flower is thought to resemble a face in deep contemplation. In Victorian times pansies codified "I think of you" in the language of flowers.

Pansies are a cheerful addition to the spring garden. Pansies are related to violets and Johnny-jump-ups, two other edible flowers. Pansies have been hybridized for over a hundred years; there are innumerable cultivars available in a wide range of colors. Commonly seen are single-colored pansies in bright hues ranging from purple, blue and deep maroon, to yellow, red, orange and white. The bicolored or tricolored pansies resemble faces and are sometimes clownlike in appearance. The flat flowers, two to five inches across, grow from six to nine inches tall.

Pansies have a slightly sweet green or grassy flavor. If you eat only the petals, the flavor is extremely mild, but if you eat the whole flower, there is a wintergreen overtone. When you eat very dark-colored pansies, your tongue turns dark—don't worry it is temporary. Use them as garnishes, in fruit salads, desserts or in soups.

CULTURE

Pansies thrive in cool weather, bringing bright color to the spring garden, fading in the heat of summer, only to rebloom in the cool of autumn. Some of the newer cultivars are heat-resistant.

Pansies prefer rich, loamy, well-drained soil that is on the moist side. Grow in full sun or in light shade. Shaded soil does not dry out nearly as quickly as soil in full sun, an added benefit when gardeners are conscious of water usage.

In cold areas, start seeds indoors ten to twelve weeks before last frost date. Transplant outdoors as soon as the soil can be worked. Pansies also can be started from seed in late summer and kept over winter in a cold frame. In areas where the temperature does not go below twenty degrees Fahrenheit, pansies can be planted in fall and lightly mulched for the winter, allowing for a very early spring bloom.

Keep picking the flowers to extend the period of bloom. Pick pansies soon after the flower opens. They keep several days in the refrigerator, but are best when freshly picked.

VEGETABLE TREE WITH CASHEW PANSY DIP

Tree:

eggplant or Styrofoam tree form for base of tree

lettuce

endive

toothpicks

cherry tomatoes

carrots, cut into 1/2-inch rounds

cauliflower, broken into florets

broccoli, broken into florets

olives

celery, cut into 1/2-inch pieces

Cut bottom off eggplant and stand upright on serving platter to create the tree form (or use a Styrofoam tree form). Attach lettuce and endive leaves with toothpicks. Using toothpicks to attach them to the tree, cover the greens with cherry tomatoes, carrots, cauliflower, broccoli, olives and celery arranged to look like a flowering tree.

If not serving immediately, mist lightly with water, cover with plastic wrap and refrigerate. Guests often remark that this is too pretty to eat, so you may have to demonstrate the edibility of this attractive centerpiece. You can create a holiday tree that looks like a snow-covered evergreen with bright red balls by using cherry tomatoes, broccoli and cauliflower.

Dip:

1 cup sweet orange juice

8 ounces cashew butter

15 to 20 pansies, petals shredded

5 whole pansies

Blend juice and cashew butter together until smooth. Gently mix in shredded pansies. Garnish with whole pansies.

Serves 12 to 16.

Hint: Increase juice to 2 cups for a flavorful salad dressing.

FENNEL SALAD WITH PANSIES AND NASTURTIUMS

1 bulb fennel

1 teaspoon balsamic vinegar

1 tablespoon orange juice

2 tablespoons extra virgin olive oil

1 tablespoon rice wine vinegar

15 pansy flowers

15 nasturtium flowers

Slice the fennel into thin pieces. In a small bowl, mix balsamic vinegar, orange juice, olive oil and rice wine vinegar. Whisk to emulsify. Toss in fennel slices. Add flowers and gently toss.

This colorful and flavorful salad is a nice accompaniment to a winter stew or soup.

Serve 4.

TRICOLOR THREE P SALAD (PASTA WITH PEPPERS AND PANSIES)

10 ounces vegetable rotini (three-colored spirals give the best
  color effect)
2 tablespoons olive oil
1 sweet red pepper, sliced in strips
1 sweet yellow pepper, sliced in strips
1 sweet bell pepper, sliced in strips
3 scallions, cut on the diagonal in 1/2-inch slices
3 or 6 pansies of different colors
salt and pepper to taste

Cook rotini al dente. Drain, put into a large bowl and toss with 1 tablespoon oil. Heat remaining olive oil in heavy frying pan. Add sliced peppers and scallions. Toss and cook for 2 to 3 minutes until vegetables are just wilted, not browned. Toss vegetables with pasta. Season to taste. Garnish with pansies before serving.

PANSY POTATO SALAD

4 medium potatoes, steamed,
  cooled and cut into chunks
2 tablespoons olive oil
2 cloves garlic, crushed
1 tablespoon balsamic vinegar
2 tablespoons parsley, finely
  chopped
2 chive flowers, broken into
  florets, chopped
15 pansies (reserve 3 whole for
  garnish), chopped
salt and freshly ground pepper
  to taste

In a large bowl, mix all ingredients together. Let stand for at least 30 minutes at room temperature for flavors to meld. Garnish with whole pansies.

Pansies come in such a range of colors, you can create different effects using different colored pansies—a rainbow of different colors, sunny yellows and oranges, cool blues, vibrant reds and purples.

Serves 4.

PANSY RAVIOLI

from Barry Marcus, St. Louis, Missouri

Dough:

1/2 cup durham flour
1/4 cup semolina flour
1 egg, beaten
1/2 teaspoon salt
1/2 tablespoon olive oil
pansies

Stuffing:

1/3 cup ricotta cheese
1 teaspoon chives, chopped
1/4 teaspoon ground pepper
3 slices white bread, crumbed
1/2 teaspoon nutmeg
15 to 20 basil leaves, chopped
1 teaspoon salt
1/2 teaspoon Tabasco

Put the flour in a bowl, making a well in the center. Add egg, salt and olive oil to the center of the well. Slowly mix in flour. Continue to mix until ingredients are thoroughly combined. Knead the dough for 5 minutes.

Wrap the dough with plastic wrap and refrigerate for several hours. Using a pasta machine, knead the dough until it is elastic. Roll the dough out to desired thickness. Gently pull the petals from the pansies. Place them on the dough, reforming the shape of the flower as best as you can. Space the flowers at least 1 inch apart. Roll the dough one more time.

Mix all ingredients together.

Lay the dough out and place 1 rounded teaspoon of the stuffing on top of each flower. Cover with another layer of dough. Cut and seal ravioli. Boil in salted water for 1 minute.

Serves 4.

EDIBLE FLOWERS

PANSIES IN PASTA WITH LANGOSTINES

from José Gutierrez, executive chef, Chez Philippe, Peabody Hotel, Memphis, Tennessee

Pasta dough:
1 pound bread flour
5 egg whites
1 teaspoon salt
1 teaspoon water
pansies

In a large bowl, mix all ingredients except pansies together well. Knead for several minutes. Wrap dough in plastic wrap. Allow to rest in the refrigerator for at least 2 hours. Roll dough out to 1/8-inch thickness. Place pansies at least 2 inches apart on half of the dough. Fold the other half of the dough over the pansies and roll again as thinly as possible. Cut pasta in squares between the pansies—at this point they will have rolled out to be quite large, up to 4 or more inches across. Cook in boiling salted water for 30 seconds as soon as the rest of the dish is ready.

Fish stock:
4 pounds fish bones
1 pound shrimp heads
4 sprigs thyme
1 large onion, chopped and braised
1 cup white wine
1 quart cold water (enough to cover above ingredients)
1 fresh tomato, chopped and seeded
2 sprigs basil

In a stock pot, combine fish bones, shrimp heads, thyme, braised onion and white wine. Add cold water just to cover. Bring slowly to a boil. Skim off scum from the boiling liquid. Add tomato and basil. Gently simmer for 20 minutes, skimming occasionally. Strain through cheesecloth with a ladle.

Langostines:
2 langostines, cut in half
2 tablespoons olive oil

Sauté langostines quickly in hot olive oil. Drain. Serve with hot fish stock in which pansy pasta has been floated.

Serves 6.

BLACK PANSY SYRUP

———

from David Feys, co-chef, Sooke Harbour House, Sooke, British Columbia, Canada

2 cups granulated sugar

1 cup water

1 cup black (or dark purple) pansy petals, loosely packed

Put pansy petals into a food processor fitted with the steel blade. Add 1/3 cup sugar. Grind pansies into sugar by pulsing 4 times, then process for about 30 seconds.

Combine sugar, pansy/sugar mixture and water in a small, nonaluminum saucepan. Over medium heat bring the mixture to a boil. Stir once and reduce the heat to low. Allow to simmer and cook to a syrup stage. (If you have a candy thermometer, do not allow the mixture to go over 220°F.) When the mixture reaches a syrup stage, remove it from the heat and pour into a heat-proof container. Allow to cool.

The rich dark color is a wonderful contrast when poured over vanilla ice cream.

Makes about 1 cup syrup.

rOSE

ROSE
Rosa spp.
Rose family
Rosaceae
Perfumed flavor
Shrub
Rich, well-drained soil
Full sun

Fossil evidence indicates that roses have existed for more than forty million years, predating man. Man has been enchanted by the rose for thousands of years. The Greek poet Sappho summed it all up more than twenty-five hundred years ago when he called roses the "Queen of Flowers." In the language of flowers, roses denote love; deep red means bashful modesty; white means "I am worthy of you"; withered white rose denotes infidelity; yellow means jealousy.

There are more than two hundred species of roses and twenty thousand hybrids that man has created. The figures are not so staggering when you consider that roses were first cultivated during the Shen Nung Dynasty in China from 2737 to 2697 B.C. The Western world did not become truly enamored of the rose until the Romans cultivated them for beauty, fragrance and their purported medicinal qualities. The Romans can

be credited with the first greenhouses using hot water pipes that kept the plants warm enough to bloom in winter.

As the Roman Empire declined, so did the rose. By the 1200s the church, which had looked unfavorably on roses as examples of Roman excesses, embraced the symbolism of the rose—white for the Immaculate Conception and red for Christ's blood. Rosary beads were traditionally made from a heated mixture of chopped rose petals, salt and water that was rolled to the desired shape and then strung together to form a complete rosary.

Roses are native to all areas of the world north of the equator. Although they grow perfectly well south of the equator, none are indigenous to the southern latitudes. Depending on the type of rose, hardiness varies from zones 3 to 8. With the myriad choices—old garden, species, rambler, climber, miniature, antique, shrub, hybrid tea, floribunda, grandiflora and miniature—roses have a place in every garden. For those without a garden, many miniatures are well suited to growing indoors under lights.

The Romans can be credited with introducing eating rose petals to Europe. This was much to the chagrin of the peasants who customarily used the rose hips. If you pick the flower, no hip will grow, as the hip is the fruit of the pollinated rose.

With all the roses to choose from, how do you pick those to eat? First, seek out *Rosa rugosa alba*—the most delicious rose, with *Rosa rugosa* coming in a strong second. Many old roses are delicious. Try the Damask rose (*Rosa damascena*) and Apothecary rose (*Rosa gallica*). When choosing hybrids remember that only fragrant roses have flavorful petals. Some, however, leave a metallic aftertaste, so sample all roses before using them in the kitchen. Among my favorite modern roses are Tiffany, Mirandy, Double Delight, Fragrant Cloud, Perfume Delight and White Lightnin. The flavors are varied, all on the sweet side, with overtones ranging from apple to cinnamon to minty.

CULTURE

Roses need full sun. They prefer moist, rich, sandy, well-drained soil. Make sure the plants get at least one inch of water per week, more in very hot weather and when they are newly planted. If at all possible, water at ground or root level using soaker hoses or a drip-irrigation system. If you must use an above-ground sprinkler, water early in the day so that the leaves have a chance to dry and do not remain wet during the night. Proper watering techniques can reduce the incidence of black spot and mildew in roses.

Plant roses in the spring. For bare-rooted roses or those in cardboard containers (first remove the cardboard container), soak the roses for at least six hours in tepid water. Dig a hole larger than the container the rose is in. Add to the soil removed from the hole: one-half cup bonemeal, one-half cup blood meal, two cups compost (or well-rotted manure), one-half cup organic fertilizer, one-half cup greensand and one-half cup rock phosphate. Mix well. Meanwhile, fill the hole with water to make sure it drains within fifteen minutes. If not, dig deeper, loosening more soil. Replace one-third to one-half of the amended soil into the hole, mounding to form a cone shape. Fan the roots out around the cone and hold the rose so that the bud union (large bump on the stem just above the roots) is at the proper level. (In areas with freezing winters, the union should be one to two inches below ground level. In warm areas, the union should be up to two inches above soil level.) Add soil, filling two-thirds of the hole. Add water to the top of the hole and allow it to soak in. Fill in the rest of the hole with soil, gently firming by hand. Mulch well with an organic mulch.

For roses purchased in containers, follow the directions as above, but do not soak the rose. After digging the hole and amending the soil, remove the rose from the container. Loosen some of the soil around the roots, especially if it seems potbound. Replace several inches of amended soil in the hole. Then place the rose, with the bud union at the correct level for your area. All container grown roses have the bud union above soil level. That makes it easier for growers to ship them anywhere in the country. Replace the rest of the amended soil, water and mulch.

Although there are many pests and diseases that can affect roses, do not be misguided into thinking that you need an array of chemical controls. I have been successfully growing roses organically for nearly twenty years. Insecticidal soap is a backbone of my regimen. I use a mixture of 1 tablespoon of baking soda dissolved in a gallon of water with three drops of Ivory liquid soap and spray on both sides of the leaves every four to seven days to control black spot. I have applied milky spore to all cultivated areas (lawns and gardens) to control Japanese beetles. When I need to, I set out Japanese beetle traps thirty feet or more away from the roses or other plants to which they are attracted.

Roses are heavy feeders. My established roses each get a "spring tonic" every year, consisting of a top dressing of three cups of compost or well-rotted organic matter (manure or leaf mold), one-half cup of rock phosphate, one-half cup of bonemeal, one-half cup of blood meal and one-half cup of greensand. This is a gallon of water to which 1 tablespoon of Epsom salts has been added. During the growing season I give the plants a liquid foliar (leaf) feeding every two to four weeks until August (follow the package instructions for proper dilution).

In cold areas, roses need winter protection. Once the weather is steadily cold (in the forties), mound up eight or more inches of soil around the base of the rose. Once it gets cold enough for that to freeze, cover the mound with several inches of mulch. Once the weather begins to warm in the spring, remove the mulch and begin to feed and prune your plants.

All roses benefit from pruning. Heavy pruning is done in the spring. Pruning is to be avoided in the fall. Always cut at a forty-five–degree angle toward an outward facing bud. Cut flowers down to the lowest five or seven leaflet group, again toward an outward facing leaflet. This encourages new growth outward, away from the plant, allowing for optimal air circulation. Most modern roses (climbers and tree roses are an exception) benefit from a severe pruning (down to twelve to eighteen inches) in the spring just as growth begins. Believe me, pruning is much more traumatic to you than to the plant.

It is most important that you choose the right rose for your area. Learn about the particular rose that interests you before you buy it. It may not be suited for your locale. If black spot or mildew is a problem where you live, look for varieties that are resistant to those diseases. See what your friends and neighbors are growing successfully. Visit a local botanic garden or arboretum. You are likely to get more honest advice than at a nursery or garden center.

WARNING

Notice that when you remove the petals from the flower, the base of the petal is whitish. Remove that part as it is bitter.

As tempting as it may be, never accept a rose (for culinary purposes) from another garden unless you are 100 percent sure it has been grown organically.

Even with organic controls, I like to wait several days after application before harvesting roses. Wash them well before using.

WILD ROSE PETAL, ROSE HIP AND LAVENDER VINEGAR

from Peter Zambri, co-chef, Sooke Harbour House, Sooke, British Columbia, Canada

1/2 cup wild rose petals, tightly packed
1/2 cup rose hips
5 flowering sprigs lavender
1-1/2 cups white wine vinegar (or rice vinegar)

Place the rose petals, rose hips and lavender sprigs in a 1-pint jar. Warm the vinegar over low heat, being careful not to bring it to a boil. Pour the warm vinegar over the flowers and hips. This should cover all the contents. Seal the lid. Let sit for 24 hours, unrefrigerated. Once the jar is opened, keep it refrigerated.

Makes 1-3/4 cups.

ROSE PETAL FUSION CRISPS

from Charmaine Eads, chef, Manor Farm Inn, Poulsbo, Washington

rice paper, 7-inch round sheets *
bowl of cold water
sesame oil
canola oil
rose petals, coarsely chopped
black sesame seeds
white roasted sesame seeds
cilantro leaves

Preheat oven to 350°F. Dip one sheet of rice paper in water for 15 seconds. Remove from water and drain excess water against side of bowl. Place rice paper on a wooden cutting board. Add several drops of sesame seed oil to 1/2 cup canola oil in a small bowl. Lightly brush the rice paper with the oil mixture. Sprinkle on rose petals, black and white sesame seeds and cilantro leaves. Dip another sheet of rice paper in water, brush one side with oil, and place oiled side face down on top of other rice sheet. Gently press the rice paper down onto the bottom sheet.

Preheat a sauté pan. Brush pan lightly with canola oil. Place the rice paper into the pan and sauté over medium heat for 2 minutes on each side. Do not allow to brown. Remove from pan, and, with a scissors, cut the fusion cracker into 8 equal pie-shaped wedges. Place wedges on a cookie sheet in the oven for 5 minutes. Remove from oven and pat off any excess oil with a paper towel or cloth. Place crisps on a cooling rack and allow to cool completely. Store in an airtight container in a cool, dry place for up to 5 days.

CARROT SLAW WITH ROSE PETALS

4 large carrots, grated
1 small zucchini, grated (optional)
1/2 cup raisins
1/4 cup mayonnaise
1 teaspoon celery seed
1 tablespoon balsamic vinegar or other herbed vinegar
rose petals
lettuce

Mix all ingredients except rose petals together. For best flavor, refrigerate for at least several hours before serving. Serve on a bed of rose petals atop a bed of dark green or red leaf lettuce. Cream-colored roses look especially elegant. Spoon a small amount of slaw onto a rose petal, pop into your mouth and enjoy.

Serves 4.

* Available in Oriental markets, sometimes sold as rice sheets.

SPINACH SALAD WITH ROSE VINAIGRETTE

———

from Anoosh Shariat, executive chef, Remington's, Louisville, Kentucky

4 slices white bread, crust removed and cut into 1/2-inch pieces

1 tablespoon melted butter

2 teaspoons cinnamon

1-1/2 pounds fresh baby spinach, cleaned and trimmed

1/2 cup roasted walnuts

1/2 cup rose petals

Dressing:

1 egg white, at room temperature

1/3 cup shallots, chopped

1 tablespoon honey

1 tablespoon rose water

1/4 cup walnut oil

3/4 cup salad oil

1/4 cup red wine vinegar

Preheat oven to 350°F. Brush bread cubes with butter and dust with cinnamon. Bake on a cookie sheet until golden brown. Remove from oven and let cool.

Divide spinach among 4 plates. Sprinkle with walnuts, rose petals and croutons. Pour dressing over salad.

Beat egg white to a soft peak in a small, deep mixing bowl. Add shallots, honey and rose water, mixing well. Start adding walnut oil slowly, then add salad oil slowly, mixing continuously. Slowly add vinegar to mixture, making sure mixture is not too thick. If it is, add a bit more vinegar until desired consistency is reached. Store at room temperature.

Serves 4.

———

ROSE PETAL SAUCE

———

from John Ash, culinary director, Fetzer Vineyards, Hopland, California

1/3 cup rose petals (preferably from deep red miniature varieties *)

1/2 teaspoon lemon juice

1/4 cup white wine vinegar

1/4 cup light corn syrup

1/2 cup granulated sugar

1/2 cup water

6 to 10 drops rose water (optional)

Combine first six ingredients and bring to a boil in a saucepan. Cool, add optional rose water and store in refrigerator for at least a week to develop color. Sauce may be used cold or hot drizzled on fresh fruit or ice cream.

Makes about 1 cup sauce.

* If using larger petaled varieties, gently cut petals in half or thirds.

JULIENNED VEGETABLES WITH GINGER ROSE VINAIGRETTE

———

from Charmaine Eads, chef, Manor Farm Inn, Poulsbo, Washington

yellow summer squash, finely julienned
zucchini, finely julienned
carrots, finely julienned
green cabbage, finely julienned
red cabbage, finely julienned
red bell pepper, finely julienned
yellow bell pepper, finely julienned
sugar snap pea pods
rose petals
1 red onion, thinly sliced and marinated 1 hour in seasoned rice vinega

Mix all julienned vegetables together. Toss with rose petals. Pour on Ginger Rose Vinaigrette (see below) and mix well. Garnish with red onion.

A wonderfully colorful and tasty presentation.

GINGER ROSE VINAIGRETTE

———

from Charmaine Eads, chef, Manor Farm Inn, Poulsbo, Washington

2 tablespoons sesame oil
1 cup peanut oil
1 tablespoon apple cider vinegar
1 tablespoon seasoned rice vinegar
1 tablespoon freshly squeezed lemon juice
2 teaspoons chili paste
1 tablespoon ginger, finely grated
2 egg yolks
2 tablespoons granulated sugar
1/3 cup rose petals
2 tablespoons black sesame seeds
2 tablespoons white sesame seeds, toasted

Whisk together all ingredients to emulsify. Adjust seasoning with salt and pepper to taste.

Makes 2 cups vinaigrette.

EDIBLE FLOWERS

CATFISH WITH ROSE VINEGAR

from José Gutierrez, executive chef, Chez Philippe, Peabody Hotel, Memphis, Tennessee

1 tablespoon olive oil

4 catfish fillets

3 cups rose vinegar

1 cup rose petals

1 cup frisee or curly endive

1 cup mâche

30 chives, 3 to 5 inches long

1 tablespoon heavy cream

4 tablespoons softened butter

salt and pepper

In a large skillet, heat olive oil. Sauté catfish in hot oil over a medium-high heat for 3 minutes on each side. Remove catfish from skillet, and keep warm. Add vinegar to skillet, and reduce to one-fourth of original volume.

While vinegar is reducing, prepare the plates. On each of 4 plates, make a bed of rose petals with frisee, mâche and chives. When vinegar has reduced, add cream. Remove skillet from heat, and add butter in small bits, whisking continuously. Season with salt and pepper to taste.

Place one catfish fillet on each prepared plate. Pour sauce over fillet and serve immediately.

You also can serve the catfish directly on a plain plate without all the fuss of the presentation. For a special occasion, the presentation is worth the effort. The long thin chive can be arranged to resemble the whiskers of the catfish.

Serves 4.

ROSE CHICKEN

1 frying chicken, cut into 8 pieces

1/4 cup rose water

1/2 cup all-purpose flour

1/2 cup graham crackers, finely crushed

3 tablespoons rose petals, finely chopped (dark-colored varieties preferable)

1/8 teaspoon salt

Place chicken in a nonmetallic dish and add rose water. Turn to coat. Cover and marinate in the refrigerator for up to 4 hours.

Preheat oven to 375°F. Mix flour, graham cracker meal, rose petals and salt together in a medium-sized bowl. Roll each piece of chicken in the flour mixture then place in a lightly greased, shallow baking pan. Bake the chicken for 35 minutes, or until done.

The slight sweetness of the coating complements the succulent chicken. Delicious hot or cold.

Serves 4.

PEAR SHERBET WITH RED CURRANT SHERBET

from Charmaine Eads, chef, Manor Farm Inn, Poulsbo, Washington

Pear sherbet:

water

3 cups granulated sugar, divided

1/3 cup pear liqueur

5 to 6 pears (Bosc or D'Anjou preferred)

1 teaspoon cinnamon

1/4 teaspoon nutmeg

1/2 cup dark-colored rose petals

Add 1 cup water and 2 cups sugar into a heavy saucepan. Bring to a boil over medium heat. Do not stir. Boil for 15 minutes. Remove from heat and allow to cool. Add pear liqueur.

Peel pears and place in a deep saucepan with enough water to cover. Add 1 cup sugar, cinnamon and nutmeg. Bring to a simmer over medium heat. Poach until pears are fork tender. Remove from heat, and remove pears from poaching liquid. Allow pears to cool.

Cut pear away from the core, discarding core. Puree pears until completely smooth. Add puree and rose petals to cooled syrup. Pour into an ice cream maker and freeze according to manufacturer's instructions. When sherbet is soft set, put in freezer.

Red currant sherbet:

water

3 cups granulated sugar, divided

1/3 cup Cassis

1-1/2 cups red currants

Add 1 cup water and 2 cups sugar into a heavy saucepan. Bring to a boil over medium heat. Do not stir. Boil for 15 minutes. Remove from heat and allow to cool. Add Cassis.

Puree currants until completely smooth. Add puree to cooled syrup. Pour into an ice cream maker and freeze according to manufacturer's instructions. When sherbet is soft set, put in freezer.

To serve, place one scoop of red currant sherbet in a dessert glass. Top with a scoop of pear sherbet. Garnish with coarsely chopped rose petals.

The sweet pear sherbet is a contrast to the tart red currant sherbet, so alternate tastes of each when eating this colorful dessert.

Serves 8.

AGE

SAGE
Salvia officinalis
Mint family
Lamiaceae (Labiatae)
Herbal flavor
Perennial
Sandy, well-drained soil
Full sun to light shade

The name is derived from the Latin *salvare*, meaning to save. For centuries sage was reputed to have great curative and healing properties. The old Latin proverb *Cur moriatur homo, ciu calvia crescit in horto?* (Why should a man die while sage grows in his garden?) pays homage to the high esteem in which sage has been held.

Sage is native to the northern Mediterranean area. It was grown in the monastery gardens in France and Switzerland and found its way to England by the fourteenth century. Sage was used for flavoring pork and other meats and fish.

Sage is an attractive perennial herb, hardy to zone 3. The stems can become woody and gnarled as the plant gets older. It grows from two to three feet tall. The gray-green leaves are oblong in shape with a pebbled texture.

Include sage in a perennial border. Keep it in mind for drought-tolerant landscapes. 'Aurea', a compact vari-ety with variegated yellow leaves, is attractive in the garden but rarely flowers. The same is true for 'Tricolor' whose lower leaves have white margins and upper leaves are tinged purple with pink margins. Unfortu-nately it is not very winter hardy. Gentian sage, *Salvia greigii*, has large (one inch), vibrant blue flowers in mid- to late summer, with an even milder flavor than culinary sage. The flowers appear in whorls with lipped corollas from late spring through early summer, bearing blue-violet flowers. The flavor of the flowers is a subtler version of the leaf flavor.

CULTURE

Sage grows best in full sun or light shade. It prefers light, sandy, well-drained soil that is evenly moist in summer but dry in winter. Start sage seed in spring or fall, transplanting into the garden when the seedlings are two to three inches tall. Set plants out early in the spring, spacing twelve to eighteen inches apart.

Lightly fertilize with organic fertilizer in early spring. Prune existing plants back by at least one-third to keep the plants bushy. Also prune back any dead wood at that time. Throw small pieces of pruned sage wood on the barbecue for an unique smoked flavor for fish, pork or poultry.

Propagate by dividing the plant in the spring, or by layering stems in the fall.

In cold climates, lightly mulch sage in the fall with several inches of shredded leaves.

SAGE BROCHETTE

___

from Ron Ottobre, chef, Mudd's Restaurant, San Ramon, California

1/2 cup cornmeal

2 cups all-purpose flour

3 tablespoons corn starch

1-1/2 tablespoons baking powder

1-1/2 tablespoons granulated sugar

1-1/2 teaspoons salt

1-1/2 cup water

1/2 cup milk

2 eggs

2 tablespoons peanut oil

24 4-inch lengths of sage (stems complete with blossoms and leaves)

oil for frying

Mix dry ingredients (except sage) together. In a separate bowl mix liquid ingredients. Gradually whisk the two together. Dip sage blossoms into the batter. Fry in hot oil 2 to 3 minutes, turning once. Drain. Serve on a bed of lettuce and garnish with a sage blossom.

The flavor is a lightly perfumed delight. Even kids will like this one. A perfect finger food—hold the stem and nibble off the flowers and leaves. Make 2-inch lengths for hors d'oeuvres. Leftovers can be reheated in the oven.

Serves 4 to 6.

SAGE PESTO

___

2 cups sage flowers

1/4 cup walnuts, roasted

1/2 cup walnut oil

1 clove garlic, peeled

4 scallions, white sections only, coarsely chopped

Add all the ingredients into a food processor and process until a smooth puree is reached. An interesting variation on the classical basil pesto for pasta. Try it as an accompaniment to roast pork or veal.

WHITE BEAN SOUP WITH SAGE

1 tablespoon olive oil

1 large onion, chopped

3 cloves garlic, minced

2 carrots, shredded

2 (1-pound) cans of white beans (great northern beans)

8 cups chicken stock

1 medium tomato, diced

1/4 cup sage flowers, chopped

salt

freshly ground black pepper

Heat oil in a large saucepan. Add onion, garlic and carrot. Sauté until onion becomes translucent and soft. Add beans, including liquid from can, and chicken stock. Stir well. Add tomato and sage flowers. Cook over a low heat until mixture comes to a boil. Simmer for 5 minutes, stirring occasionally. Season to taste with salt and pepper.

Serves 4.

ORANGE, FENNEL AND SAGE SALAD

2 heads of fennel, cored and sliced
into thin "C" shapes

1 Bermuda onion, julienned

2 navel oranges, peeled, cut in half lengthwise and cut into
semicircles

1/2 cup sage flowers

1/2 cup olive oil

1/4 cup chive or savory vinegar

leaves of Boston lettuce

Mix all the ingredients except the lettuce together in a large bowl. Adjust seasoning with salt and freshly ground pepper. Cover and let stand at room temperature for 90 minutes to allow flavors to meld. Serve on lettuce leaves.

A colorful and tasty luncheon salad.

Serves 4.

THE BIG TEN

HEARTY BEAN AND CORN STEW

1/4 cup olive oil

1 tablespoon cumin

1 tablespoon curry powder

2 sweet red peppers, chopped

6 carrots, finely grated

4 stalks celery, chopped

1 sweet Bermuda onion, finely chopped

6 tomatoes, chopped

8 cups stock (vegetable or chicken)

1 cup dried beans

2 cups corn, freshly cut off the cob

2 cups cooked chicken (optional)

1/2 cup parsley, chopped

1/2 cup sage flowers, coarsely chopped

1/4 cup basil flowers, coarsely chopped

1 cup rice

plain yogurt or sour cream for garnish

In a heavy soup pot, heat oil with spices. Add vegetables and sauté lightly. Add stock, beans, 1 cup corn, optional chicken, parsley and flowers (reserve a small amount for garnish) and bring to a boil. Reduce heat, cover and simmer gently for 2 hours. Add rice, cover and simmer for an additional hour. Adjust seasoning to taste with salt and pepper if necessary.

If stew is too thick for your taste, add additional stock or water; if it is too thin, cook it longer. Immediately before serving, add reserved cup of corn. Serve garnished with a dollop of yogurt or sour cream and a sprig of flowers.

Serves 8.

SAGE MUSHROOMS

2 tablespoons olive oil

1 teaspoon butter

2 large Portobello mushrooms, cut in slices

1/4 cup sage flowers

1/2 cup white wine

Heat butter and oil in a frying pan over a medium heat. When butter has melted and starts to sizzle, add cut mushrooms. Sauté until mushrooms become soft. Add

sage flowers, reserving some for garnish. Pour in wine and cook for several minutes. Serve garnished with reserved flowers.

The richness of the mushrooms is tempered by the sage. A delicious side dish that could be the entree in a vegetarian dinner.

Serves 4.

SAGE CRUSTED LEMON SOLE

―――

1 cup sage flowers, finely chopped

12 small mushrooms, finely chopped

3/4 cup parsley, finely chopped

1 tablespoon lemon zest, finely chopped

1/3 cup bread crumbs, processed to a fine consistency

1 egg

6 tablespoons sweet (unsalted) butter, softened to room temperature

salt

freshly ground black pepper

2 tablespoons olive oil

4 lemon sole fillets

Mix the flowers, mushrooms, parsley, lemon zest, crumbs, egg, butter, salt and pepper in a nonmetallic bowl. Preheat the broiler.

In a heavy, cast-iron (or all metal—no plastic handles) frying pan, heat the oil until hot (not smoking). Add the fillets and cook them about 2 minutes on each side, just until lightly browned. Season with salt and pepper, if desired. Spoon the crust mixture onto the fish. Smooth to evenly cover each fillet. Place the frying pan about 12 inches under the broiler and cook until the crust is crisp and lightly browned. Be careful not to burn it.

Serves 4.

SIGNET MARIGOLD

Marigolds are annuals, native from New Mexico to Argentina. Signet marigolds are related to the popular African and French marigold (which, contrary to their names, are from Central and South America). In the Victorian language of flowers, marigolds signify jealousy.

Marigolds have finely dissected, strongly scented leaves. The signet marigolds grow to form compact, ten- to twelve-inch rounded mounds. Even before the flowers open the foliage is an attractive green that looks almost like a fern. The scent of the foliage is much better than that of other marigolds; when bruised it has a lemon scent.

The signet marigolds bear diminutive, single flowers no more than one-half to one inch in diameter. 'Lemon Gem' has dainty, one-half–inch lemon-yellow flowers; 'Tangerine Gem' has vibrant one-half–inch orange blooms.

The flavor of the signets is the best of any marigolds, almost like a spicy tarragon. Remove the white part from the end of the petal where it was attached to the flower as it is very bitter.

I have tasted other marigolds over the years, and the flavor of some is actually repugnant. If you absolutely must eat a large, double marigold, I suggest trying one of the Inca series—either yellow or orange. The flavor is tangy to bitter, also with a tarragon overtone.

Marigold petals can be dried for use in the winter. Follow the same instructions as for calendula.

SIGNET
MARIGOLD
(Dwarf marigold)
Tagetes signata
(T. tenuifolia)
Composite family
Asteraceae
(Compositae)
Spicy, herbal flavor
Annual
Moist, well-drained soil
Full sun

CULTURE

Marigolds prefer full sun and moist, well-drained, moderately fertile soil.

Marigolds are easily grown from seed. Start the seed indoors six weeks before the last frost date, or direct seed them into the garden after danger of frost is past. Allow six to eight inches between plants.

Marigolds are somewhat tolerant to drought, but they do need occasional water, especially when the plants are young. Keep picking the flowers and they will bloom all through the summer and up until frost.

WARNING

Marigolds may be harmful in large amounts. Eat them occasionally and in moderation.

EDIBLE FLOWERS

MARIGOLD BUTTER

petals from 20 single marigolds
1/2 pound butter, softened to room temperature

Finely chop the petals. Mix them into the softened butter. Let sit at cool room temperature several hours. Roll into a log shape using waxed paper. Refrigerate overnight. Keeps refrigerated up to 2 weeks, frozen up to 6 months. Cut slices to garnish any grilled fish dish.

DEVILED EGGS

12 eggs
water
ice
3 tablespoons mayonnaise
1 teaspoon Dijon mustard
1/2 teaspoon mustard powder
1 teaspoon curry powder
1 tablespoon marigold petals, finely chopped
1 tablespoon dill weed, finely chopped

Place eggs in a medium saucepan. Fill with cold water to 1 inch over top of eggs. Bring water to a boil. Cover pan, lower heat and gently simmer for 20 minutes.

Plunge eggs into a large bowl filled with ice water. Crack each egg once with a wooden spoon. Leave in ice water for 15 minutes.

Shell the eggs; cut each in half lengthwise. Place the yolks in a bowl and the whites on a serving platter. Mash the yolks until smooth. Add remaining ingredients and blend well. Pipe or spoon the yolk mixture into the hollow of the whites. Garnish with additional marigold petals.

Serves 8 to 12. Allow at least 2 halves per person for hors d'oeuvres.

GREEN AND GOLD—BROCCOLI AND MARIGOLDS

1 large bunch broccoli, cut into 2-inch pieces (use florets and peeled stems)
2 tablespoons butter
juice of 1 large lemon
1 clove garlic, very finely chopped or put through a garlic press
1/4 cup marigold petals

Steam broccoli until just tender, retaining its bright green color. While broccoli is cooking, mix other ingredients in a small saucepan over a low heat. Stir frequently until butter is melted. Drain broccoli and place in serving dish. Pour on the sauce, tossing the broccoli gently to coat it with the petals. Serve immediately, or refrigerate and serve cold the next day.

Serves 4 to 6.

MORNING SUNSHINE MUFFINS

———

1-3/4 cups all-purpose flour
2 teaspoons double-acting baking powder
1/2 teaspoon salt
1/4 cup granulated sugar
2 eggs
2 tablespoons melted butter
3/4 cup milk
3/4 cup chopped dates
2 tablespoons marigold petals, chopped

Preheat oven to 425°F. Sift together flour, baking powder, salt and sugar. In a separate bowl beat eggs. Mix in butter, milk, dates and marigold petals. Add wet ingredients to dry, mixing just enough to evenly moisten. Spoon mixture into greased muffin tins, filling halfway. Bake for 15 to 20 minutes, or until tops are lightly browned. Delicious served with marigold butter.

Makes 12 muffins.

POTATO MARIGOLD SALAD

———

2 pounds small new red potatoes
6 tablespoons olive oil
3 tablespoons savory flower vinegar
6 chive flowers, broken into florets
petals from 10 marigolds
salt and pepper to taste

Steam the potatoes until tender. Whisk together olive oil, vinegar, chive florets, salt and pepper. Cut the potatoes into chunks. In a bowl, toss the potatoes with the dressing. Garnish with the marigold petals. Serve warm. A nice contrast of spicy chives, bland potatoes and slightly bitter marigolds.

Serves 4.

EDIBLE FLOWERS

SUMMER QUICHE

2 eggs

1/2 cup mayonnaise

1 tablespoon all-purpose flour

1 cup milk

1/2 teaspoon salt

1 cup Swiss cheese, finely grated

1/2 cup tomato, finely chopped

1 cup fresh corn kernels

2 tablespoons marigold petals, finely chopped

1 unbaked 10-inch piecrust (or 3 6-inch piecrusts)

Preheat oven to 375°F. Place a cookie sheet on a rack in the middle of the oven. Beat eggs in a medium-sized bowl. Mix in mayonnaise and flour. Add milk and salt.

Arrange the cheese, tomato, corn and marigold petals evenly in the pie shell. Pour in egg mixture. Place the quiche on the preheated cookie sheet in oven. Bake 30 minutes for 6-inch quiche, 45 minutes for 10-inch quiche, or until firmly set.

Serves 4 to 6.

PRIMARY PASTA

1 tablespoon extra virgin olive oil

8 ounces crimini mushrooms, sliced

1 sweet red pepper, seeded and coarsely chopped

1/4 cup cream

1/4 cup Parmesan cheese

1 pound fresh fettucine, cooked al dente and drained

2 tablespoons marigold petals, coarsely chopped

2 tablespoons borage flowers

In a large skillet, heat olive oil over a medium flame. Add mushrooms and sauté until they become soft. Add pepper and cook for 1 minute. Add cream and Parmesan cheese, stir well to mix. Slowly add pasta into the skillet, tossing with each addition to mix pasta and mushroom combination. Add marigold petals and borage flowers and serve immediately.

The primary colors in this dish—red, yellow and blue—make it especially attractive to children.

Seves 4.

ƒQUASH BLOSSOMS

Native Americans grew summer and winter squash long before the Spanish brought other varieties to America. Indians used the male blossoms in a number of ways from side dishes to desserts. The flowers of numerous varieties of both summer and winter squash can be eaten, yet the most commonly consumed is the zucchini flower.

All squash are tender annuals. In general, they are vining plants and can grow to prodigious lengths, meandering through the garden. Newer bush-type varieties of some squash have been introduced, but even they take up at least three feet square, if not more. Varieties that produce smallish fruit can be trained on a trellis. Be sure that the squash, once formed, are supported.

In general squash leaves are large and attractive. The vining types are excellent to grow on a sunny hillside. There they can run as much as they want, while providing needed erosion control and ground cover. The bush varieties are handsome in a perennial border or in a large container.

The flowers vary in size, but can get up to four inches across when fully opened. Most flowers are one to three inches deep—perfect for stuffing. Squash flowers are most often a vibrant yellow, but may be pale yellow or yellow-orange.

Some cooks prefer to use male blossoms, others female. It is easy to tell the difference. Male flowers are on long, slender stems. Female flowers are short-stemmed. Look closely and you can see the miniature squash behind the female flower. If the female is not polli-

SQUASH BLOSSOMS
Curcubita pepo spp.
Gourd family
Curcubitaceae
Vegetal flavor
Annual
Enriched soil
Full sun

nated, the flower and the little squash turn brown and fall off.

Using female flowers is one of the best ways to practice squash birth control. If you have grown zucchini, you know how the cute little four-inch squash can turn, seemingly overnight, into a baseball bat, in size and texture. You do need the males to pollinate the females. It can be attractive to have both the squash and the flower in a recipe.

The flavor of squash blossoms is best described as mildly vegetal.

CULTURE

Squash grow best in full sun. Summer squash grow so quickly it is easiest to direct seed them into the garden once all danger of frost is past. Squash that need a long growing season should be started indoors in the coldest areas.

To meet squash's heavy nutrient needs, dig a hole about a foot deep and fill it with well-rotted manure or compost. Form a hill with the soil from the hole. Plant two or three seeds in the hole. Water well throughout the growing season.

Black plastic mulch helps to warm the soil early in the season and keep out weeds. Do not use black plastic in warm climates. In warm areas, it pays to mulch, but choose an organic material such as grass clippings, hay, pine needles or cocoa hulls.

Squash are susceptible to vine borer, squash beetle and squash bug. To prevent infestation, cover the squash as soon as they germinate with spun polyester material such as Agronet or Reemay. Remove the material once the plants begin to flower or they will not get pollinated.

Mildew can be a problem, usually later in the season. At that point, it is best to simply rip the plant out, especially if it has already produced squash.

When buying seeds or plants, I look for modern hybrid varieties that are labeled as disease-resistant. I have also found that some of the heirloom varieties, by virtue of the fact that they have been around for so long, perform well, are disease-resistant and are more flavorful than the newer hybrids.

SQUASH BLOSSOMS, ITALIAN STYLE

from Teresa Costa, Main Street Fruit and Vegetable, Huntington, New York

12 to 16 squash blossoms with 1-1/2 inches of stem
2 tablespoons olive oil
2 cloves garlic, coarsely chopped
1 teaspoon oregano
salt and pepper to taste

Peel stems off squash blossoms. Heat oil in a large, heavy frying pan over a medium heat. Sauté garlic, stirring until it is lightly browned. Add squash blossoms, oregano, salt and pepper. Cook slowly, stirring frequently, about 5 to 6 minutes, or until stem is soft. Serve immediately. Serves 4 as a side dish.

SOUTHWESTERN-STYLE FRIED SQUASH FLOWERS

1/2 cup unbleached flour
1 cup milk
1/8 teaspoon salt
1/2 teaspoon chili powder
20 squash flowers
oil for frying

In a bowl, combine flour, milk, salt and chili powder to make a batter. Dip flowers in batter and drop into hot oil. Turn once and fry until golden. Drain and eat immediately.

SOUTHERN-STYLE SQUASH BLOSSOMS

Corn bread:

1 cup unbleached flour

1/4 cup whole wheat flour

3/4 cup yellow cornmeal

1/4 cup granulated sugar

2 teaspoons baking powder

1/2 teaspoon salt

1 cup milk

1/4 cup vegetable oil

1 egg, beaten

1 tablespoon hot red pepper sauce

1-1/2 to 2 cups corn kernels (freshly cut off 2 ears of corn)

1/2 cup Vidalia or Walla Walla onions, coarsely chopped

Preheat oven to 400° F. Butter an 8- or 9-inch baking pan (round or square). In a large bowl, mix dry ingredients together. In a separate bowl, beat wet ingredients together. Add mixed wet ingredients to dry, stirring until just blended. Pour mixture into greased pan. Let sit 5 minutes at room temperature. Bake for 20 to 25 until top is golden brown and a toothpick inserted in the middle comes out clean. Remove from oven and set on a rack to cool.

Stuffed squash:

2 cups corn bread, crumbled

20 squash blossoms

2 tablespoons olive oil

Stuff squash blossoms with crumbled corn bread. Add olive oil to a large skillet over a medium heat. Sauté squash blossoms, turning to brown all sides slightly. Serve immediately.

Serves 4 to 6 as an appetizer course or side dish.

SQUASH BLOSSOMS STUFFED WITH GOAT CHEESE

from Kevin Cloud, chef, Misto Caffe & Bakery, Torrance, California

1 cup goat cheese

1/4 cup sun-dried tomatoes, coarsely chopped

6 garlic cloves, roasted

1 tablespoon cream

1 teaspoon chive florets, coarsely chopped

1 teaspoon basil, coarsely chopped

1 teaspoon oregano, coarsely chopped

8 to 12 squash blossoms

1 egg yolk, beaten

1 cup fresh bread crumbs

oil for deep frying

Using the plastic blade in a food processor, mix the goat cheese, sun-dried tomatoes, garlic, cream, chive florets, basil and oregano. Pipe mixture into squash blossoms and close end of flower. Dip stuffed flowers into egg yolk and roll in bread crumbs. Deep fry until they turn light brown. Remove from oil and drain. Serve immediately.

Serves 4 to 8, depending on whether they are served as hors d'oeuvres, an appetizer or as an edible garnish.

SQUASH BLOSSOMS WITH PEPPER AND CORN

---

from Jimmy Schmidt, chef/owner, The Rattlesnake Club, Detroit, Michigan

2 tablespoons virgin olive oil

1/2 cup fresh corn kernels

3 cloves garlic, roasted and minced

1 small sweet red pepper, roasted, peeled, seeded and diced

1 small poblano chile, roasted, peeled, seeded and diced

1/2 cup white wine

salt

freshly ground pepper

1/4 cup fresh basil, chopped

20 squash blossoms, each about 3 inches long

corn or canola oil for frying

2 cups tempura batter

hot pepper sauce

1 cup Roast Pepper Vinaigrette

sprigs of fresh herbs

Tempura batter:

1 large egg yolk

2 cups ice cold water

1/4 teaspoon baking soda

1-2/3 cup all-purpose flour, sifted

Combine egg yolk with water and baking soda in a medium-sized bowl. Slowly whisk in flour. Batter should be thick enough to just coat the blossoms.

Roast Pepper Vinaigrette

1 sweet red pepper, roasted, peeled and seeded

1/4 cup balsamic vinegar

salt

1 cup virgin olive oil

freshly ground black pepper

Combine red pepper, balsamic vinegar and salt in blender. Puree until smooth. Gradually add olive oil, processing until smooth and emulsified. Season to taste with salt and pepper.

Heat olive oil in a medium skillet over high heat. Add corn and cook until tender, about 3 minutes. Add garlic, red pepper, poblano chile and white wine. Cook until wine is almost completely evaporated, about 5 minutes. Season to taste with salt and pepper. Stir in basil.

Working with one squash blossom at a time, carefully peel back one petal for filling. Stuff 1 generous tablespoon of pepper mixture into blossom, then fold petal back over stuffing. Refrigerate until ready to cook. Fill large, heavy, deep skillet with corn oil to a depth of 3 inches. Heat over medium-high heat to 350°F.

Dip stuffed blossoms into Tempura Batter, then remove to a rack set over a baking sheet, allowing excess batter to drip off. Lower blossoms into hot oil and fry until golden, about 4 minutes. Drain on absorbent paper. (Blossoms may be sautéed instead of fried.)

Arrange blossoms in the center of serving plates and spoon over Roast Pepper Vinaigrette. Garnish with herbs and serve immediately.

Serves 4 to 5.

THE BIG TEN

STUFFED SQUASH FLOWERS—TWO WAYS

———

from Rita Cohen and Jerry Rippa, Long Island, New York

Stuffing 1:

1 tablespoon olive oil

1/2 cup eggplant, cut in short strips

1/2 cup mozzarella cheese, cut in short strips

4 anchovies, cut in short strips (optional)

squash flowers, stems and stamens removed

Heat olive oil in skillet. Add eggplant strips and sauté until eggplant is tender. Drain excess oil and set aside.

In a bowl, mix together mozzarella cheese strips, sautéed eggplant and anchovies. Stuff mixture into squash flowers. Dip flowers into batter and fry in hot vegetable oil until golden on both sides. Drain and serve hot.

Stuffing 2:

1/2 cup mozzarella cheese, cut in short strips

6 sun-dried tomatoes, drained and cut in short strips

1 tablespoon capers

squash flowers, stems and stamens removed

vegetable oil for frying

In a bowl, mix together mozzarella cheese strips, sun-dried tomatoes and capers. Stuff mixture into squash flowers. Dip flowers into batter and fry in hot vegetable oil until golden on both sides. Drain and serve hot.

Batter (enough for approximately 8 to 10 flowers):

1 cup all-purpose flour

1 teaspoon baking powder

2 eggs

salt and pepper to taste

beer

Mix dry ingredients together in a bowl. Beat eggs in a separate bowl. Add dry mixture to eggs. Stir and add enough beer to make the mixture the consistency of pancake batter.

EDIBLE FLOWERS

MAMA TERESA'S SQUASH FRITTERS

from Teresa Costa, Main Street Fruit and Vegetable, Huntington, New York

2 large eggs
1/2 cup Italian parsley, chopped
1/4 cup Romano cheese, grated
1/4 cup Parmesan cheese, grated
salt and pepper to taste
15 squash blossoms, coarsely chopped
oil for deep frying

In a large bowl, mix eggs, parsley, cheeses, salt and pepper. Beat well. Add squash blossoms. Heat oil in a deep frying pan. Drop fritters into oil by well rounded tablespoons. Deep fry until golden brown, turning once. Drain and serve.

Serves 4 for lunch or a side dish.

ZUCCHINI PASTA

from Bonnie Blair Hegeman, Brookville, New York

3 tablespoons butter, divided
1 tablespoon olive oil
1 medium onion, coarsely chopped
2 cups zucchini, sliced
1 cup zucchini petals
1 pound pasta, cooked al dente
1/2 cup freshly grated Parmesan cheese
salt and pepper to taste

In a medium frying pan, melt 1 tablespoon butter in the oil over a medium heat. Add onion and zucchini, sauté until lightly browned. Add petals and remaining butter, and cook for 1 minute. In a large bowl, toss the sautéed mixture with the hot pasta. Add cheese and toss. Adjust flavor with salt and freshly grated pepper.

Serves 4.

HAVASUPAI INDIAN SQUASH BLOSSOM PUDDING

kernels from 3 ears of green corn
water
2 to 3 cups squash blossoms, destemmed
salt

Place green corn kernels in a saucepan. Add just enough water to cover corn. Cook over a medium-low heat for half an hour. In another saucepan, place squash blossoms. Cover with water and bring to a boil. Cook until tender. Drain blossoms, and mash. Stir mashed blossoms into green corn and continue to cook until thickened. Season to taste with salt.

Serves 4.

$\mathcal{E}$XPANDING YOUR PLEASURES

After trying the Big Ten, you are ready to broaden your culinary and horticultural horizons and expand your gustatory pleasures using edible flowers. This section encompasses all the other edible flowers, listed alphabetically by common name.

As you read, keep in mind the flavors you like in cooking. In general, the edible flowers of herbs have the same flavor as the leaf but less intense. From mildest to strongest flavor they include: borage, rosemary, basil, dill, oregano, Greek oregano, thyme, coriander and hyssop. Flowers with a sweet flavor are: sweet woodruff, red clover, dandelion, yucca,

pineapple sage and elderberry. Other flowers have a more floral flavor: pea, apple, lilac, dianthus, honeysuckle, pineapple guava and scented geranium. Lavender and violet flowers give a perfumed flavor to food. Lemon, orange and tuberous begonia flowers lend a citrusy tang.

Johnny-jump-up and bee balm have a minty flavor. For a touch of anise use fennel or anise hyssop. Redbud, tulip and runner beans have a beanlike flavor. Nodding onion, society garlic or garlic chives are oniony. For a biting, spicy flavor, look to arugula, mustard, radish, broccoli and winter and summer savory. A bitter tang is imparted to foods by chicory, English daisy, chrysanthemum, shungiku, safflower and sunflower. Hibiscus, roselle, okra and rose of Sharon are mild-flavored flowers. Chamomile, linden and jasmine are used in beverages.

Now that you are thinking edibility instead of just beauty, take another look at the flowers you grow and see which ones you can harvest to try out in some of these recipes. As you expand your culinary use of flowers, you will gain confidence using flowers for the unique flavors and pizazz they add to even the simplest dishes.

ANISE HYSSOP

ANISE HYSSOP

Agastache foeniculum
(A. anethiodora)
Mint family
Lamiaceae (Labiatae)
Anise flavor
 Perennial, self-seeding
Any well-drained soil
Full sun to light shade

Anise hyssop is a tender perennial that grows three to four feet tall. Like other members of the mint family, the stems are square. The three- to four-inch ovate leaves have serrated edges. They appear opposite on the stems.

The upright branching plant has dense, deep lilac-colored, terminal flower spikes five to six inches long that begin to bloom in midsummer. Look closely at the spikes and you can see the small, two-lipped flowers. As the flowers fade from the spikes, cut the spikes down to the nearest leafing branches. You will be rewarded with more flowers later in the season, although the spikes will not be as showy as the earlier ones. The flowers produce abundant nectar that yields a light, fragrant honey.

The entire plant has a lovely anise scent to it, indicative of the flavor of both the flowers and the leaves. Although anise hyssop is not one of the best known herbs, the flavor of the flowers is wonderful. When I eat an anise hyssop flower, I am carried back to the days of my childhood, at a thirty-five-cent Saturday movie matinee, eating Good 'n' Plenty candies.

CULTURE

Anise hyssop prefers full sun, but will grow in light shade in any well-drained soil.

It grows easily from seed. Plant outdoors as soon as all danger of frost is past, or sow seeds indoors at least six weeks before the last frost. Transplant outdoors, allowing at least twelve to fifteen inches between plants. Unlike many perennials started from seed, anise hyssop will flower the first summer. You can sow anise hyssop directly in the garden in the fall in warm climates.

Anise hyssop dies back to the ground after a killing frost. Anise hyssop is late to come up in the spring. The second year I had it, I despaired of it coming back and purchased four new plants. I stuck them in the garden and then saw the tiny emerging leaves of my one-year-old plants. Never one to waste anything, I dug them up and shared them with friends. I also saw several others coming up nearby; anise hyssop does self-seed.

ANISE HYSSOP MUSHROOM PIZZA

Pizza dough:

5 cups all-purpose flour

1 packet quick-rising yeast

1 teaspoon salt

1 cup lukewarm water

1 tablespoon olive oil

Add four cups of flour, yeast and salt to a bowl. Mix together. Slowly stir in water. Continue to stir. As mixture becomes doughy, add olive oil. Add additional flour if needed. Knead until firm adding flour if necessary to keep the dough from being sticky. Form dough into a ball, cover with a towel and allow to rise in a warm place until doubled in bulk.

Punch the dough down and knead briefly. Roll dough out into a circle and place on a lightly oiled pizza pan. Bake in a preheated 450°F oven for 4 to 6 minutes to cook through, but do not let it brown. Remove from oven.

Topping:

12 ounces mushrooms, sliced

1 tablespoon olive oil

1/2 cup anise hyssop florets, divided

1/2 cup Monterey Jack cheese, shredded

Sauté mushrooms in olive oil over a medium heat just until mushrooms are cooked through, but not browned. Toss in 1/4 cup anise hyssop florets. Spoon mushrooms onto cooked pizza dough. Sprinkle with cheese. Bake at 450°F for 4 to 7 minutes, or until cheese begins to lightly brown. Remove from oven, sprinkle with remaining anise hyssop florets and serve.

Serves 4.

SALMON WITH ANISE HYSSOP BEURRE BLANC

———

2-1/2 cups Riesling wine, divided

3 tablespoons dill florets

4 salmon fillets

1 cup fish stock

1 tablespoon shallots, minced

1 clove garlic, minced

1 tablespoon rice wine vinegar

6 tablespoons butter

1 cup anise hyssop florets

Pour 2 cups Riesling wine into a large skillet. Add dill florets and enough water to just cover salmon fillets. Bring liquid to a boil, add salmon fillets. Poach salmon over a low heat until just cooked through, about 10 to 15 minutes, depending on thickness of fillets. Remove fillets from poaching liquid and keep warm.

While the salmon is cooking, prepare the sauce. Pour fish stock and 1/2 cup Riesling wine into a skillet. Add shallots, garlic and vinegar. Cook over a medium heat, stirring occasionally. Reduce to about 1/4 original volume. Remove pan from heat. Whisk butter in to sauce, 1 tablespoon at a time. Add anise hyssop florets and mix. Serve over salmon.

Serves 4.

ANISE HYSSOP BUTTER COOKIES

———

1 cup all-purpose flour

1/4 cup plus 2 tablespoons confectioners' sugar

pinch of salt

7 ounces sweet (unsalted) butter, cold and cut into small pieces

1 teaspoon vanilla

2 tablespoons anise hyssop flowers, minced

Fit a food processor with the plastic blade. Add flour, sugar and salt. Add the butter and process until ingredients are just combined, about 2 minutes. Add vanilla and anise hyssop flowers, processing for an additional 2 minutes. Remove the dough from the processor and shape it into a ball. Roll it into a 1-inch thick log and wrap it with waxed paper. Refrigerate for 1 hour.

Preheat oven to 375°F. Unwrap log and slice it into 1/4-inch rounds. Place cookies on a ungreased cookie sheet. Bake for 7 to 10 minutes, or until lightly golden. Delicious right from the oven.

Makes 36 cookies.

ANISE HYSSOP FLOWER CUSTARD WITH BLACK PANSY SYRUP

from David Feys, co-chef, Sooke Harbour House, Sooke, British Columbia, Canada

Custard:

1 cup whole milk

1 cup whipping cream

6 tablespoons anise hyssop flowers

1/4 cup granulated sugar

2 large eggs

3 large egg yolks

Garnish:

2 cups Black Pansy Syrup (see page 49)

6 teaspoons anise hyssop flowers

6 anise hyssop leaves

6 black pansy flowers

Combine milk and cream. Pour half of this mixture into a small saucepan with sugar and the anise hyssop flowers. Scald the mixture over a low heat. Remove from heat and add remaining milk mixture. Stir well and set aside to cool. Cover and refrigerate overnight, if possible. The length of time allotted to let the anise hyssop steep in this mixture will greatly affect the finished product.

Preheat oven to 350°F. Prepare a 9-by-13-inch Pyrex or aluminum pan with enough hot water to reach halfway up the sides of custard molds. Put this prepared bain marie into the oven.

In a medium-sized bowl, beat the eggs and egg yolks well. Add the cooled infused milk mixture. Combine well and pour equal amounts into 6 clean, dry custard molds.

Bake custard in the bain marie for 25 to 30 minutes. To test for doneness, insert a small knife into the center of a custard. If clean when removed, it is properly cooked. Use a pair of tongs to remove custard molds from the bain marie to a cooling rack. Allow to cool completely. Refrigerate for at least 1 hour.

Remove the custard by running a small knife around the edge of the mold and inverting directly onto a serving plate. Pour the syrup over the top of the custard. Decorate each plate with 1 teaspoon anise hyssop flowers, 1 anise hyssop leaf and 1 black pansy flower.

Serves 6.

APPLE

APPLE
Malus spp.
Rose family Rosaceae
Floral flavor
Tree
Deep, fertile soil
Full sun

The botanic name for apple is derived from the Latin *Malum*, meaning apple. Most modern apples are descended from *Malus pumila*, which was the original apple. Apples are among the oldest of all cultivated fruits. They are known to have been in cultivation since prehistoric times. The first written record of the apple is in the book of Genesis in the Bible. Despite being the temptation that drove man out of Eden, apples have continued to enjoy popularity throughout the millennia.

The pharaohs grew apples along the Nile in Egypt more than three thousand years ago. In ancient Greece apples were a rare commodity. A bride and groom, by law, could share one apple between them on their wedding day. In the Victorian language of flowers, apple meant preference.

The modern apple is native to the Caucasus mountains of western Asia. Like many of the herbs, it was brought to England by the Romans in the third and fourth centuries. Apples were first brought to the New World in 1623 by William Blackstone, an Episcopal priest. No one has done more to popularize apples than Jonathan Chapman (a.k.a. Johnny Appleseed). He was known as a missionary nurseryman who gave away apple seeds to everyone he met as he journeyed from Pennsylvania to Illinois.

Apples are generally rounded trees that can grow to fifty feet tall, but are usually much smaller, especially in cultivation, where the average height is twenty to twenty-five feet. Dwarf (up to six feet tall) and semi-dwarf trees (up to fifteen feet) are regular trees grafted onto dwarfing stock. Genetic dwarfs are the smallest of all fruit trees. Recently introduced, they are dwarf as a result of breeding, not grafting. For the home garden, these are more practical. The trees are attractive, with elliptical, leathery leaves with serrated edges. The leaves are a smooth bright green above while paler underneath.

Flowers appear in early spring at about the same time the leaves emerge. The flowers are about two inches across with five petals that are white flushed with pink. Flowers grow in groups of three to six at the tips of young leaves. Although a lone apple tree will flower, two or three compatible varieties (that bloom at the same time) must be planted for cross-pollination and resulting fruiting. If the flower is pollinated, the fruit will grow, ripening in late summer or fall, depending on the variety.

The flowers have a mildly sweet, floral flavor. They are a nice accompaniment to fruit dishes and can easily be candied to use as garnish later in the season.

CULTURE

Apples must grow in full sun for good flowering and fruit production. They prefer deep, fertile, moist, well-drained soil.

Check with your local Cooperative Extension Service to find the apple varieties that are best suited for growing in your area. Plant the trees only when they are dormant, in early spring for zones 3 to 7, and in fall for zones 8 to 10. Allow twenty feet between standard trees, twelve feet between semi-dwarf varieties and eight feet between dwarf trees. Genetic dwarfs are suitable for planting in containers that are at least two to two and one-half feet in diameter.

Do not fertilize at the time of planting; it can burn the roots. Add two to four inches of light organic mulch around the base of the tree. Do not mulch right up to the trunk of the tree.

WARNING

Apple flowers should be eaten in moderation as they may contain cyanide precursors.

STRAWBERRIES AND KIWI WITH APPLE BLOSSOMS

1 pint strawberries, cleaned, stemmed and cut in half
2 kiwis, peeled and sliced
apple petals

Place kiwi around the sides of individual glass dessert bowls. Add strawberry halves in the center. Top with apple petals.

An elegant-looking dessert that is quick and easy to make. For added richness, serve with a dollop of Sweet Woodruff Yogurt Custard (see page 208).

Serves 4.

ARUGULA

ARUGULA (Rocket,
Roquette, Rugola,
Rocket salad, Rucola)
Eruca vesicaria sativa
Mustard family
Brassicaceae (Cruciferae)
Spicy flavor
Annual
Well-drained soil
Full sun to light shade

Arugula is native to the Mediterranean. It was long believed to be an aphrodisiac.

Arugula is an annual herb. In the past decade, it has gained in popularity as a pungent addition to green salads. The leaves grow in a loose form to a length of ten inches or more. For best flavor, pick leaves when they are several inches long. The leaves can be picked individually or the entire plant can be cut back to within a half inch. It is a cut-and-come-again green that will regrow after a severe pruning.

Those who grow arugula for the greens know that they get bitter as the plant goes to flower. The flowers grow on the ends of stalks that rise six to twelve inches above the leaves. Like other members of the mustard family, arugula flowers have four petals in a crosslike pattern. The flowers are less than one inch across and are off-white with some striation toward the center. The flowers have a piquant, spicy flavor.

CULTURE

Arugula is easily grown from seed. Cool weather is best for leaf formation. As the weather warms, arugula goes to flower. This is a problem if you want to eat the leaves, but not if you want the flowers. I found that by continually picking the flowers, new ones formed all summer long from a small planting. For the greens, I make successive plantings throughout the growing season.

Sow the seeds directly in the garden. In areas with cold winters, sow it as soon as the soil can be worked in the spring. In warmer climates, it can be grown virtually year round. Space seeds a half inch apart in shallow furrows. Arugula grows quickly, sprouting within four to six days. After three weeks, thin the bed, removing every other plant. Those thinnings do not go into the compost pile, rather they are lovely greens to be used in salads. Young arugula is one of the plants usually included in a mesclun mix. Leaves can be harvested continually once they reach a length of about four inches. Once the plant flowers, the leaves become unpalatably bitter, so just enjoy the flowers for their flavor. Arugula can easily be grown in a container—try some in a small pot or even a window box.

SPRING SALAD WITH BACON

1 bunch watercress, cleaned, washed and dried
1 small loose-leaf lettuce (red leaf or Boston)
4 slices of thickly sliced bacon
2 tablespoons red wine vinegar
1 clove garlic, crushed
Petals from 30 arugula flowers

Tear the lettuce and watercress in small pieces into a large bowl. Cut the bacon into 1/2-inch pieces and put in a frying pan over low heat. Cook the bacon slowly, turning often, until it is crispy and brown. Remove the bacon from the pan and set aside. Pour the vinegar into the pan with the bacon fat and allow to boil for 30 seconds. Add the garlic and stir, making sure to get any brownings off the pan. Spoon the hot dressing over the greens. Top with bacon pieces and arugula petals. Serve immediately.

Serves 4.

NAVAJO SALAD

from Robert Werst, chef/owner, y.e. coyote, Hicksville, New York

1 endive
1 head radicchio
1 bunch arugula
8 strawberries, sliced
1 tablespoon 'Lemon Gem' and 'Tangerine Gem' marigold petals,
  coarsely chopped
2 tablespoons arugula petals
4 slices smoked cheddar cheese, cut into triangles

Raspberry Vinaigrette
1/4 cup raspberry vinegar
1/2 cup extra virgin olive oil
1/4 cup sweetened lime juice
1 tablespoon garlic, finely chopped
1/2 tablespoon chili powder
salt and freshly ground black pepper

Whisk all ingredients together in a bowl.

Makes 1 cup of dressing.

Break off leaves of endive, radicchio and arugula. Wash several times to remove all grit. Dry well. Arrange leaves attractively on plates. Add strawberries, marigold petals, arugula petals and cheese triangles in an artistic manner. Drizzle Raspberry Vinaigrette on salad.

Serves 4.

BASIL

BASIL
Ocimum basilicum
Mint family
Lamiaceae (Labiatae)
Herbal flavor
Annual
Well-drained, rich soil
Full sun

Both in folklore and in medicine basil has had a duplicitous reputation, for good and evil. Modern pharmacology has upheld Pliny's (first century A.D. Roman naturalist) contention that basil relieves flatulence. In Italy, basil is considered one of the symbols of love. One lover gives it to another as a token of fidelity. In India basil has long been revered as a sacred plant. Even today the Hindu grow basil in memory of a beloved departed one.

Basil is one of the most popular culinary herbs. It is grown for the one- to two-inch shiny green leaves that have a somewhat spicy flavor when fresh, sweetening as they dry. Originally native to tropical Asia, basil is now widely cultivated throughout the world.

Often grown in the garden as a companion plant with tomatoes, it repels whiteflies and gnats, two insect pests of tomatoes. Basil is also an excellent culinary companion for tomatoes. Their intermingling flavors in a salad or on a slice of crusty bread with a touch of olive oil, salt and pepper says summer to my palate.

Basil grows with one upright stalk that branches on all sides. Two leaves are at every joint on the branches. In general, basil flowers are small and white or lavender, growing on a tubular spike that rises above the leaves. The flowers begin to appear in midsummer. Gardeners are taught to pinch the center stem to prevent the plant from flowering. Indeed, when the plant flowers, leaf production decreases. In order to have both flower and leaf, I wait until the stem begins to flower, then I cut it back, below the flowers. In an attempt to reproduce itself, the plant then sends up a new flower stalk, and I repeat the process.

Basil has recently enjoyed an explosion of interest within the horticultural field, the result being a wide range of different-flavored cultivars. I like to grow a variety, both for the flavor and the look in my garden. One of the most unique to be introduced in recent years is Spicy Globe basil, a small, bushlike plant that grows in a rounded shape up to ten inches tall. Even untrimmed, its growth habit makes it look like a small topiary. With its diminutive size, it is perfect for growing in containers. Unlike the other basils, its flowers are not spiked, but grow close to the leaves. Even the leaves are great for the lazy cook—so small they do not need chopping before use.

Italian basil (*Ocimum basilicum crispum*) is also known as lettuce leaf basil. It is the most prolific of all basils, with the characteristic flavor in large (three to five inches) leaves on a plant up to three feet tall and equally wide.

It is nice to have some color variation within a plant, and the dark opal or purple basil (*Ocimum basilicum purpurascens*) provides that. It is often offered as an ornamental, but grow it for its flavor as well. The plant is a bit smaller than the standard basil, growing eighteen to twenty inches high.

Lemon basil (*Ocimum basilicum citriodorum*) has a twist of lemon that differentiates its flavor from the other basils. It also grows no more than twenty inches high.

I am always interested in trying new colors and flavors of basil and other edibles in the garden, as should you. Look for cinnamon basil, anise basil and other varieties to sample.

Like many of the other herbs with edible flowers, the flavor of the flower is a milder version of the flavor of the leaf. Basil can best be described as a combination clove and mint that is both strong and sweet.

CULTURE

Basil, a tender annual, grows in a bush form to about two feet tall. Plant basil in a sunny location in well-drained, fairly rich soil.

Basil is easily grown from seed. In all but the warmest temperature zones, seed can be started indoors about four to six weeks before the last frost date. In warm areas, it can be directly seeded into the garden. Because of its tenderness, it should not be planted out into the garden until night temperatures are above fifty degrees Fahrenheit. Space tall basils twelve inches apart, dwarf varieties at least six inches apart and Italian basil plants fifteen inches apart. Within four to six weeks of transplanting, you can begin to harvest leaves.

Basil benefits from fertilization several times during the growing season. I usually foliar feed when I transplant it, after I have harvested the first leaves, and again a month or six weeks later.

As temperatures begin to drop in the fall, compact varieties of basil can be transplanted into a container for indoors. Basil is an annual and will not keep growing all winter, but this will give you a bit more time to enjoy this flavorful herb.

BASIL TOMATO SOUP

from Charmaine Eads, chef, Manor Farm Inn, Poulsbo, Washington

1-pound can tomato sauce
1 cup cream
1 cup half-and-half
2 tablespoons granulated sugar
1/3 cup basil flowers, reserve some for garnish
2 tablespoons Pernod (optional)

In a large saucepan, heat tomato sauce, cream, half-and-half and sugar over a medium-low heat. Add sugar and basil flowers. Do not allow to boil. Just before serving, add Pernod. Garnish with reserved basil flowers.

Serves 4 to 6

BASIL CORN CHOWDER

1 medium Walla Walla onion, coarsely chopped
1 tablespoon olive oil
1/2 cup basil flowers
8 medium red potatoes, cut into 1-inch cubes
kernels from 8 ears corn, divided
6 cups vegetable stock (or chicken stock or water)
salt and pepper to taste

In a large saucepan, sauté onions in olive oil until translucent. Add basil flowers, potatoes and half the corn. Continue to cook for 3 minutes. Pour in the vegetable stock, and bring to a boil. Lower heat, cover and simmer for 15 minutes or until potatoes are tender.

Remove from heat and allow to cool for 15 to 20 minutes. Pour half of the soup into a blender or food processor. Process until smooth. Pour back into saucepan. Reheat and add remaining corn. For a smoother soup, puree all of the soup, for a chunkier soup, process for less time. If you like soup thinner, add more vegetable stock. Adjust seasoning with salt and pepper.

This soup has the taste and consistency of a traditional milky or creamy rich chowder. The secret is pureeing part of the soup—a great calorie saver. If you must, you can add up to 1 cup of milk or half-and-half. This soup keeps for at least 6 months in the freezer.

Serves 8 to 10.

BASIL FLOWER PESTO

1 pound fresh tomato-basil linguine, cooked al dente and drained
2 tablespoons olive oil
1 cup basil leaves, coarsely chopped *
1/3 cup pine nuts
1 cup basil flowers

In a large skillet, heat olive oil over a medium heat. Add basil leaves and toss in oil for 2 minutes. Add pine nuts and continue sautéing for 2 minutes. Add basil flowers and toss to mix. Using salad tongs, add the pasta to the skillet in small batches, tossing after each addition. Serve hot or at room temperature.

Serves 4.

*Lemon basil is delicious in this dish, but any other basil is satisfactory.

SPICY TOMATO SALAD

6 ripe tomatoes
2 scallions
8 basil leaves
20 basil flowers
20 rosemary flowers
1/4 cup extra virgin olive oil
juice of one lemon
salt and black pepper (optional)

Cut tomatoes into large, bite-sized chunks or wedges and place in a large nonmetallic bowl. Mince scallions, tear basil leaves into small pieces and toss with tomatoes. Add basil and rosemary flowers. Drizzle with olive oil and lemon juice. Season with salt and pepper to taste. Serve immediately.

Serves 4 to 6.

PASTA WITH BASIL—ORIENTAL STYLE

1 pound fresh herb pasta, cooked al dente and drained
2 stalks celery, cut into 1/2-inch sections
1 medium cucumber, peeled, seeded and cut into 1/2-inch cubes
1 sweet red pepper, seeded and cut into 1/2-inch pieces
10 to 12 small artichoke hearts, cut in half
8 sun-dried tomatoes cut into quarters

Dressing:
1/2 cup wine vinegar
1/3 cup canola oil
1 teaspoon soy sauce
1 teaspoon sesame oil
1 teaspoon brown sugar
1/4 cup basil flowers *

Toss all ingredients together in a large bowl. Add dressing and toss to mix well. Allow to sit at room temperature for at least 1 hour to allow flavors to meld and infuse the pasta.

In a small bowl add all dressing ingredients and whisk well.

This can be served warm—I prefer it cold or at room temperature for a quick and easy summer dinner.

Serves 4 as a main course, 8 as a side dish.

* Experiment with different flowers—anise basil, lemon basil and cinnamon basil—for different flavors.

EASTERN BASIL CHICKEN WITH COUSCOUS

2 tablespoons extra virgin olive oil

1 broiler/fryer chicken, cut into 8 pieces

1 cup mushrooms, sliced

1/2 cup onion, chopped

1/3 cup basil flowers, coarsely chopped

16 ounce can whole tomatoes, drained, cut into bite-sized pieces

3 tablespoons basil vinegar

1/4 teaspoon granulated sugar

salt and freshly ground pepper

2 tablespoons cornstarch dissolved in 1/4 cup water

1-1/2 cups water

1/4 teaspoon salt

2 tablespoons butter

1 cup couscous

basil flowers for garnish

Heat olive oil in a large skillet. Add chicken and brown evenly on all sides. Remove chicken from skillet, set aside. Reserve 2 tablespoons of pan drippings, discard the rest.

Return the drippings to the skillet and sauté mushrooms and onions over a medium heat. Add basil flowers, tomatoes, sugar, salt and pepper to taste. Stir well. Return chicken to skillet, lower heat, cover and gently simmer for 30 to 35 minutes. Stir occasionally.

Bring water to a boil with salt and butter in a medium saucepan. Stir in couscous. Remove from heat, cover and let stand for 5 minutes. Fluff couscous with a fork before serving.

Remove chicken to serving platter. Surround with couscous. Add cornstarch mixture to skillet, stir until thickened. Pour sauce over chicken and serve. Decorate with additional basil flowers.

Serves 4 to 6.

BEE BALM

Bee balm is so named as evidence of bee's love for the flower's nectar. Oswego Indians made a tea from bee balm, which they shared with the American colonists. After the Boston Tea Party, bee balm tea was the beverage of choice. Even today it is still popular. Bee balm is also known as Oswego tea, named for the Indian tribe who, like the Shakers, favored it above others. The name bergamot comes from the similarity between the fragrance of bee balm and that of the bergamot orange.

Bee balm distinguishes itself as one of the few native American herbs. It grows wild in moist woods, thickets along stream banks from Michigan to New York and south to Tennessee and Georgia, especially in upland areas. A distinctive perennial herb, bee balm grows two to three feet tall with a large ragged head of bright crimson flowers and reddish bracts from late June to September. Like other members of the mint family, it has square stems and opposite leaves. The brilliant flowers make this a good choice to plant in a perennial border.

The flavor can be described as citrusy, sweet, hot and minty.

Monarda fistulosa, wild bergamot, is distinguished by its pinkish or pale lavender flowers with lilac tinged bracts. Its flavor can be quite intense, spicy and minty at the same time. It is commonly used in the Pacific Northwest as a spicy garnish to salads or vegetables.

CULTURE

Bee balm grows best in partial shade or full sun in rich, moist soil.

BEE BALM (*Oswego tea, red bergamot*) *Monarda didyma*
Mint family
Lamiaceae (Labiatae)
Mint flavor
Perennial
Moist, rich soil
Partial shade to full sun

Start the seed in a cold frame in mid-summer. By the following spring it will be strong enough to be transplanted. An alternative is to direct seed bee balm into the garden in November. The seeds will germinate in the spring. By the second year it will reach its mature size.

Bee balm can be propagated from root divisions. It usually needs dividing about every three years. Dig up the fibrous roots in early spring. Divide and replant the outer roots, which are the newer roots, and discard the center. Allow at least eighteen inches between plants.

To get the largest blooms, the plant should not be allowed to flower the first year. Cut back any flower heads as they form. The second and subsequent years, cut the flower head back after it blooms, and you may be rewarded with a second flowering in the fall.

After a killing frost, cut back the stalks almost to ground level and mulch the plant well. In spring, remember to remove the mulch.

EDIBLE FLOWERS

MONARDA SNAPPER

2 tablespoons butter

1 clove garlic, minced

1 tablespoon lemon thyme flowers, coarsely chopped

1/2 cup bee balm flowers, coarsely chopped

olive oil

4 red snapper fillets

1/4 cup Riesling wine or other light white wine

Melt butter in a skillet. Add garlic and sauté for 2 minutes. Add flowers and sauté for 1 minute. Remove from heat.

Heat a large skillet. Pour in just enough olive oil to lightly coat pan. Add red snapper. Cook over a medium heat for 3 minutes on one side. Turn fillets over and pour on sauce. Continue to cook until fish just turns opaque. Remove to a serving platter.

Return skillet to heat. Add wine to deglaze pan, stirring continually. Pour liquid over fish fillets. Serve immediately.

Serves 4.

BEE BALM ICE CREAM

1 cup milk

1-inch length vanilla bean

2 tablespoons red bee balm flowers, cut into 1/4-inch lengths

1/4 cup granulated sugar

1-1/2 cups cream

3 egg yolks

Mix a small amount of the hot liquid into the beaten yolks, then pour the warmed yolks into the milk. Continue to stir over a low heat until liquid thickens and coats a wooden spoon.

Remove from heat and let cool to room temperature. Remove vanilla bean. Process in an ice cream maker according to manufacturer's directions. This ice cream has a surprisingly nutty flavor. It takes a bit of time to make, but is well worth the effort.

Serves 4 to 6.

Pour milk into a heavy saucepan and place over a low heat. Add vanilla and flowers. Stir until milk is lukewarm. Add sugar, stir and heat slowly until mixture is hot. Do not let it boil. Add cream, heat until mixture is hot, not to a boil. Beat egg yolks until frothy.

EXPANDING YOUR PLEASURES

BEE BALM POUND CAKE

1 cup butter

2 cups granulated sugar

2-1/4 cups all-purpose flour

6 eggs

juice of 1 lemon

1 teaspoon vanilla

1/2 cup bee balm flowers, coarsely chopped

1/8 teaspoon salt

Preheat oven to 325°F. Cream together butter and sugar until mixture is light and fluffy.

In a separate bowl, sift and then measure flour. Alternate adding flour and eggs (one at a time) to the creamed sugar, beating continually. Add lemon juice, vanilla, bee balm flowers and salt. Mix for 1 minute.

Pour batter into a buttered and floured tube pan and bake for about 1 hour and 20 minutes, or until a toothpick inserted in the center comes out clean. Take cake out of the oven and put on a rack to cool for 10 minutes. Remove cake from pan and allow to cool completely on rack.

Serves 15 to 20.

BEE BALM TEA

2 tablespoons bee balm flowers, chopped

4 cups water, boiling

Steep flowers in water for 5 to 10 minutes. Strain and serve.

Serves 4.

BEE BALM TARTLETS

Filling:

1 cup freshly squeezed lemon juice

1 cup granulated sugar

3 eggs

3 egg yolks

10 tablespoons butter, cut into small pieces

1/4 cup bee balm flowers, coarsely chopped

In the top of a double boiler, mix lemon juice and sugar. Heat until the sugar is dissolved, stirring occasionally with a wooden spoon. Add eggs and egg yolks, stirring continually for about 10 minutes until the mixture thickens and coats the back of the spoon. Add butter, stirring until completely combined. Stir in bee balm. Remove from heat, transfer to a glass or stainless steel bowl and refrigerate overnight or until set.

Tartlets:

6 tablespoons butter, softened and cut into small pieces

5 tablespoons granulated sugar

2 tablespoons water

1 egg

1 egg yolk

2 cups all-purpose flour

flour for dusting board

Fit a food processor with the plastic blade. Add butter and sugar; cream together. Add water, egg and egg yolk. Process until just mixed. Add flour, processing until well mixed. Remove dough from processor bowl. Divide dough in half, wrap each half in waxed paper and refrigerate for at least 2 hours.

Remove dough from refrigerator. Dust a wooden board with flour. One at a time, roll the dough halves out to a thickness of 1/8 inch. Cut with a 3- to 4-inch cookie cutter (use a glass if you don't have a cutter). Fit each piece of cut dough into 2-inch tartlet pans or miniature muffin tins. This should make 24 tartlets. Prick the bottom of each with a fork and refrigerate for 1 hour.

Preheat oven to 375°F. Remove tart pans from refrigerator and bake on a cookie sheet for 7 to 8 minutes, or until they just turn golden. Remove from oven and set aside to cool.

Just before serving, spoon filling into cooled tartlet shells. Garnish with additional flowers.

Makes 24 tartlets.

BORAGE

The word borage is likely a derivation from the Latin *burra* meaning a shaggy garment, referring to the rough foliage of this lovely herb. Borage was once believed to have great powers. According to Pliny it brought happiness and joy where it grew. In *Gerard's Herball*, he quotes the belief that had been carried down from the ancient Greeks and Romans, "I, Borage, bring always courage." In the Victorian language of flowers, borage means bluntness.

Borage is an annual herb with dark gray-green, hairy leaves with a cucumber flavor. Borage is native to the Mediterranean area. Cultivated in northern Europe, it was brought by settlers to America. It was purportedly planted by Columbus' men on Isabella's Island. It was first listed in an American seed catalog in 1806. In the past, it was grown more as a medicinal than a culinary herb, but now its subtle flavor is becoming more appreciated.

Borage grows eighteen to twenty-four inches, but I have seen it up to four feet tall in California, with prickly hairs covering virtually the entire plant. The leaves are large and oval with wavy edges, growing alternately along hollow, somewhat succulent, branched stems. The small (one inch) star-shaped, brilliant blue (rarely rose) flowers, borne in clusters from April to November (depending on the area of the country) are very attractive to bees. In midsummer a plant may seem to be abuzz with all the activity.

BORAGE
(Bee Bread, Starflower, Common Bugloss)
Borago officinalis
Borage family
Boraginaceae
Herbal flavor
Annual, self-seeding
Light, poor, dry soil
Full sun

The flavor of borage, both petals and leaves, is mildly like cucumber. Traditionally borage flowers were used to flavor wine drinks. Candied, the flowers were popular sweets in the last century. Lift the flowers from the hairy sepals before using them. The flowers are beautiful frozen in ice cubes then floated in a refreshing summer drink.

As you can see from the recipes, borage pairs well with nasturtiums. Not only are their colors complementary—sky blue and bright orange—their flavors harmonize well.

CULTURE

Borage grows best in full sun and will tolerate a range of soils, but it prefers a light, poor, dry soil.

EDIBLE FLOWERS

Direct seed borage into the garden after all danger of frost is past. The roots are very delicate, making borage difficult to transplant. Once planted the seed germinates quickly. Allow at least twelve inches between plants, more in warmer climates. Unless you harvest all the flowers, you usually do not have to worry about planting borage in subsequent years as it self-seeds freely.

Consider planting borage at the top of a hill or mound or on sloping ground where you can view it from below. An upward view of the plant best shows off the beauty of the drooping flowers.

WARNING

Borage can have a diuretic effect, so it should not be eaten in great quantity,

BURGUNDY BORAGE PUNCH

from Pat Lanza, Shandelee Herb Garden, Livingston Manor, New York

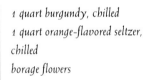

1 quart burgundy, chilled
1 quart orange-flavored seltzer, chilled
borage flowers

Mix burgundy and seltzer in a punch bowl. Float borage flowers on the punch. For a festive look, freeze borage flowers in ice cubes and float these in the punch.

Serves 12 to 16 (small punch glasses).

BENEDICTINE

from Bob Holmes, Creation Gardens, New Albany, Indiana

1 8-ounce package cream cheese, softened to room temperature
1 large cucumber, peeled, seeded and grated on medium grater, drained
1 teaspoon onion, finely grated
1/4 teaspoon salt
2 teaspoon dill, finely chopped
1 teaspoon young borage leaves, finely chopped
2 to 3 drops green food coloring
15 to 20 borage flowers
sprigs fresh dill

Mash the cream cheese until it is softened and of a uniform texture. Add cucumber, onion, salt, dill and borage leaves, and mix. Add green food coloring, mixing well to thoroughly blend. Decorate with borage flowers and fresh dill sprigs.

Makes about 1 to 1-1/2 cups of dip.

EXPANDING YOUR PLEASURES

BORAGE AND CUCUMBERS IN SOUR CREAM DRESSING

―――

from Renee Shepherd, Shepherd's Seeds, Felton, California

3 medium cucumbers

salt

1 cup sour cream or plain yogurt

2 tablespoons rice vinegar

1/2 teaspoon celery seed

1/4 cup scallions, chopped

1 teaspoon granulated sugar

salt and freshly ground pepper

1/4 cup very young borage leaves, finely chopped

borage flowers for garnish

Wash, score and slice the cucumbers very thin. Salt lightly and let stand in a colander for 30 minutes to drain. Rinse off the salt and pat dry. In a bowl, mix remaining ingredients, adding salt and pepper to taste. Add cucumbers and toss lightly. Refrigerate for 1 hour before serving. Garnish with borage flowers.

Serves 6 to 8.

―――

WHITE BEAN SALAD

―――

from Applewood Seed Company, Golden, Colorado

1 cup dried white beans

2-1/4 cups cold water

1/2 teaspoon salt

1/2 green bell pepper, chopped

1/2 sweet red pepper, chopped

1 tablespoon chives

4 leaves basil, chopped

1 teaspoon summer savory

1 large clove garlic, finely minced

1/3 cup pine nuts

1 cup Nasturtium Vinaigrette (see page 39)

15 borage flowers

Rinse beans and discard any imperfect ones. Add beans to cold water in a saucepan. Bring to a boil. Simmer for 2 minutes. Remove from the heat, cover and allow to stand for 1 hour. Add salt, return pan to the stove and gently simmer, covered, for 1 hour or until beans are tender. Remove from heat and cool. Add green and red peppers, chives, basil, summer savory, garlic, pine nuts and Nasturtium Vinaigrette. Mix well. Allow to stand at room temperature for 45 minutes, then refrigerate for 1 to 2 hours before serving. Garnish with borage flowers just before serving.

Serves 6.

PASTA SALAD

Salad:

2 cups tricolor pasta (rotini or macaroni), cooked al dente

1 cup sugar snap peas, stringed and cut in thirds

1 cup sweet red pepper, cut in thin slices

4 scallions, coarsely chopped

1/4 cup plus 3 tablespoons borage flowers

Dressing:

3 tablespoons safflower oil

2 teaspoons rose vinegar

1 tablespoon grated ginger

1 clove of garlic, crushed

1 tablespoon tamari

Toss salad ingredients (reserving 3 tablespoons borage flowers) together with dressing. Allow to stand at room temperature for several hours. Just before serving, garnish with remaining borage flowers.

Whisk all ingredients together.

FLORAL TOSTADAS

from Dale Engleborn, Sebastopol, California

10 flour tortillas, deep fried

4 cups pinto beans, cooked and mashed

1/2 cup nasturtium leaves, chopped

1 cup tomatoes, chopped

2 avocados, sliced

1/2 cup black olives, pitted and chopped

1 cup carrots, grated

2 cups cheddar cheese, grated

1/2 cup hot sauce

1 cup borage flowers

1 cup nasturtium petals

Assemble ingredients on tortillas in layers, starting with the mashed beans and ending with the flowers. Add hot sauce to taste.

Serves 4 to 6.

STUFFED NASTURTIUMS

———

1/2 cup whipped cream cheese

1/4 cup ricotta cheese

2 tablespoons plain yogurt

1/4 cup walnuts, finely chopped

1/4 cup currants, finely chopped

1 tablespoon lemon zest, finely chopped

1 teaspoon vanilla

1 tablespoon maple syrup

15 borage flowers, coarsely chopped

20 to 25 nasturtium flowers

20 to 25 whole borage flowers

Mix all ingredients except nasturtiums and whole borage flowers together. Refrigerate for 1 hour. Shape the stuffing into small balls and gently place in the flowers. Garnish with borage flowers.

BLUEBERRY, STRAWBERRY AND CUCUMBER COMPOTE

———

1/3 cup brown sugar

2 cups sour cream

1 pint blueberries, washed and stemmed

1 pint strawberries, washed, stemmed and cut in half

2 medium cucumbers, peeled, seeded and cut into 1/2-inch pieces

borage flowers

Combine brown sugar and sour cream. Add berries and cucumber. Refrigerate until time to serve. Garnish generously with borage flowers.

BROCCOLI

BROCCOLI Brassica oleracea
(Botrytis group)
Mustard family
Brassicaceae (Cruciferae)
Spicy flavor
Annual
Rich, well-drained soil
Full sun

Broccoli and other cole crops including cabbage, cauliflower and kale are descended from the wild cabbage, *Brassica oleracea*. After eons of cultivation, it has become an extremely complex species, so scientists have arbitrarily divided it into different groups.

Broccoli is a vegetable that is really a biennial, but it is grown as an annual. The leaves are gray-green. Fleshy, edible stems end in large tight heads of densely clustered flower buds, called curds. Typically the curds are green or blue-green, but purple and purplish-green varieties are also readily available. Sprouting broccoli (Italica group) is similar to broccoli, but has no central head.

As the weather warms, and if the heads are not harvested, the buds will open and small yellow flowers appear. They are less than one inch across with four petals in a cross formation. The flavor is not as piquant as other members of the mustard family, but they do have a gentle spicy bite to them.

CULTURE

Broccoli needs full sun. It grows best in rich, well-drained soil.

Start seeds indoors six weeks before last spring frost date. Transplant outdoors after danger of frost is past. Allow twelve to eighteen inches between plants.

Young plants are readily available at nurseries and garden centers in the spring.

In warm climates, broccoli can be seeded directly into the garden in late summer for a fall and winter harvest.

TANGY LETTUCE CARROT SALAD

1 loose-leaf head of lettuce (Bibb or Boston), torn into bite-sized pieces
10 baby carrots, thinly sliced
4 tablespoons olive oil
2 tablespoons chive vinegar
1 teaspoon honey
1 clove garlic, crushed
salt and freshly ground pepper to taste
20 to 30 broccoli flowers, petals only

Toss lettuce and carrots in a bowl. Whisk together oil, vinegar, honey and garlic. Season with salt and pepper to taste. Pour the dressing on the salad and mix together with the flower petals. A nice contrast of flavors with the sweet carrots, buttery lettuce and tangy flowers.

Serves 4.

CHAMOMILE

Chamomile has been cultivated for over two thousand years as an ornamental groundcover. In the Victorian language of flowers, it denotes energy in adversity, perhaps from its ability to rise again after being stepped on in the garden.

Chamomile is a creeping perennial herb, the plant itself growing only about one inch high. The leaves are fernlike and can form a mat around the rooting spot of the creeping plant stem. When in bloom, the flowering stems reach up to twelve inches in height. The flowers are small and daisylike with white petals surrounding a conical yellow disc. With successive pickings, the flowers will grace the garden from midsummer until they are killed by the frost of autumn.

The dried flowers are used in their entirety to make tea. Long used by herbalists as a calmative for the stomach and nerves, chamomile does indeed have mild sedative properties.

CULTURE

Chamomile grows best in moist, well-drained soil in full sun or partial shade, but it will survive in poor soil as long as it is well drained. Chamomile is easily grown from seed planted in the spring. Once established, chamomile will self-seed. In an established planting, you can divide the runners in early spring.

CHAMOMILE
(English Chamomile) Anthemis
nobilis
Composite family
Asteraceae (Compositae)
Sweet apple flavor
Perennial
Moist, well-drained soil
Full sun to partial shade

Harvest the flowers just when the petals begin to droop slightly. Lay the flowers on a sheet or a screen (with a cloth below to catch whatever falls through) in the sun so they can dry quickly. As they are drying, remove the leaves and stems. Once completely dried, store the flowers in a tightly covered container in a cool dry place.

WARNING

Ragweed sufferers may also be allergic to chamomile. Chamomile contains thuaone and should be drunk in moderation—no more than one cup of tea a day.

CHAMOMILE TEA

1 teaspoon dried chamomile flowers
1 cup boiling water

Let flower steep in water for 3 to 5 minutes.

CHICORY

CHICORY
Cichorium intybus
Composite family
Asteraceae (Compositae)
Bitter flavor
Perennial
Almost any soil
Sun to shade

When the Swedish botanist, Carolus Linnaeus, who introduced botanical nomenclature, planted a floral clock, he included chicory as it reliably opens and closes it petals at the same time every day.

Chicory is a perennial herb originally native to Europe. Today it has naturalized throughout most of temperate North America, growing in waste areas and fields, roadsides and vacant city lots.

The plant usually grows to three feet tall, but can reach up to six feet in height. Chicory has a tough, long taproot, making it difficult to remove. Even along roadways where the verge is mowed, chicory will quickly regrow. Often the plant, with a basal rosette of dandelionlike leaves, is not even noticed until the flowers open. The flowers grow at the base of the smaller leaves along the stiff stem.

In spring the young leaves are used in salads. (Belgian endive is a cultivated cousin of this handsome weed.) Most commonly, chicory roots are dried and roasted and, especially in the South, blended with coffee, giving it a slightly bitter flavor while cutting down on the caffeine.

It flowers from July through November with two-inch, sky-blue flowers. The flower head actually consists of fifteen to twenty ray flowers. The ends of the flowers are squared off and slightly toothed. Chicory has a pleasant, mild-bitter flavor.

CULTURE

Chicory is often considered a weed, giving an indication that it will grow in almost any type of soil. In humid areas the growth is more profuse than in dry areas.

Direct seed chicory in the garden after the last frost date. Be warned that once you have it in your garden, it will most likely be there for the duration.

WARNING

The plant can cause dermatitis in sensitive individuals.

CHICORY RICOTTA

from José Gutierrez, executive chef, Chez Philippe, Peabody Hotel, Memphis, Tennessee

1 gallon milk

1 tablespoon salt

1 quart buttermilk

1/2 teaspoon salt

1 teaspoon white pepper

1/3 cup 'Lemon Gem' marigold petals, coarsely chopped

1/3 cup chicory petals, coarsely chopped

1 tablespoon thyme petals

2 tablespoons chopped chives

1/4 cup dill flowers

2 tablespoons heavy cream

Bring milk and salt to a boil in a large saucepan. Add buttermilk and bring to a boil again. Remove from heat. Add salt and pepper. Strain in a colander lined with several layers of cheesecloth. Gently toss in flowers and chives, reserving some for garnish. Add cream. Return to strainer, press down firmly to shape and release liquid. Refrigerate until serving.

Serve on toast points or melba toast, or stuff into vegetables or other flowers. Makes about 2 cups.

CRAB SPREAD

from Applewood Seed Company, Golden, Colorado

12 ounces crab meat, coarsely chopped

1/2 cup water chestnuts, coarsely chopped

1/4 cup scallions, finely chopped

2 tablespoons soy sauce

2/3 cup plain yogurt

1/3 cup mayonnaise

2 tablespoons chicory petals

Gently toss crab meat with water chestnuts and scallions. In a separate bowl, blend yogurt, mayonnaise and soy sauce. Add the yogurt mixture to the crab meat and mix well. Garnish with chicory petals.

Delicious spread on melba toast or crackers, or used to stuff celery.

RED, WHITE AND BLUE SALAD

feta cheese
cherry tomatoes
vinaigrette dressing
petals from 10 chicory flowers
red leaf lettuce

Crumble feta cheese into a nonmetallic bowl. Slice cherry tomatoes in half, mix with cheese. Add vinaigrette and toss gently. Refrigerate for several hours to allow flavors to blend. Just before serving, pull petals off flowers and add to tomato-cheese mixture. Serve on a bed of red leaf lettuce with a chicory flower in the center.

A red, white and blue salad—perfect for the Fourth of July.

CHRYSANTHEMUM

We know that common names for plants are not reliable. A plant may be known by one name in one locale and another in a different part of the country. For that reason, it is better to refer to plants by their botanic names, which are universally understood. There is a rub, however, when names get changed. Although *Chrysanthemum x morifolium* (the common garden variety chrysanthemum) was officially changed to *Dendranthema grandiflorum*, it may be a long time before the new name is universally recognized. For that reason, any name changes are followed by the former name in parenthesis. Will the common name change as well over time, so that a mum becomes an ema?

Chrysanthemums have been cultivated in China since 500 B.C., where they were not only prized for their beauty but also as a food. In the Victorian language of flowers, red chrysanthemums signify love, white mums mean truth, while yellow mums imply slighted love.

The garden mums we enjoy today are the result of hundreds of years of breeding and selection in Europe, Asia and North America. Perennial chrysanthemums are hardy to zone 5. Chrysanthemums originally ranged from nine to fifteen inches tall. With a great deal of hybridization, however, some varieties grow up to four feet tall. Most chrysanthemums are vigorous clump-formers. The stems are greatly branched and may be upright or sprawling. The thick leaves are usually dull green and lobed, giving off a characteristic chrysanthemum odor when bruised.

CHRYSANTHEMUM
(Garden mum)
Dendranthema grandiflorum
(Chrysanthemum x morifolium)
Composite family
Asteraceae (Compositae)
Bitter flavor
Perennial
Rich, moist, well-drained soil
Full sun

Hybridization has not just affected the size of the plant. Flower heads range greatly in size and form, from one-inch button mums to eight-inch spider mums. There are simple single flowers, doubles, and pom-poms. Petal form runs the gamut from quills to spoon shaped to long, narrow spiders. Every color except blue is represented in modern mums. The National Chrysanthemum Society has divided the flower types into thirteen classes.

Chrysanthemums bloom in late summer and fall, adding a much-needed boost of color to the garden. Grow them in containers, in perennial borders and in rock gardens. With the myriad varieties from which to choose, there are chrysanthemums for every garden.

The tang or bitterness of chrysanthemum varies among the hundreds of varieties. Chrysanthemum petals are traditionally brewed into a revitalizing tea.

CULTURE

Chrysanthemums grow best in full sun. They prefer rich, moist, well-drained soil. They are shallow rooted and heavy feeders, so they benefit from regular feedings and watering. Side dress with compost or well-rotted manure several times during the growing season.

Chrysanthemums are usually grown from cuttings or purchased as plants. Be aware that the large flowering plants you purchase in the fall may not be hardy, although they will give you a beautiful show of color for many weeks.

For beauty year after year, buy rooted cuttings or small plants in early summer. Plant them out before the weather turns hot in warm climates or after all danger of frost is past in colder climates. For a bushy, compact plant, pinch the stems back to six or seven leaves until the beginning of July in short-season climates and until the beginning of August in long-season climates.

After the plant has gone dormant for the winter, lightly mulch with hay or leaves to protect it in cold climates. To maintain vigor, divide the plants every few years and replant in rich, well-drained soil.

WARNING

The base of the petal is bitter. Remove this before eating.

AUTUMN BLESSING SALAD

———

1 tablespoon salt

4 cups water

1/2 cup chrysanthemum petals (a mixture of red, yellow and orange for best effect)

1 gallon ice water

2 teaspoons granulated sugar

1-1/2 cups sliced fresh mushrooms

3 carrots, grated

2 cups Romaine lettuce, torn into bite-sized pieces

1 cup red leaf lettuce, torn into bite-sized pieces

1 cup Boston or Bibb lettuce, torn into bite-sized pieces

1/4 cup raisins

In a saucepan, bring salted water to a boil. Quickly dip chrysanthemum petals into boiling water, then plunge them into ice water to stop any cooking action. Drain petals and toss with sugar.

In a large bowl, toss together mushrooms, carrots, lettuces and raisins. Sprinkle sweetened chrysanthemum petals on top of salad. Try this colorful salad without dressing. The range of flavors and textures of the ingredients can best be appreciated as they are. If you must, add just a touch of light salad oil and vinegar.

Serves 4.

CHRYSANTHEMUM LAMB

———

from Yujean Kang, chef/owner, Yujean Kang's, Pasadena, California

1/2 pound lamb tenderloin, sliced 1/4 inch thick against the
  grain

2 quarts salad oil

6 ounces shiitake mushrooms, julienned

3/4 teaspoon cornstarch blended with 1/2 teaspoon water

6 ounces enoki mushrooms

1 cup yellow chrysanthemum petals (marinated with a dash of
  vinegar, granulated sugar, a pinch of salt and 4 to 5 ounces
  sesame oil)

4 pieces prosciutto di parma, sliced thin, deep fried until crispy

Marinade:

1 teaspoon rice wine

1 teaspoon ginger juice

1 teaspoon garlic, minced

1 egg

1 tablespoon soy sauce

1 tablespoon cornstarch

2 tablespoons salad oil

pinch of salt

pinch of Szechwan peppercorns, freshly ground

Mix together.

Mix lamb with marinade. Marinate for 30 minutes.

Heat wok or large, deep frying pan over a medium heat.
Add 2 quarts of salad oil. When oil is hot, add marinated lamb to wok, stir until it turns color. (This
method is like deep frying, but with a very low temperature because the lamb has been marinated with

whole egg and cornstarch, therefore the lamb will be
seared without burning. This keeps the lamb moist and
very tender.) Add shiitake mushrooms, continue to fry
a few seconds. Drain into a strainer placed over an
empty pot.

Sauce:

1/2 teaspoon ginger, minced

3 tablespoons plum wine

1 teaspoon kirsch

1 tablespoon light soy sauce

1 teaspoon oyster sauce

1 teaspoon granulated sugar

1 teaspoon Shanghai black vinegar

1/2 oil infused with shallots

1/2 teaspoon sesame oil

1/2 teaspoon oil infused with Szechwan peppercorns

Mix together.

Reheat wok to a very high heat. Add minced garlic, stir,
then add sauce. Thicken with cornstarch until sauce is
almost caramelized. Do not burn. Add lamb, shiitake
mushrooms and enoki mushrooms. Toss to coat evenly.

To assemble the plates, arrange chrysanthemum petals
around the edges of 9-inch plates. Place lamb and
mushrooms in center. Top with slices of prosciutto di
parma.

Serves 4.

CORIANDER

Pliny first named this aromatic herb "coriandrum" from the Greek *koris* meaning bug.

Coriander was one of the first culinary herbs and spices. Records indicate that the Chinese used the seeds as a flavoring for beverages, cakes and candies more than five thousand years ago. It is even mentioned in the Old Testament several times. Coriander was introduced throughout northern Europe and into England with the spread of the Roman empire.

Seeds have been found in ancient Egyptian tombs. The Chinese believe it conferred immortality. In the Victorian language of flowers, coriander symbolizes hidden worth.

Coriander is a fast-growing annual herb, reaching a height of two feet. Notice how the plant changes as it grows. The first and lower leaves are deeply lobed. Harvested at this point for the leaves, it is called cilantro or Chinese parsley. With their unique flavor somewhat reminiscent of sage and lemon peel, the cilantro leaves are favored in Chinese, Thai and Mexican cooking. As the plant grows, the upper leaves are narrow and fern-like. The white to pale-pink flowers grow in umbels like other members of the parsley family. If the flower is not cut, seeds form. When harvested, the seeds are called coriander seed. They are yellowish brown, only one-eighth to one-fourth inch in diameter.

The flavor of the flower is difficult to describe and is somewhat different from both the leaves and the seed, more like a pungent mix of anise, cumin, sage and orange.

CORIANDER
(Cilantro, Chinese parsley)
Coriander sativum
Carrot family
Apiaceae (Umbelliferae)
Herbal flavor
Annual
Fairly rich, well-drained soil
Sun

CULTURE

Coriander tolerates a range of growing conditions, but prefers well-drained, fairly rich soil in a sunny location.

Coriander grows and germinates quickly. Plant the seed about one inch deep, directly in the garden after any danger of frost is past. Allow twelve to fifteen inches between plants. Coriander has a delicate root system and does not transplant well. Expect flowering within nine weeks of sowing. Since it grows so quickly, make successive plantings every two to three weeks. If allowed to go to seed, coriander will quickly self-sow.

CORIANDER BEAN DIP

---

from Eileen Mendyka, Good Thyme Farm, Bethlehem, Connecticut

1 1-pound can white kidney beans
1 to 3 fresh chilies, seeded (or 4-ounce can chopped green chilies)
3 cloves garlic
2 tablespoons coriander flowers
1/4 cup red onion, coarsely chopped
3 tomatoes, seeded and chopped

Combine beans, chilies, garlic and coriander flowers in a food processor. Puree. Remove to a nonmetallic bowl and stir in onion and tomatoes. Refrigerate for at least 1 hour to allow the flavors to meld. Garnish with additional coriander flowers and serve with tortilla chips or pita wedges.

Makes 2 cups.

CORIANDER CHICKEN IN A CLAY POT

---

lidded clay baking pot (Romertopf type)
small roasting chicken, 3 to 4 pounds
salt and pepper
3 carrots, cut into 1-1/2-inch lengths
4 medium red potatoes, cut into 6 pieces
1/4 cup coriander flowers, coarsely chopped
3 tablespoons cornstarch dissolved in 3/4 cup water

Soak clay pot in water for 15 minutes, or according to manufacturer's directions.

Rub chicken with salt and pepper and place in bottom half of pot. Place carrots and potatoes around chicken.

Sprinkle with coriander flowers. Cover and place in a cold oven. Turn the oven on to 425° F. Bake for 1 hour and 15 minutes. Remove pot from oven, being careful to put it on a wood (not metal or glass as pot may crack) surface. Remove chicken and vegetables from pot and place on a serving platter.

Pour juices from pot into a saucepan. Heat until boiling. Slowly pour in cornstarch, stirring constantly. When sauce turns translucent and thickens to desired consistency, remove from heat. Carve chicken, serve with vegetables and sauce.

Serves 4 to 6.

CUCUMBER CORIANDER SALAD

4 ounces pecan halves or pieces

2 medium cucumbers

10 to 15 coriander flowers, broken into florets (reserve 1 or 2 whole flowers for garnish)

6 tablespoons plain yogurt

1 clove garlic, crushed

Toast the pecans in a small frying pan over a medium-high heat. Cut the cucumbers into quarters lengthwise. Remove the seeds and cut the remaining cucumber into 1/2-inch pieces. Mix the coriander flowers, yogurt and garlic in a bowl. Toss in the cucumber pieces and the toasted pecans. Garnish with whole coriander flowers.

Serves 4.

SOUTHWESTERN CHICKEN

1 tablespoon olive oil

3 tablespoons chive florets

4 chicken breast cutlets

2 tablespoons chive flower vinegar

1/2 cup tomatoes, peeled, seeded and cubed

1 cup corn

1/3 cup chicken broth

1/2 cup cream

2 tablespoons coriander flowers, chopped

Heat oil in a skillet over a medium-high heat. Add chive florets and chicken cutlets. Sauté 4 to 5 minutes on each side, until chicken is lightly browned. Remove chicken from skillet and keep warm.

Lower heat to medium. Pour in chive flower vinegar to deglaze the pan. Stir well. Add tomato cubes, corn, chicken broth, cream and coriander flowers. Cook for several minutes but do not allow it to come to a boil. Place chicken breasts on plates and spoon sauce around them. Serve immediately.

Serves 4.

DANDELION

DANDELION
(Pissabed, Pries' Crown, Telltime)
Taraxacum officinale
Composite family
Asteraceae (Compositae)
(Cichorium Tribe)
Sweet flavor
Perennial
Rich, well-drained soil
Cool, sun

The name is derived from the French *dent de lion*, which translates to lion's tooth, denoting the toothed edges to the leaves. The diuretic effect is evidenced from one of the common names, pissabed. In the language of flowers, dandelion denotes love's oracle.

Often looked upon disparagingly as the scourge of the perfect, well-manicured American lawn, dandelions were cultivated in European kitchen gardens for hundreds of years. The dandelion was purposely brought from Europe to the New World by the settlers.

Native Americans and the American pioneers made great use of all parts of the plant. Even today, the dandelion's versatility is widely enjoyed. Flowers are brewed into tea, wine and beer. The young leaves are delicious in salads or cooked as a green. The roots are often roasted and ground into a coffee substitute. Medicinally, the tea is used as a mild calmative.

Dandelions appear in the spring. The leaves are in a basal rosette, growing up to 12 inches long. The flowers are bright, buttercup yellow, borne singly on hollow stems that range in height from one to eighteen inches. Flower heads also vary in size from one-half to two and one-half inches in diameter, with several concentric rows of short yellow bracts.

Dandelion blossoms have a sweet, honeylike flavor when picked young. As the flowers mature, the flavor becomes bitter. The green sepals can also be somewhat bitter and should be removed for any recipe in which emphasis is placed on the sweet nature of the plant and for any brewed beverage. The flowers open in the morning and close at night, so pick dandelions immediately before using them as the flowers close quickly after picking.

CULTURE

The dandelion is a cosmopolitan herb. It was introduced from Europe to North America so long ago it is considered by some to be a native plant. Dandelions can be found growing wild throughout most of North American in grassy waste areas and on open ground.

For best leaf and flower production, sow seeds in the spring in rich, well-drained soil. Plant twelve inches apart in hills or drills. Seed can be collected from choice plants growing in the wild, although the purity is not guaranteed. For serious cultivation purposes, it is best to rely on purchased seed. I have noticed more and more dandelions appearing on lawns over the past two springs. This is in direct correlation with a decreased use of herbicides. With their bright flowers, they lend a cheery note to the otherwise stern appearance of formal lawns.

Dandelions are temperature and weather sensitive. Flowers appear in abundance during the cool clear days of mid-spring, and disappear when the weather gets hot. In the cool of autumn, a second flush of bloom appears.

Dandelions have long taproots, making them difficult to control. Digging up a portion of the plant while leaving any part of the root does not succeed in killing it. Pick the flowers before they go to seed to prevent additional seeding by the wind. Or, if you wish to spread dandelions, gently blow on the seed head and watch the featherlike seeds take flight.

WARNING

Contact dermatitis has been reported from handling dandelions. This is most likely from the latex in the leaves and stems.

Do not eat dandelions from lawns that have been chemically treated with herbicides, preemergents or weed-and-feed type fertilizers.

DANDELION WINE

4 quarts dandelion flowers (remove stem and sepals)
4 quarts granulated sugar
4 quarts boiling water
juice from 2 lemons
juice from 1 orange
1 yeast cake

Add dandelion flowers to a large stone crock or jar. Cover with sugar. Add boiling water. When water has cooled to lukewarm, add the lemon juice and orange juice. Break up the yeast cake and add to the liquid. Stir well. Cover loosely and let stand for 24 hours. Strain through cheesecloth and discard solids. Return liquid to the crock, loosely cover and let stand for 3 days.

Strain through several layers of cheesecloth. Return liquid to crock and allow to ferment. Bottle when all fermentation action stops. Keep at least 3 to 4 months before drinking.

Makes 1-1/2 gallons of wine.

EDIBLE FLOWERS

DANDELION "MUSHROOMS"

15 dandelion flowers, rinsed in water, but still slightly moist

1/2 cup all-purpose flour

2 tablespoons butter

Dredge the moist flowers in flour. Heat the butter in a heavy frying pan. Add flowers and fry quickly, turning to brown all sides. Serve hot. Close your eyes and pop one of these crisp goodies into your mouth. Would you believe it was a dandelion and not a fried mushroom?

Serves 4.

CORNMEAL DANDIES

1 egg

1 teaspoon water

1 cup cornmeal

1/4 cup Parmesan cheese, finely grated

1/4 cup peanut or vegetable oil

15 to 20 dandelion flowers

Beat eggs with water in a small bowl. Mix cornmeal and cheese in a small bowl. Heat oil in a heavy frying pan until it begins to sizzle. Dip each flower into the egg mixture, then place it in the cornmeal-cheese mixture and gently toss until all surfaces are covered. Gently drop the coated flower in the hot oil, turning frequently, until it is evenly golden. Drain on paper towel.

May be served immediately or later at room temperature.

This is a variation of a Native American dish. The slight bite of the cheese is a fine contrast to the sweetness of the flowers. A versatile recipe, serve the battered blossoms as a side dish, crunchy garnish or hors d'oeuvres.

DANDY EGGS

1 tablespoon sweet (unsalted) butter

20 dandelion buds

4 eggs

1 tablespoon water

4 dandelion flowers

Melt the butter in a 10-inch frying pan over a medium heat. Add the dandelion buds, cooking until they start to open into flowers. Whisk the eggs and water until the mixture is light and frothy. Slowly pour the eggs into the cooked buds, stirring gently as the eggs set. Cook to desired consistency. Serve garnished with dandelion flowers.

DIANTHUS

Dianthus literally means flower of the gods. In the Victorian language of flowers clove pinks mean make haste. Pinks were especially popular in kitchens of England and France in the sixteenth and seventeenth centuries. They were used in cordials, syrups, vinegars, butters and other culinary creations.

Wild clove pinks are native to the western Mediterranean. They are the horticultural parents of modern carnations.

Clove pinks are perennials hardy to zone 8. In most regions of the country they are grown as annuals. They range from one and one-half to three feet tall. Their foliage is an attractive gray blue. Pinks flourish in the cool weather of spring and fall and give out in the heat of summer.

Dianthus deltoides (maiden pink) has very small, narrow green leaves. It is low growing, forming a lovely mat in the garden. It is hardy to zone 4. The forked stalks (four to twelve inches tall) bear red or pink (occasionally white with crimson eye) three-fourths-inch flowers.

Depending on the climate, the semi-double rose-purple or white flowers bloom in spring or fall. Dianthus flowers have a sweet clove flavor that is quite versatile in the kitchen.

CULTURE

Clove pinks grow best in full sun. They will grow in ordinary garden soil as long as it is very well drained.

Dianthus are readily available in nurseries and

DIANTHUS
(Clove Pink, Pinks, Carnation, Gillyflower)
Dianthus caryophyllus
Pink family
Caryophyllaceae
Sweet clove flavor
Annual—tender perennial
Ordinary garden soil, well drained
Full sun

garden centers. Set out the plants in the spring after any danger of frost is past. Allow eight to twelve inches between plants.

Dianthus can be grown from seed sown outdoors in late spring or early summer. Seed can be sown indoors four weeks before the last frost date in spring. Seeds take two to three weeks to germinate.

Do not mulch dianthus as they need good air circulation around their roots.

Established plants can be divided in spring and replanted. You can wait and divide and replant in summer after they finish blooming.

Encourage repeat bloom by cutting off all faded flowers.

WARNING

Remove the narrow base of the petal (usually white in color) as it is often bitter.

REX SOLE WITH DIANTHUS BEURRE BLANC

1 tablespoon extra virgin olive oil
4 Rex sole, cleaned and skinned *
petals from 10 dianthus flowers, cut in half, divided
1/2 cup white wine
1 tablespoon butter, softened to room temperature

In a large skillet, heat olive oil over a medium heat. Add half of the dianthus petals and the sole. Sauté about 3 minutes on each side, until lightly browned. Remove sole from skillet and keep warm.

Remove skillet from heat while pouring in wine. Return the skillet to the heat and deglaze the pan, stirring to dissolve any brownings from the bottom. Add the rest of the dianthus petals and cook for 1 minute. When liquid has reduced by half, add butter a bit at a time, whisking continuously. Place sole on plates and pour on sauce. Garnish with dianthus petals.

Serves 4.

DIANTHUS TEA

1 tablespoon dianthus petals,
  chopped
1 cup boiling water

Steep petals in a cup of water for 3 to 5 minutes. Strain.

Serves 1.

* This is a small fish. If it is not available, use Dover or lemon sole fillets, allowing about 4 ounces per person.

PINK MARMALADE

———

1 cup granulated sugar

1 cup water

2 cups dianthus petals, coarsely chopped

Put sugar and water into a heavy, nonaluminum saucepan. Bring to a boil and simmer until it thickens to a syrup consistency. Add chopped petals and gently simmer, stirring frequently, until pulpy. Pour into sterilized jars and allow to cool to room temperature. Refrigerate for up to 3 weeks.

DIANTHUS SORBET

———

2 cups water

1/4 cup granulated sugar

1/2 cup dianthus petals, coarsely chopped

Pour water into a nonaluminum saucepan. Add granulated sugar and petals, stirring well to dissolve sugar. Bring liquid to a boil, turn down heat and allow to simmer for 5 minutes. Remove from heat and let cool to room temperature. Pour into an ice cream maker and process according to manufacturer's directions. Freeze until ready to serve.

Serves 4 to 6.

DILL

DILL (Dillweed, Dillseed)
Anethum graveolens
Carrot family
Apiaceae (Umbelliferae)
Herbal flavor
Annual/biennial
Well-drained soil
Full sun

Dill derives its name from the Old Norse word *dilla*, meaning to lull. Indeed the oil derived from the seed has long been used in potions to soothe colicky babies and settle adult digestive upsets.

The ancient Egyptians and Romans used dill as a medicinal herb, with documentation dating back five thousand years. The ancient Greeks and Romans wove dill into garlands to crown the foreheads of their conquering heroes. The Romans wove the yellow flowers into wreaths that served a double duty in their banquet halls. The lovely decorations had a peculiar aroma which was at the same time fresh and spicy.

Today dill is cultivated chiefly as a culinary herb. The leaves can be used fresh or dried, often in salads and with fish. The seeds are the flavoring that give dill pickles, which originated in Germany, their name and characteristic flavor.

Originally native to Asia, dill has naturalized throughout most of temperate Europe and North America. It grows along roadsides and in waste places. Dill is a hardy annual or biennial herb, averaging three or more feet in height. One hollow green stem branches to leafstalks bearing fine, feathery bluish green leaves. Yellow flowers on slightly domed umbels appear at the ends of the branches in midsummer, spreading to look like miniature umbrellas. The flowers are followed by the seeds, which are actually fruits, distinguished by their prominent ribs. Like many of the herbs, the flowers of dill have a milder yet similar flavor to the leaves. The flowers are lightly pungent and sharp-tasting.

CULTURE

Dill can grow in poor soil, as long as it is well drained, but prefers fairly good, well-drained soil. In mild climates, sunny, open areas are best for cultivating dill. In more temperate areas, protect dill's willowy stems from the wind. Do not plant near fennel, as cross-pollination will occur.

Grow dill from seed in late spring or early summer. Dill has delicate roots and does not transplant well, so seed it directly into the garden. Thin plants to about twelve to fifteen inches apart. Planted on the north side of the garden, it will not shade any lower growing plants.

With its fernlike foliage, dill is beautiful in the garden. Consider planting it against a wall at the back of the border. Don't restrict this beautiful herb to the vegetable or herb garden.

DILLY SOUP

1 tablespoon olive oil

1 tablespoon curry powder

1/4 teaspoon freshly grated ginger

1/4 cup onion, finely chopped

2 cups zucchini, thinly sliced

4 cups chicken stock

1 tablespoon dill florets, coarsely chopped

1 cup half-and-half

Heat olive oil in a medium saucepan. Add curry powder, ginger and onion. Sauté until onion becomes translucent. Stir in zucchini and cook for 4 minutes. Add chicken stock and dill florets. Simmer gently for 15 minutes. Allow soup to cool for 15 minutes. Puree soup in a blender or food processor. Return to saucepan and add half-and-half. Reheat but do not boil. Serve garnished with additional dill florets. Delicious hot or cold.

Serves 4 to 6.

DILLED POTATO SALAD

from Pat Lanza, Shandelee Herb Garden,
Livingston Manor, New York

8 medium red potatoes

1/4 cup onion, coarsely chopped

1/4 cup celery, coarsely chopped

1/4 cup walnuts, coarsely chopped

1 hard-boiled egg, coarsely chopped

1 cup mayonnaise

1/8 cup dill flowers, coarsely chopped

salt and pepper to taste

Boil potatoes until tender. Cool and dice into 1-inch cubes. Toss potatoes with all other ingredients in a large bowl. Refrigerate for at least 1 hour to allow the flavors to meld.

Serves 8 to 12.

MUSSELS WITH TOMATO AND DILL FLORETS

from José Gutierrez, executive chef, Chez Philippe, Peabody Hotel, Memphis, Tennessee

20 mussels

1 cup onion, coarsely chopped

1 cup white wine

1 teaspoon garlic, finely chopped

3 tablespoons dill florets, divided

1 teaspoon sweet red pepper sauce (available in Oriental markets) or red pepper puree

1 cup cream

salt and pepper

1/4 cup tomato strips

Rinse mussels through several changes of water until there is no grit left. Discard any open mussels that do not close when gently tapped. Place onion and mussels in a large skillet with white wine and garlic. Cover and cook over high heat for 5 minutes, until it boils and the mussels open. Remove the mussels from the skillet and set aside.

Return the skillet to the heat, adding 1 tablespoon dill florets, red pepper sauce and cream. Stir and add salt and pepper to taste. Boil for 2 to 3 minutes. Strain liquid. Add remaining dill florets (reserving some for garnish) and tomato strips. Remove top shell from mussels and arrange tastefully on a large soup plate. Pour sauce over mussels and serve immediately.

Serves 1 for dinner or 2 as an appetizer.

ELDERBERRY

The word elder is derived from the Anglo-Saxon *aeld*, meaning fire. The hollow branches of the plant were blown through to increase the flames of fires. Pliny used the name *Sambucus* to describe this plant two thousand years ago. It is derived from the Greek *sambuca* referring to the Roman woodwind instrument. It is interesting to note that western American Indians called it (*Sambucus caerulea*) "the tree of music," as they bored a hole through the pith to make a flute. They also used the long shoots for arrow shafts.

Mythically, the elder is considered to be the witch's tree. Supposedly it is a favored form for a witch to assume. You could tell if your plant was a witch, as it would bleed if it were cut. Many superstitions surrounded the plant; people were hesitant to cut one down or burn it. Some people planted elderberries around their houses to protect against witches or in graveyards to guide happiness to the deceased.

Evidence of elderberry cultivation has been found in Stone Age sites in Switzerland and Italy. Elderberry (*Sambucus canadensis*) can be found growing wild in rich soils from Nova Scotia to Georgia and Texas to Manitoba. *Sambucus caerulea* grows in open areas from California to western Canada.

Elderberry is a large deciduous shrub, which can easily grow to ten feet in height. The stems have a thick white pith. The leaves are compound, growing opposite on the branches. Each leaflet is oval and toothed, with five or seven comprising a leaf.

ELDERBERRY
Sambucus canadensis and
Sambucus caerulea
Honeysuckle family
Caprifoliaceae
Sweet flavor
Shrub
Rich, well-drained soil
Full sun

The small white or off-white flowers, often called elderblow, appear in flat umbrellalike clusters in June and July. By late summer the berries ripen, turning purplish black.

The flowers are delightfully sweet scented and sweet tasting. When harvesting elderberry flowers, do not wash them as that removes much of the fragrance and flavor. Instead, check them carefully for insects.

CULTURE

Elderberry prefers moist, sheltered areas in which to grow. Plant in full sun in rich, moist, but well-drained soil.

Plants can be purchased at nurseries or garden centers. Water well after planting. Once established, an elderberry needs little care.

EDIBLE FLOWERS

The leaves, bark, branches and roots of elderberries contain poisonous alkaloids. Only the flowers, not even the stems of the recommended elderberriess, should be eaten. The berries should only be eaten after they have been cooked or processed as with wine or jam, never eaten raw. Even the flowers should not be consumed directly from the plant.

The tea can act as a mild laxative or promote sweating in some individuals; drink it in moderation.

ELDERBLOW TEA

elder blossoms
water to cover
lemon wedges
honey

In a nonmetallic container, cover the elder blossoms with cold water. Allow them to soak for 24 hours. Strain and discard the flowers. Dilute with water to taste. Serve with a squeeze of lemon and sweeten with honey to taste.

ELDERBLOW MINT TEA

1 cup elderblow
3 sprigs mint
4 cups water

Add elderblow and mint to boiling water. Steep for 10 minutes. Strain. Delicious served hot or cold. This drink is supposedly good to calm a queasy stomach.

ELDERBLOW MUFFINS

1 cup unbleached flour, sifted
2 teaspoons baking powder
1/2 teaspoon salt
1/4 cup granulated sugar
1 1/2 cups elderblow
2 tablespoons sweet (unsalted)butter, melted
1 egg, beaten
1/2 cup buttermilk
1/2 cup orange juice

Preheat oven to 400°F. Sift together dry ingredients into a bowl. Toss in flowers. In a separate bowl, mix butter, egg, buttermilk and orange juice. Add wet mixture to dry, stirring only until dry ingredients are moistened.

Grease muffin tins. Fill each cup 2/3 with batter. Bake 20 to 25 minutes until muffins are lightly brown.

Makes 24 muffins.

ELDERBLOW CORN FRITTERS

2 eggs, separated

3/4 cup beer

4 tablespoons vegetable oil, divided

1/2 teaspoon salt

1 cup all-purpose flour

1/3 cup elderblow

1 cup fresh corn kernels

In a bowl, whisk together egg yolks, beer, 2 tablespoons vegetable oil and salt. Add flour, stirring until batter is smooth. Mix in elderblow florets and corn kernels. In a separate bowl, beat egg whites until they are stiff. Gently fold egg whites into batter.

Heat a frying pan over medium-high heat. Add oil. Drop batter by rounded tablespoonfuls into the pan. Turn over when bubbles on top of fritters break. Fritters are traditionally deep fried—these are equally delicious without the added fat.

Serves 4 as a main dish for lunch or 6 as a side dish.

ENGLISH DAISY

ENGLISH DAISY
Bellis perennis
Composite family
Asteraceae (Compositae)
Bitter flavor
Perennial/biennial
Moist soil
Full sun

Despite its name, the English daisy is native to Eurasia. It has been widely cultivated in northern Europe and England.

This plant is to the English what the dandelion is to Americans, a rather invasive lawn weed. Ironically, in England dandelions are cultivated plants widely available in nurseries, while in America, English daisies are cultivated. In California and the Pacific Northwest, however, the weather is mild enough for these perennial beauties to seed themselves into lawns occasionally, yet they are still not looked upon as a scourge the way dandelions are.

English daisies are perennials that grow to six inches tall. The leaves are at the base of the plant, forming a tuft. The flower heads grow singly on thin stalks. Flower heads average between one and two inches across with white,

pink or red ray flowers surrounding the center of yellow disk flowers. English daisies bloom in the spring and early summer. Single, semi-double and double flowers are available.

The ray flowers have a mildly bitter taste and are more commonly used for their looks than their flavor.

CULTURE

English daisies prefer to grow in full sun and moist soil. They thrive in cool weather.

Although they are technically perennial, in cold areas they are often treated as tender annuals or biennials. In warm areas, they are treated as hardy biennials.

In warm areas with mild winters, sow seed directly in the garden in late summer. This will give a lovely show of color for winter and spring. In areas with cold winters, start the seeds indoors in midwinter. Grow them in temperatures between fifty-five and sixty-five degrees Fahrenheit. Transplant into the garden as soon as the soil can be worked. Place a light mulch of soil over the plants until all danger of frost is past. In this manner, you will have a show of color for late spring.

Pick off spent flowers. If the summer is cool, a second flush of bloom can occur in late summer or early autumn.

BAVARIAN BEANS

———

1 pound string beans, cut into 1-1/2–inch pieces

1 small sausage or wurst, crumbled

2 tablespoons parsley, finely chopped

1 tablespoon summer savory flowers, coarsely chopped

1 ounce pasta, cooked al dente, drained and cut into 1-1/2–inch pieces

2 tablespoons English daisy petals

Steam beans until they turn bright green and are still crispy. Drain.

While beans are steaming, cook sausage bits in a skillet over a medium-high heat. Sauté until the sausage begins to brown. Drain excess fat from pan. Add parsley and summer savory flowers and cook with sausage over a low heat for 2 minutes. Toss in beans and pasta and cook until everything is completely heated through. Garnish with English daisy petals and serve immediately.

Serves 4 to 6.

SUNSHINE CAKE

———

from Applewood Seed Company, Golden, Colorado

2-1/4 cups all-purpose flour, sifted
2-1/2 teaspoons baking powder
1 teaspoon salt
2/3 cup butter, softened
1-1/2 cups granulated sugar
3 eggs
1 cup milk
1-1/2 teaspoons vanilla
2 9-inch round cake pans, greased and floured

Preheat oven to 350°F. In a bowl, sift together flour, baking powder and salt. Set aside. In a separate bowl, cream butter and sugar until the mixture is light and fluffy. Add eggs, beating thoroughly. Alternately add flour and milk, beating well after each addition. Stir in vanilla. Pour into prepared pans. Bake 20 to 30 minutes or until a toothpick inserted in the center of each cake comes out clean. Place pans on a cooling rack for 10 minutes. Remove cakes from pans, cool completely on rack.

Frosting:
1/2 cup butter, softened
8 ounces cream cheese, softened
4 cups confectioners' sugar, sifted
1 teaspoon vanilla
1 teaspoon jasmine essence (optional—available in Middle-Eastern or Oriental markets. If not available, substitute orange flower water or rose water.)
English daisy petals

In a bowl, cream together butter and cream cheese. Gradually add sugar, beating continually. Add vanilla and jasmine essence. Beat until smooth. Frost cake. Garnish cake with English daisy petals.

fENNEL

One of the superstitions surrounding fennel is that anyone who eats it will have clearer vision. Like dill, fennel was also a symbol of victory to the ancient Greeks and Romans. For centuries fennel was used ritualistically, and later medicinally. It was not until the fourteenth century that fennel seed began to be appreciated as a culinary herb. The rich used it to flavor fish and vegetables, while the poor used it as an appetite suppressant on fast days.

Originally native to the Mediterranean area, fennel is now cultivated worldwide. Fennel was first brought to North America by Spanish priests, evidenced by it growing wild around old missions. Today fennel has also naturalized along roadsides from Connecticut to Florida, and from Nebraska to Michigan. In the Southwest, especially in California, it has become a common weed.

Fennel is a perennial herb that is often grown as an annual. Fennel and dill are sometimes confused, but a closer look reveals the differences. Both are graceful looking plants to have in the garden. Fennel's stems are blue-green, glossy and somewhat flattened at the base. The foliage is bright green and feathery. The clusters of tiny yellow flowers in flat-topped umbels do not appear until the summer of the second year. By fall the flowers have matured, producing one-quarter-inch gray green seeds (actually fruits) that are much used in Indian and other cookery.

The plant itself gives off a strong anise scent. It is beautiful in flower arrangements and keeps its scent for days.

CULTURE

Fennel grows happily in average garden soil. Fennel can grow four to six feet tall. Plant it along the

FENNEL
Foeniculum vulgare
Carrot family
Apiaceae (Umbelliferae)
Anise flavor
Annual/perennial
Average garden soil
Partial shade to full sun

north side of the garden to keep it from casting shade on other plants.

In mild areas of the country, sow seed of fennel in early spring. In colder areas, seed fennel into the garden in July. Of course, like many of the other herbs, small plants are available at nurseries and garden centers. They can be planted anytime in spring after danger of frost is past. Allow at least eight inches between plants.

Bronze fennel is somewhat lower growing than wild fennel and more compact in its habit. A row of it is very handsome in the vegetable garden. I have seen a grouping of three or more bronze fennel in a perennial border—the effect is striking, indeed. In western gardens, bronze fennel really thrives as a hardy perennial.

The flavor of fennel flowers is mildly anise.

WARNING

Fennel or the seed oil may cause contact dermatitis in sensitive individuals.

EDIBLE FLOWERS

MARA'S PLEBEIAN DIP WITH FENNEL

from Carole Saville, Los Angeles, California

1 7-ounce can lima beans

1 clove garlic, minced

juice of 1 lemon

3 fennel flowers, minced

pepper to taste

small jar black caviar (the inexpensive kind is fine)

Drain lima beans. In a bowl, crush lima beans with a mortar or the back of a spoon so each bean is mashed. Do not use a food processor or blender as the result will be too uniform in consistency. Add minced garlic, lemon juice and fennel flowers. Season with pepper to taste. Mix well. Fold in caviar, taking care not to crush eggs. Cover and refrigerate for several hours or overnight to allow the flavors to meld. When ready to serve, scoop mixture into a serving dish and garnish with fennel leaves and flowers.

Serve with melba toast as a unique hors d'oeuvres.

Serves 8 to 12.

PINK CAULIFLOWER

1/2 cup chicken broth

1 tablespoon tomato paste

1 tablespoon olive oil

1 cauliflower, broken into florets

5 to 10 fennel flowers, broken into florets

Mix the broth, tomato paste and olive oil in a saucepan. Bring to a boil over a medium heat. Add the cauliflower and fennel, stirring to coat all parts of the cauliflower. Cover and cook for 5 minutes. Turn the cauliflower, and cook for about 5 minutes more, or until just tender. An unusually colored dish with great flavor.

Serves 4.

POPPYSEED CHICKEN

—

4 tablespoons olive oil

1/3 cup orange juice

2 cloves garlic, crushed

4 chicken breast pieces, boned and skinned

1/4 cup fennel florets

1/2 cup fresh bread crumbs

2 tablespoons poppy seeds

Mix the oil, orange juice, garlic and fennel florets together in a large bowl. Add the chicken pieces. Turn the chicken so it is well coated with the marinating liquid. Cover the bowl with plastic wrap and refrigerate for at least 4 hours, turning the chicken at least once.

Preheat the oven to 375°F. Place chicken in a flat baking dish and bake for 20 minutes. While the chicken is cooking, add the bread crumbs and poppy seeds to the remaining marinade. Spoon this mixture on top of the chicken and bake for an additional 15 to 20 minutes, until crumbs become brown and crispy.

Serves 4.

APPLE PIE

—

1/2 cup granulated sugar

1/3 cup brown sugar

2 tablespoons all-purpose flour

2 tablespoons fennel florets, finely chopped

6 tart apples, peeled and sliced thin

pastry for a 9-inch pie crust in pie pan

2 tablespoons butter

Preheat oven to 375°F. In a bowl, combine sugar, brown sugar, flour and fennel florets. Toss in the apples. Add mixture to pie pan. Cut butter into small pieces and dot over apples. Bake for about 35 to 45 minutes, or until apples are cooked.

The Fennel flowers give this traditional dish a new twist.

Serves 6 to 8.

GARLIC CHIVES

GARLIC CHIVES
(*Chinese chives*)
Allium tuberosum
Amaryllis family
Amaryllidaceae
Onion flavor
Perennial, self-seeding
Well-drained soil
Full sun

Garlic chives are a perennial, hardy to zone 4. The long, flat, narrow, gray-green leaves grow about twelve inches tall. The leaves are grasslike in appearance, but solid enough to be upright. The edible leaves have a strong garlic flavor.

Besides its use as an edible herb, this is an attractive plant in the perennial border. The flowers are bright, showing up well against a dark background. The most striking planting of garlic chives I have ever seen was a crescent moon-shaped garden. The entire garden was about twelve feet long. In late summer, when I viewed it, the planting was simple but nonetheless eye-catching. The entire border of the garden was lamb's ears (not edible, alas) and the rest of the garden was garlic chives. With a full moon hanging over it, it was quite a sight.

The flower stems reach eighteen to thirty inches high, topped with a flat-headed cluster of white flowers in summer. Each individual flower has a piquant garlic-onion flavor with a slight crunch.

CULTURE

Garlic chives grow best in full sun. Plant from mid-spring through summer. Allow twelve inches between plants.

Garlic chives can be aggressive. Plants can be divided and thinned whenever necessary. It also self-seeds. Keep picking the flower heads as they mature and before they drop seeds.

If the plant starts getting too woody-looking, trim the foliage back to within an inch of the ground. As traumatic as it may seem, it will benefit from such a severe pruning.

WARNING

These pretty little flowers pack a lot of flavor. Use individual florets for garnish, not the entire flower cluster.

TOSTADA WITH GARLIC CHIVES

1 teaspoon butter

1 teaspoon olive oil

florets from 4 garlic chive flowers, chopped

10 ounces mushrooms, sliced

4 8-inch flour tostadas (flour tortillas, deep fried to crisp)

1 cup red leaf lettuce, shredded

1 cup Romaine lettuce, shredded

1 can red kidney beans, drained

1/3 cup black olives, sliced

1 cup Monterey Jack cheese, grated

florets from 1 garlic chive flower for garnish

In a small frying pan, melt butter in olive oil over a medium heat. Add chopped garlic chive florets and mushrooms. Sauté until mushrooms soften, but do not let them brown. Place tostadas on 4 plates. Add shredded lettuces to each tostada, covering all but the outer edge of the tortilla. Spoon on the kidney beans, followed by sautéed mushrooms, cheese and olives. Garnish with garlic chive florets. A lighter version of the typical tostada without meat, guacamole or sour cream—still very tasty.

Serves 4.

SCALLOPS WITH PEPPER SAUCE

1 tablespoon olive oil

1 tablespoon butter

3 garlic chive flowers, broken into florets and chopped

1 sweet red pepper, seeded and coarsely chopped

1 pound sea scallops

2 tablespoons cream

In a skillet, heat the oil and butter over a medium heat. Add garlic chive florets and peppers. Sauté about 5 minutes. Do not let the peppers or flowers brown. Add scallops and cook an additional 5 minutes. Remove scallops from skillet and keep warm. Over a high heat, reduce liquid in skillet by half, stirring frequently. Add cream and cook for 1 minute. Divide scallops between 2 plates and spoon sauce over them. Serve immediately.

An interesting contrast of sweet peppers and spicy garlic chives.

Serves 2.

COYOTE CHICKEN

from Robert Werst, chef/owner, y.e. coyote, Hicksville, New York

4 small chicken breasts, split (8 pieces)
1/2 cup olive oil
1/2 cup sweetened lime juice
1/4 cup mild chili powder
2 tablespoons garlic, finely chopped
6 to 8 chipotle peppers (smoked jalepeño peppers, available in
* gourmet food shops)*
salt and freshly ground pepper
1/2 cup garlic chive florets

Place chicken breasts in a shallow glass baking dish (do not use metal). Mix the rest of the ingredients in a bowl. Pour over the chicken. Turn chicken to coat all sides. Cover chicken with plastic wrap and refrigerate overnight or up to 24 hours, turning occasionally.

Mesquite grill or broil chicken about 7 minutes per side or until done. Mesquite grilling gives the chicken a smoky, nutty flavor that you miss with broiling.

Serves 4.

GRILLED LAMB WITH GARLIC CHIVES AND MUSTARD

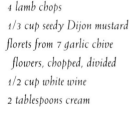

4 lamb chops
1/3 cup seedy Dijon mustard
florets from 7 garlic chive
* flowers, chopped, divided*
1/2 cup white wine
2 tablespoons cream

Brush all sides of lamb chops with mustard. Press garlic chive florets into the mustard. Heat a large nonstick frying pan. When pan is hot add chops. Cook about 5 minutes on each side—lamb will still be pink when done. Remove chops from pan, set aside and keep warm.

Remove the pan from the heat while adding the wine to deglaze the pan. Return to a medium-high heat and stir well to loosen any brownings. Cook for 2 to 3 minutes, lower heat and add cream. Cook for 1 minute more. Place chops on serving plates and spoon sauce over them. Garnish with garlic chive florets. Serve immediately.

Serves 4.

VEAL MEDALLIONS WITH ANISE AND GARLIC

from Jim Bain, executive chef, East Hill Woods, Southbury, Connecticut

1 bulb garlic (yes, entire bulb, not 1 clove)
4 veal chops or 4 slices of veal loin 1/2-inch thick
salt and freshly ground black pepper
1/3 cup all-purpose flour
1-1/2 teaspoons sweet paprika
8 tablespoons butter, divided
1/3 cup dry white wine
1 cup garlic chive florets, coarsely chopped
1-1/2 teaspoons Pernod or other anise-flavored liqueur

Peel the garlic and cut into matchstick-sized strips. Place in a pot of cold water. Bring to a boil. Drain immediately and set garlic aside.

Trim all fat from the veal chops. Season to taste with salt and pepper. Combine flour and paprika in a bowl. Dredge veal chops in flour mixture.

In a skillet, melt 4 tablespoons of butter over a medium heat. Add veal chops and brown for 5 minutes. Turn chops, sprinkle with the garlic pieces and cook for 5 minutes longer. Remove the veal from the pan and set aside.

Pour the wine into the skillet and bring to a boil. Deglaze the pan, scraping and stirring. Add garlic chives and stir. Add Pernod to pan and flame. Add remaining butter in small bits, whisking continually.

Place veal chops on plates. Spoon sauce over chops. Garnish with additional garlic chive florets. Serve immediately.

Serves 4.

GREEK OREGANO

GREEK OREGANO
(Oregano)
Origanum heracleoticum
Mint family
Lamiaceae (Labiatae)
Herbal flavor
Perennial
Rich, moist soil
Sun

Greek oregano is a beautiful perennial. In colder climates it is treated as an annual. In warm climates it may grow to three feet tall. The half-inch oval leaves are gray green and slightly pungent. It is commonly used in Italian sauces and sprinkled on pizza. Large clusters of pale purplish pink flowers bloom through the summer months. In a warm climate, it can make an attractive edible hedge.

The flavor of Greek oregano flowers is also a more pungent herb than the common oregano or pot marjoram already discussed.

CULTURE
Unlike its cousins, Greek oregano prefers a rich, moist soil. See pages 154 and 155 for detailed *Origanum* culture.

CORNY SALAD

———

4 ripe tomatoes, cut into bite-sized pieces
1 cup raw corn, cut fresh from the cob
2 stalks celery, cut into bite-sized diagonals
1 sweet pepper (red, yellow or orange for color interest), diced
1 teaspoon Greek oregano flowers
1 teaspoon basil flowers
1 teaspoon thyme flowers
1 avocado, well mashed—save the pit
juice of 1 lime or lemon

Mix all ingredients together in a nonmetallic bowl. If not serving right away, refrigerate with the avocado pit; this keeps the avocado from turning brown. Garnish with herb florets.

Stuff mixture into a hollowed-out tomato or sweet pepper or in a tulip flower for a sensational and delicious presentation. Avocado is a good source of protein, making this a great hot weather main course.

Serves 4.

VEAL CUTLET WITH OREGANO FLOWERS

———

4 veal cutlets
1/2 cup all-purpose flour
1 tablespoon butter
2 tablespoons olive oil
1 red onion, finely chopped
2 cloves garlic, crushed
1/2 cup sherry
1/2 cup beef broth or stock
1/4 cup oregano flowers

Place each cutlet between 2 pieces of waxed paper and pound to a thickness of 1/4 inch. Dredge the cutlets in the flour. Heat butter and oil in a frying pan over medium-high heat until butter starts to sizzle. Put the cutlets in the pan, turning to brown both sides quickly. Remove them from the pan and set aside.

Lower the heat. Put onion and garlic in the pan, and cook until just softened and glistening (not browned). Add sherry and broth and bring the mixture to a boil. Add oregano flowers and stir to mix into the liquid. Return the cutlets to the pan. Cover and simmer for 20 minutes. Spoon the thickened sauce over each cutlet.

Serves 4.

HIBISCUS

Hibiscus rosa-sinensis is among the most widely cultivated of the more than three hundred different species of hibiscus. Native to tropical Asia, hibiscus is now found growing in tropical and subtropical areas worldwide.

Chinese hibiscus is an evergreen, growing as a small tree or large shrub. In the wild it can grow to thirty feet high; in cultivation it grows to a more controllable four to fifteen feet. The deep green, glossy, oval leaves are somewhat pointed and slightly toothed on the edges. Leaves range from one to four inches long.

The flowers are large and exotic looking. When fully open the flared, five-petaled flower can be four to six inches across with brilliantly hued petals of orange, red or purplish red. The reproductive parts of the flowers stick out on a long filament, adding to their exotic beauty. Usually each flower only lasts for a day or two, but new buds are constantly produced, making the hibiscus almost ever blooming.

Hibiscus' main culinary contribution is the luscious red color and mild citrus/cranberry flavor that it imparts to teas.

CULTURE

Hibiscus rosa-sinensis is hardy in zone 10. Elsewhere it must be grown in a container. It can be taken outdoors for the summer. As it is not frost hardy, it must be brought back inside before the cold weather sets in. It can be kept indoors year-round in a greenhouse.

Hibiscus grows best in full sun and well-drained soil. Protect it from the wind by growing it in a sheltered location. To achieve a full, lushly formed plant, prune the hibiscus stems back by one-third of their length each spring.

There is a good choice of hibiscus cultivars available commercially, subsequently hibiscus is not often propagated by amateur growers. Softwood cuttings can be taken in the summer. Because most hibiscus are hybrids, growing them from seed does not often result in plants true to the parent.

EXPANDING YOUR PLEASURES

HIBISCUS TEA

1 tablespoon hibiscus petals, fresh or 1 teaspoon dried

1 cup boiling water

honey (optional)

Steep petals in water in a cup for 5 minutes. For additional sweetness add honey, if desired.

Serves 1.

CALIFORNIA ROLL—HAWAIIAN STYLE

16 hibiscus flowers

1 cup cooked sushi rice

1 avocado, cut into 1/2-inch cubes

1/4 pound crab meat, cut into small pieces

black and white sesame seeds

soy sauce or tamari

wasabi

Place a teaspoonful of rice into each flower. Add a piece of avocado and a piece of crab meat. Sprinkle with sesame seeds. If desired, have soy sauce or tamari and wasabi (Japanese horseradish sauce) for dipping. A beautiful appetizer or hors d'oeuvres.

Serves 4 to 8.

HONEYSUCKLE

HONEYSUCKLE (Wild
honeysuckle, Japanese
honeysuckle)
 Lonicera japonica
Honeysuckle family
Caprifoliaceae
Floral flavor
Perennial vine
Any soil
Full sun

In the Victorian language of flowers, honeysuckle denotes affection. If, as an adult, you try to recreate some wonderful childhood memory it often falls short of your expectation. Not only that, but the less than wonderful adult experience manages to tarnish the childhood memory. I had not tasted honeysuckle in over thirty years. It was with more than slight trepidation that I went to try this childhood favorite. As I bit into the end of the flower, I could sense the presence of the nectar. The aroma and sweet flavor were just as I had remembered. That is the good news about honeysuckle.

Honeysuckle was imported into America from Japan around the turn of the century. It was highly touted as a decorative climber. Indeed it is both decorative and climbing, however, now it is considered to be a pernicious weed. It is described as an evergreen, twining vine that climbs or covers the ground, self-rooting as it goes. The vine can easily grow to thirty feet in length. The stems are slightly hairy. The two to three-inch leaves, which grow opposite on the stems, have a somewhat narrow heart shape. The leaves are deep green, often downy below, but less commonly downy above.

The flowers appear in May and continue to bloom sporadically through late summer. When the first flush of bloom is on the vine, the scent wafts through the air, especially at night. That is the time to discover where the honeysuckle is growing; its sweet perfume will lead you to the plant. The flowers are trumpet-shaped, growing in pairs. The flowers start off white, occasionally tinged purple, and turn buff yellow as they mature.

At the base of the flower is the cache of nectar, which is actually what gives the sweet flavor. Carefully break a tiny piece at the base of the flower, without breaking the filament. Slowly pull the piece away from the flower, bringing the filament toward you. Just as it reaches the base of the flower you see a drop of golden nectar. Touch it to your tongue. What a sensual delight! That is the same flavor you get when you eat the entire flower, a floral, nectarous delectation.

In Japan, the flowers are used to make a beverage tea, available commercially in Asian markets.

CULTURE
There is more information in the literature on how to control and eradicate Japanese honeysuckle than there is on trying to grow it. Although it is

beautiful to grow up a trellis or bower, the risk is too great that this plant will get out of bounds. Once it does, it can spread rapidly in open sunny areas or under (and around and up) trees as well, strangling anything in its path.

Don't grow it, but take advantage of it where you do find it and enjoy the flowers. Share them with your children and your parents. Everyone should know the joy of tasting a honeysuckle.

WARNING

Only *Lonicera japonica* is edible. Although the many other varieties of honeysuckle are recommended as ornamental in the garden, do not eat them.

HONEYSUCKLE STRAWBERRY SORBET

1/2 cup honeysuckle flowers
3 cups strawberries, cleaned, hulled and cut in half

Cut pistils and stamens out of honeysuckle flower, being careful not to remove the nectar at the base of the flower. Put flowers and strawberries into the bowl of a food processor fitted with the metal blade. Process until smooth.

Pour mixture into an ice cream maker and freeze according to manufacturer's directions. Serve garnished with several honeysuckle flowers.

An ambrosial dessert with no added sugar. The honeysuckle is in peak bloom at the same time the local strawberries are ripe, making a wonderful marriage of flavors.

Serves 6 to 8.

HYSSOP

HYSSOP Hyssopus officinalis
Mint family
Lamiaceae (Labiatae)
Strong herbal flavor
Perennial
Well-drained soil
Partial shade

Hyssop is an evergreen herb native to the Mediterranean. It has been prized since ancient times for its medicinal value. Because of the strong aroma of the leaves, European women supposedly pressed them in the pages of their prayer books to keep them awake during services. Pungent flavors are not as popular as they were it the past; the culinary use of hyssop has declined since the Middle Ages. Monks used to use the herb for seasoning soups and sauces. Romans used it as a base for an herbal wine. In the Victorian language of flowers, hyssop means cleanliness.

Hyssop is native to Eurasia. Early settlers brought it to America for its medicinal qualities. It was much used as a treatment for respiratory problems. Today it has naturalized from Quebec west to Montana and as far south as North Carolina.

This multistalked herb usually grows from twelve to twenty-four inches tall. It is interesting to see that the new stems are square, rounding off as they flower. The leaves are small, narrow and pointed or lance-shaped. The blue (sometimes pink or white) flowers appear in spikes in the leaf axils from July to October.

Hyssop has been described as aromatic, hot and bitter. To me it tastes like tonic. With such an unusual flavor, a little bit can go a long way, so use it sparingly. Experiment with it, if it doesn't appeal to you, that's all right, there are many better tasting flowers for you to try. Hyssop is used as a flavoring for the liqueur Chartreuse.

CULTURE

Hyssop is the plant you have all been waiting for—an edible flower that thrives in partial shade and ordinary soil. If the soil is good and rich, the plant will grow luxuriantly, but flavor and aroma are sacrificed.

Sow the seeds in early spring in light, well-drained soil in partial shade. Transplant them, if necessary, in early summer, allowing twelve inches between plants. As it blooms, keep cutting it back. It will keep blooming for a long period, and new tender leaves will be produced. Once established, hyssop will self-seed in the garden.

Hyssop is very effective as a small hedge in a formal herb garden.

EXPANDING YOUR PLEASURES

AVOCADO AND PAPAYA SALAD WITH HYSSOP VINAIGRETTE

from Carole Saville, Los Angeles, California

1 small head Nappa cabbage
1 papaya
1 avocado
1 teaspoon hyssop flowers, finely chopped

Shred Nappa cabbage and set aside. Peel and cut papaya into crescent slices, saving the rind. Set sliced papaya aside. Over a bowl, squeeze the papaya rind to express any extra juice. With a whisk, incorporate the juice into the Hyssop Vinaigrette. Pit and cut avocado into crescents and set aside. In a salad bowl, toss the cabbage with 2/3 of the vinaigrette.

Divide cabbage among 4 salad plates. Arrange both avocado and papaya slices artfully atop the cabbage. Spoon the remaining vinaigrette over the papaya and avocado. Garnish with hyssop florets and serve.

Serves 4.

Hyssop Vinaigrette

2 tablespoons white wine
 vinegar
5 tablespoons canola oil
1 tablespoon extra virgin olive
 oil
1 teaspoon hyssop flowers,
 finely chopped
salt and white pepper

In a bowl, pour in white wine vinegar, then whisk in canola oil and extra virgin olive oil until emulsified. Add hyssop flowers, and salt and pepper to taste.

Makes 1/2 cup.

HYSSOP STUFFED PORK

1 tablespoon extra virgin olive oil
2 shallots, finely chopped
1 stalk celery, finely chopped
2 mushrooms, finely chopped
3/4 cup chicken broth
1 tablespoon hyssop flowers, finely chopped
1-1/2 cup fresh bread crumbs
4 thick-cut pork chops (or substitute chicken breast cutlets), cut
 in half up to the bone

Preheat oven to 375°F.

Heat oil in a skillet. Add shallots, celery, mushrooms and sauté for 4 minutes, stirring frequently. Add chicken broth and hyssop flowers. Remove from heat. Toss in bread crumbs, until evenly moistened. Stuff pork chops. Heat skillet. Add pork chops and sear both sides. Place chops in a shallow baking pan and bake for 20 to 30 minutes, or until done.

Serves 4.

JASMINE

JASMINE

(Arabian jasmine) Jasminum sambac
Olive family
Oleaceae
Vine hardy zone 10
Sweet perfumed flavor
Well-drained soil
Bright light

The roots of Arabian jasmine are probably in tropical Asia, but it has been cultivated for thousands of years and its true history has become lost.

Jasmine is a vining plant, hardy only in zone 10. In all other areas, it can be grown as a houseplant that blooms in winter.

The tubular, white flowers are borne in clusters in the winter. The flowers are intensely fragrant and are traditionally used for scenting tea.

CULTURE

Grow jasmine in bright light, with several hours of full sun a day. It prefers temperatures of sixty degrees Fahrenheit at night and eighty degrees Fahrenheit during the day. Keep the plant lightly moist in spring and summer; feed every two weeks. In fall and winter, allow the soil to dry out a bit between waterings; do not fertilize. In spring, prune the stems back and repot the plant. Jasmine can be propagated from tip cuttings in summer or fall.

WARNING

Do not confuse jasmine the the poisonous Carolina jasmine (*Gelsemium sempervierens*) or Jessamine (*Sestrum* spp.).

JASMINE TEA

tea leaves (choose a strongly flavored tea)
jasmine flowers

For a mildly fragrant tea, use 6 to 8 parts tea to 1 part jasmine flowers. Mix tea leaves with jasmine flowers in a bowl. Place in a jar and cover with cheesecloth and allow to stand for a week or more in a cool, dry area or until jasmine flowers have dried out and infused the tea with their perfume.

JOHNNY-JUMP-UP

In the Victorian language of flowers, the three colors of the Johnny-jump-up—purple, white and yellow—denote memories, loving thoughts and souvenirs. Sent to ease the hearts of separated lovers, it acquired the name heartsease. It also was a regular ingredient in love potions.

Johnny-jump-ups were introduced to America from their native Europe. They have escaped from gardens and now grow in fields, wastelands and along forest edges throughout much of North America.

Although Johnny-jump-ups are annuals, they seem to be perennial. They produce numerous seeds that germinate quickly, ensuring that this feisty plant will continue in the garden year after year. Notice that this year's plants may be in different parts of the garden from last year—Johnny has jumped up again.

They grow from four to twelve inches high with toothed leaves, rounded near the bottom of the plant, oblong higher on the plant. The five-petaled flowers resemble cute little (one-half to one inch) faces, smiling at you from the garden.

The petals by themselves have almost no flavor. If the flower is eaten in its entirety (including green sepals), there is a distinct wintergreen flavor to the flower. One grower remarked that it tasted just like Pepto-Bismol. The flowers are beautiful candied or floated on punch. The mild flavor makes them versatile and at home in a fruit salad or on a veal chop.

JOHNNY-JUMP-UP
(Heartsease, Field Pansy)
Viola tricolor
Violet family
Violaceae
Mint flavor
Annual/self-seeds
Ordinary soil
Full sun to shade

CULTURE

In warm areas of the country, sow seed in fall for bloom throughout the winter. In areas that get frost, seed sown in fall will germinate early in spring. In the cold areas, seed can also be directly sown in the garden early in spring. Seed can be started in winter indoors and the plants transplanted outdoors in spring. Once established in the garden, Johnny-jump-ups will self-seed and delight you with their cheery countenances for years.

Johnny-jump-ups like cool weather and bloom profusely in the spring. Keep them deadheaded, and if the summer is not too hot they may revive in the fall.

WARNING

Johnny-jump-ups contain saponins and may be toxic in large amounts.

HERB AND FLOWER CHEESE TERRINE

from Renee Shepherd, Shepherd's Seeds, Felton, California

1 pound cream cheese, softened

3/4 pound sweet (unsalted) butter, softened

1 cup grated Asiago cheese (or very fresh Parmesan)

2 large cloves garlic, finely chopped

3/4 cup fresh basil, finely chopped (or 6 tablespoons dried basil)

1/4 cup fresh oregano, finely chopped (or 2 tablespoons dried)

2 teaspoons Worcestershire sauce

3/4 teaspoon white pepper

3/4 cup toasted pine nuts (or pecans), coarsely chopped

3/4 cup parsley, finely chopped

1/2 to 3/4 pound provolone cheese, thinly sliced

100 to 150 Johnny-jump-up flowers (more if you have them)

various other edible flowers, if available, for garnish

Cream together the softened cream cheese, butter and Asiago cheese. Add the garlic, basil, oregano, Worcestershire sauce and pepper, combining thoroughly. Add the pine nuts and chopped parsley and mix again. It's messy, but the best way to mix is to use your hands.

Butter a loaf pan or terrine. Line with waxed or parchment paper. Layer bottom of pan with provolone cheese slices, then add a layer of the soft cheese mixture and a sprinkling of Johnny-jump-up flowers. Continue to alternate layers of provolone, soft cheese mixture and flowers, ending with provolone. For a good effect, try to get about 5 layers. Cover with plastic wrap and refrigerate overnight.

Remove from refrigerator and let stand about 15 minutes before turning out on serving platter. Remove paper and garnish with more Johnny-jump-ups and other flowers as available. Serve in slices. It is also delicious served on crackers for hors d'oeuvres. This recipe freezes very well, and slices can be cut off and used when needed.

Serves 15 to 20 as a rich appetizer; serves 50 to 75 for hors d'oeuvres.

VICHY SQUASH

from Bonnie Blair Hegeman, Brookville, New York

2 tablespoons canola oil
1 medium onion, finely chopped
3 cups zucchini chunks
2-1/2 cups chicken broth
1-1/2 cups plain yogurt
1/2 cup Johnny-jump-up flowers

Heat oil in a saucepan over a medium-low heat. Add onion and sauté until translucent and glistening (not brown). Add zucchini and continue to sauté. As zucchini begins to soften, pour in chicken broth. Bring to a boil, then remove from heat. Allow to cool to room temperature. Puree in a blender or food processor. Add yogurt. Mix in half of the Johnny-jump-ups. Refrigerate until cold. Serve garnished with remainder of flowers.

For a richer soup with less tang, use milk or half-and-half. For more tang, substitute buttermilk.

Serves 4.

SPRING FRUIT SALAD

2 oranges, peeled, sectioned and cut into bite-sized pieces
1 medium bunch of green seedless grapes
1 pint strawberries, stems removed, cut in half
1 tart apple, cut into bite-sized pieces
2 kiwis, peeled and sliced thinly
20 Johnny-jump-up flowers

Mix fruits in a nonmetallic bowl several hours before serving, allowing the flavors to meld. Serve garnished with the Johnny-jump-up flowers.

Serves 4.

JOHNNY-JUMP-UP VEAL CHOPS

from José Gutierrez, executive chef, Chez Philippe, Peabody Hotel, Memphis, Tennessee

1 white turnip, peeled and cubed

1 tablespoon olive oil

4 veal chops

2 cups Johnny-jump-up flowers

Preheat the oven to 400°F. Steam turnip until quite tender. Cool and puree. Heat olive oil in a large frying pan. Sauté veal chops until browned on both sides. Finish the chops in the oven for 15 minutes or until pink inside. Remove chops from oven. Cover each chop with a thin layer of the turnip puree. Press flowers into the puree, covering all but the bone of the chop with flowers.

Serves 4.

LAVENDER

The word lavender comes from the Latin *lavare*, meaning to wash. The ancient Greeks and Romans used lavender for its fresh clean scent in washing water, in soaps and for perfuming sheets. These uses have persisted for several millennia. During the Middle Ages it was a popular strewing herb. Much legend surrounds lavender, and over the years it has been imbued with certain powers by diverse peoples. In North Africa lavender is used to protect the Kabyle women from being mistreated by their husbands, while in Tuscany it protects small children from the evil eye. Its ability to soothe and calm, merely from its scent, is supposed to work on animals and humans alike. To the Victorians in their language of flowers, lavender meant distrust.

Lavender is originally native to the Mediterranean mountains and coast. Lavender is a shrubby plant, multibranched with woody branches and narrow leaves. The fragrant flowers appear on the ends of long spikes. The conquering Romans first brought lavender to England, where it continues to grow happily. Bees are attracted to lavender; lavender honey is a gourmand's delight. The most popular use of lavender is for fragrance. It is used in perfume, soap and toiletries. Sachets line linen closets and lingerie drawers throughout the world.

Lavandula angustifolia, English or true lavender, is the best for eating. This same plant has been known as *Lavandula officinalis* and *Lavandula vera*. It is a hardier

LAVENDER
Lavandula spp.
Mint family
Lamiaceae (Labiatae)
Perfumed flavor
Tender shrub
Light, dry, well-drained soil
Full sun

perennial than the French lavender (*Lavandula dentata*). English lavender has blunt, narrow, grayish-green leaves. In warm climates it can grow to three feet or more. The small lavender flowers are grouped in whorls of six to ten.

French lavender (*Lavandula dentata*) has long, narrow, grayish green leaves. Its flowers are a rich dark purple. It is smaller, growing to about twelve inches tall, and thrives in warm climates.

Lavender flowers have a sweet, perfumed flavor with a lemon overtone. Lavender can be very intense so use it sparingly. Too much can give a soapy flavor.

CULTURE
Lavender prefers a sunny location and light, dry, well-drained soil. It is an ideal plant for a large rock garden.

The easiest way to grow lavender is to purchase a young plant from a nursery in the spring. Set it out in the garden after any danger of frost is past. Allow at least twelve to eighteen inches between plants. In the first year, cut off any flowering stems as they appear. This encourages the plant to grow more foliage and become bushier. Such treatment seems severe, but in the long run you will have a healthier, more vigorous plant.

If you are patient, however, you can grow it from seed. In the Northeast, where I live, I have not had great luck with lavender from seed, with a successful germination rate of about twenty-five to forty percent. Not all the plants that germinated survived, but I am particularly proud of those that did. Plant seed in late fall. It is slow to germinate, so don't give up. In northern areas, the seeds may not germinate until the following spring. By summer, the seedlings can be transplanted.

Lavender is marginally hardy in cold areas. Mulch the plants well in late autumn to protect them through the winter. Space permitting, plants can be moved indoors for the winter and grown on a sunny windowsill or under lights. Lavender often begins to look ratty after about four years. The simplest solution is to replace the plant.

Lavender flowers can be used fresh or dried. To dry, pick the flower stems when the buds begin to open or when in full bloom. Place them on a clean cloth stretched over a screen. Dry the tops in the shade. Stems can also be hung upside down to dry, wrapped in a layer of cheesecloth, in a shady place. Once dried, it is easy to pluck the flowers from the stems. Store flowers in a tightly covered container in a dry place, or freeze for future use.

WARNING

Lavender oil may be poisonous. No more than two undiluted drops should be taken internally.

LAVENDER BLUEBERRY SOUP

from John Ash, culinary director, Fetzer Vineyards, Hopland, California

4 quarts fresh or frozen blueberries
1 cup hearty red wine
3 cups water
12 ounces honey (or to taste)
4 ounces orange juice concentrate
2-1/2 tablespoons dried lavender flowers
juice and rind of 3 medium lemons
2 cinnamon sticks
1 teaspoon freshly ground black pepper
1/2 teaspoon ground cloves
1 teaspoon salt

Put all ingredients into a stock pot. Bring just to the boil, then reduce heat and simmer 10 minutes. Garnish with a dollop of crème fraiche and a sprinkling of fresh blueberries and lavender florets. Serve hot or cold. An excellent soup for a summer luncheon.

Makes about 4-1/2 quarts.

LAVENDER APPLE CHUTNEY

from Darcy Ward, sous-chef, Mudd's Restaurant, San Ramon, California

2 cups apple juice

2 cups granulated sugar

1 cup apple cider vinegar

1 red onion, coarsely chopped

1 cinnamon stick

1/8 teaspoon red pepper flakes

2 cups Granny Smith apples, peeled, seeded and diced

1/2 cup lavender flowers, chopped

1/2 cup sweet red pepper, chopped

1/2 cup golden raisins

Combine apple juice, sugar, cider vinegar, red onion, cinnamon stick and pepper flakes in a saucepan. Simmer until a syrup starts to form. Add the apples and cook over a low heat until tender. Remove the apples, set aside. Reduce the syrup until it thickens. Add the apples, lavender flowers, red pepper and raisins. Cook for 5 minutes.

This is a spicy-sweet condiment that is delicious with poultry or pork.

RED SNAPPER WITH LAVENDER AND NASTURTIUM BEURRE BLANC

1/2 pound sweet (unsalted) butter, softened to room temperature

24 nasturtium flowers

4 tablespoons shallots or scallions, finely chopped

1-1/2 cups white wine (chardonnay or other light wine)

24 sprigs lavender

1 cup heavy cream

6 red snapper fillets

Place 1/4 pound butter in a small bowl. Mix in 20 nasturtium flowers. Set aside.

Use two small saucepans. (To simplify matters, let's call one pan L and the other N.) Put 3/4 cup wine and 2 tablespoons shallots in each pan. Add 12 lavender sprigs to pan L. Over a medium heat, reduce the liquid in both pans to approximately 1/3 cup. Add 1/2 cup cream to each pan. Lower heat and reduce again to

about 1/3 cup. Remove from heat. With a whisk, gradually work in the plain butter in small bits into pan L, and the nasturtium butter into the pan N.

Cut the fish fillets in half lengthwise. Sauté, skin side down for about 3 or 4 minutes. Turn and cook the other side until fish has turned translucent (flaky is overcooked).

Arrange 3 pieces of fish on each plate with the nasturtium and lavender sauces around them. Garnish with reserved flowers.

In this recipe you are making both a lavender and nasturtium beurre blanc for an impressive presentation.

Serves 4.

EDIBLE FLOWERS

LAVENDER TUNA

1 tablespoon lavender flowers, finely chopped
1 tablespoon fennel florets, finely chopped
1 teaspoon freshly ground black pepper
4 tuna steaks

Preheat grill or broiler. Mix lavender flowers, fennel florets and pepper together in a small bowl. Rub the tuna with the flower mixture, lightly coating all sides. Grill to desired doneness. (Try fresh tuna cooked rare—it is quite a taste delight.)

Serves 4.

LAVENDER COOKIES

from José Gutierrez, executive chef, Chez Philippe, Peabody Hotel, Memphis, Tennessee

2/3 cup granulated sugar
3/4 cup all-purpose flour
4 egg whites
1/2 cup butter, melted
1/2 teaspoon vanilla
3 tablespoons lavender florets, chopped

Preheat oven to 450°F. In a mixing bowl, blend sugar and flour. Whisk in egg whites, one at a time. Whisk butter into mixture. Add vanilla. Refrigerate for 10 minutes.

Lightly oil a cookie sheet. For simple cookies, pour 1 to 2 teaspoons of batter onto cookie sheet, allowing 1 inch between each cookie. For curlicues, pipe the batter, using a pastry bag, onto the cookie sheet, making 9-inch-long strips 1/4 inch wide, allowing 1 inch between each strip. Bake in preheated oven 1 minute. Remove from oven and sprinkle florets on each cookie, once the batter has spread out. Return to oven and bake for several minutes until very lightly browned. Remove one cookie at a time, wrapping it around a 1-inch diameter cylinder (large pencil). Cookies cool quickly and become brittle.

ORANGE AND LAVENDER SORBET

from José Gutierrez, executive chef, Chez Philippe, Peabody Hotel, Memphis, Tennessee

1 quart freshly squeezed orange juice, divided

9 ounces granulated sugar

1 tablespoon lavender flowers, finely chopped

In a nonaluminum saucepan heat 2 cups of orange juice with the sugar. Stir to mix. Add lavender flowers and bring to a boil. Lower heat and simmer for 15 minutes. Strain. Pour the liquid into the remaining 2 cups of orange juice and mix. Pour the mixture into an ice cream maker and process according to manufacturer's instructions. Scoop into glasses and serve garnished with additional chopped lavender. Pour a splash of Cointreau on top for an interesting variation.

Serves 6 to 8.

LAVENDER ICE CREAM

1-1/2 cups milk

1-1/2 cups cream

1-inch section of vanilla bean, sliced lengthwise

6 egg yolks

1/3 cup granulated sugar

2 tablespoons lavender flowers, finely chopped

In a saucepan, heat milk and cream to a scald. Add vanilla bean. Remove pan from heat and allow to cool slightly. In the top of a double boiler, whisk egg yolks and sugar. Slowly pour in the milk, whisking constantly. Continue to cook until the mixture begins to thicken and coats a spoon. Add lavender flowers. Remove from heat and allow to cool to room temperature for at least 1 hour. Chill in the refrigerator for an hour. Strain liquid and pour into an ice cream maker and freeze according to manufacturer's instructions.

Serves 4 to 6.

LEMON

LEMON
Citrus Limon
Rue family
Rutaceae
Citrus flavor
Tree-hardy in zones 9 and 10
Light, fertile loam
Full sun

The name is derived from the Arabic and Persian word *limun* used for all citrus fruits. In the Victorian language of flowers, lemon means fidelity.

Lemons were believed to have been introduced into the western world from India in the tenth century. Recently lemons have been identified in the ruins of Pompeii, leading to the assumption that lemons had been cultivated by the Romans.

Lemons are small trees, ranging from ten to twenty feet in height, hardy to zones 9 and 10. In cooler climates dwarf varieties can be grown in containers in a greenhouse in the winter and brought outside in the summer. Their growth habit is open, with lightly thorned branches. The semi-glossy green leaves are elliptical with crenated edges. It is an attractive landscape tree in warm areas. Lemons are usually cultivated for their fruit.

Lemon flowers are very fragrant. They appear star-shaped and are less than one inch in diameter, white inside, streaked with violet outside. The flavor is citrusy and sweet.

CULTURE

Lemons need full sun. They prefer light, well-drained, fertile loam rich in organic matter.

Plant lemons in late winter or early spring. They are usually purchased from a nursery. Choose your plant well. Look for trees suitable for your climate. When planting allow twenty to thirty-five feet around the tree. Lemons need plenty of water until well established. Water every two to five days in hot dry areas; in more humid areas, every week or two. Mulch well around the tree, taking care not to mulch right up to the trunk. Apply citrus fertilizer as directed, but do not feed after midsummer.

Lemons adapt readily to container cultivation. In cooler climates grow the plants outdoors during the warm months and indoors during the cool months. Indoors, they require bright light and cool days and nights, not over sixty-five degrees Fahrenheit for flower production. Do not allow the soil to dry out.

LEMONCELLO

from Georgene McKim, Palos Verdes, California

8 to 10 lemons
1 liter of 80- or 90-proof vodka
3 cups granulated sugar
4 cups water
20 lemon flowers

Zest lemons. Mix vodka and lemon zest. Pour into a large bottle. Cover loosely and let infuse for 1 week.

Put sugar and water in a medium saucepan. Bring to a boil. Do not stir. Boil for 15 minutes. Add lemon flowers. Allow syrup to cool to room temperature. Combine vodka with syrup and stir well. Strain into bottles and cork. Let age for 2 weeks.

Store in the freezer. Serve icy cold in thimble-sized vodka glasses, garnished with a fresh lemon flower.

Substitute lemon flowers in any of the orange flower recipes.

LILAC

LILAC
(Common lilac)
Syringa vulgaris
Olive family
Oleaceae
Floral flavor
Shrub
Well-drained, alkaline soil
Sun to partial shade

The word lilac is actually an Old English word which is derived from the Arabic *laylak* and Persian *nilak* meaning blue. *Syringa* is Greek for tube, referring to the shape of the individual flowers. In the language of flowers lilacs symbolize memory and humility; white lilacs symbolize innocence.

The common lilac is native to southeastern Europe. It is a beautiful flowering shrub, hardy to zone 4. It needs a period of winter cold and dormancy, and consequently cannot grow in zones 8 to 10.

Lilacs can grow, if unpruned, up to fifteen feet tall, usually in a shrubby habit. The heart-shaped leaves are an attractive green.

Lilacs are grown for the colorful fragrant display they give in spring. The individual flowers, which have four petals, are clustered together to form a spike. Flowers come in a range of purples, mauves and, of course, light purple (lilac). Hybridization has brought white flowers. Although lilacs are commonly grown and there are many cultivars, most people have no idea which variety lilac they have in their yard. The flavor of lilacs varies from plant to plant. I have sampled many lilac flowers. Some have no flavor at all. Others have a decidedly green or herbaceous flavor. Some start out with a green flavor but have a perfumed floral aftertaste. The best lilacs are those that have a straight floral, perfumed flavor of lilac.

CULTURE

Lilacs prefer full sun but will tolerate partial shade. They grow in almost any type of soil as long as it is well drained and not alkaline. Acidic soil will prevent it from flowering.

Lilacs are widely available in the nursery trade. Plant in the spring or fall. Suckers can be dug out and replanted in early fall. Allow at least six feet between plants. Mulch lilacs with four to six inches of well-rotted manure every two years in autumn. This is the best fertilizer for these shrubs.

Lilacs benefit from regular pruning. Cut back any obviously dead wood in the winter. Remove all weak wood that does not have large flower buds or that still has the past year's fruit on it. In the spring, the number of blooms will not be great, but each cluster will be large. The second year more flowers and bigger flowers will be produced. By the third year the clusters will be more plentiful, but will be getting smaller. Repeat the pruning process every three years.

LILAC CHICKEN

1/2 cup lilac flowers, divided
water
white wine
2 chicken breasts, split and boned (4 pieces of chicken)
1 tablespoon butter
1 tablespoon all-purpose flour
salt and pepper

Place lilac flowers (reserving 2 tablespoons for garnish) in a large covered frying pan. Add 1 inch of water and 1/2 inch of wine to the pan. Bring to a boil. Gently place chicken in liquid. Cover and poach over a low heat 4 to 5 minutes. Turn chicken and cook an additional 4 to 5 minutes, until barely cooked through. Remove chicken to a warm platter.

Boil to reduce poaching liquid by half. Remove flowers and discard. In a separate saucepan, make a roux from the butter and flour. Melt the butter, then stir in the flour. Let cook for 5 minutes over a low heat, stirring often to keep it from sticking. Add the reduced liquid gradually to the roux, continually stirring with a whisk. Cook over a low heat several minutes, or until it reaches the desired thickness. Adjust seasoning with salt and pepper to taste. Spoon sauce on the chicken. Garnish with reserved lilac florets.

Lavender flowers can be substituted for lilac flowers. The flavor is a bit stronger, so fewer flowers are needed.

Serves 4.

LILAC TEA SANDWICHES

———

1/2 cup lilac flowers, divided
4 ounces whipped cream cheese
8 slices white bread, crusts removed

Mix the flowers into the cheese, reserving 2 table-spoons for garnish. Let sit for at least 1 hour to allow flavors to meld.

With a cookie cutter, cut each slice of bread into attractive shapes—hearts, diamonds, flowers. You should try to get 3 pieces from each slice. Without a cookie cutter, you can make triangles by cutting the bread twice on the diagonal. Spread the pieces of bread with the lilac cream cheese. Garnish with reserved flowers.

This recipe can be adapted for almost any flower. Sweet flowers lend themselves more for tea sandwiches, while savory flowers are better for crackers or with crudités for hors d'oeuvres. Large petals should be cut into 1/4- to 1/2-inch pieces.

Serves 4 to 6 for tea.

LILAC YOGURT

———

1 pint frozen vanilla yogurt
1/4 cup lilac blossoms

Soften yogurt slightly and mix in flowers. Serve garnished with flowers.

This is quick and easy to prepare just before serving. If refreezing any of the yogurt, be aware that the flowers may turn brown. It will not affect the flavor, but it looks unattractive.

Serves 4.

LINDEN

The name is derived form the Greek *ptilon*, meaning wing. This refers to the large bract from which the flower arises.

American linden (*Tilia americana*) is native to most of the eastern half of North America, growing as far north as Canada, south to Florida and west to Texas. Other lindens include European linden (*Tilia x europaea*), small-leaved linden (*Tilia cordata*) and broad-leafed linden (*Tilia platyphyllos*). The different species of linden can interbreed, so it is common to find natural hybrids. For the same reason it may be difficult to identify a linden with complete accuracy.

Lindens are handsome deciduous trees that grow from forty to eighty feet or more in height. The heart-shaped leaves have sharp edges and range in size from three to nine inches. Small flowers, white to yellow in color, appear in early summer. The flower stalk comes out of a leaflike bract; the flowers are delightfully fragrant and have a honeylike flavor.

CULTURE

All lindens need full sun. *Tilia americana* grows in a range of soils; *Tilia cordata* grows best in cool, deep,

LINDEN
(*Basswood, Lime Tree*)
Tilia spp.
Linden family
Tiliceae
Sweet honey flavor
Tree
Moist loam
Full sun

moist loam; and *Tilia platyphyllos* prefers light soil and humid conditions. Purchase a young tree from a reputable nursery or mail-order catalog. Plant in spring or fall. Mulch well around the base of the tree but not right up to the trunk. Remember to take into account how large it will eventually grow.

WARNING

Recent studies indicate that frequent consuption of linden flower tea may cause heart damage.

LINDEN TEA

1 tablespoon linden flowers
1 cup water, boiling

Steep the flowers in water for several minutes.

Serves 1.

MARJORAM

*MARJORAM (Oregano,
Common Marjoram,
Wild Marjoram, Pot Marjo-
ram) Origanum vulgare
Mint family
Lamiaceae (Labiatae)
Herbal flavor
Perennial/annual
Dry, alkaline, well-drained soil
Full sun*

The botanic name and one of the common names come from the same Greek derivations. *Oros* is mountain and *ganos* is joy. Oregano or *Origanum* is a joy of the mountain. The purplish red tufts of flowers are a joy to behold. Imagine the native Mediterranean hillsides with wild marjoram in bloom. (Actually there are more than thirty species of fragrant *Origanum* native to the area.) Such a sight must evoke a smile. Indeed, wild marjoram has long been considered a symbol of happiness. In both ancient Greece and Rome the bride and groom wore wreaths of wild marjoram to symbolize the joy of their union. According to the Victorian language of flowers, marjoram signifies blushes.

Wild marjoram is native to southern Europe and has naturalized in North America from Ontario and Quebec south as far as North Carolina and west to California and Oregon. It grows wild in borders of cornfields and in well-drained stony soil. While it is a perennial in mild climates, in colder areas it is usually treated as an annual.

This hardy perennial herb has a creeping underground root that produces erect purplish-brown, woody, square-stemmed stalks with small dark green leaves. The stems grow from one to three feet tall. Both the stem and flower stalks are hairy. The small (one-quarter inch), purplish-red flowers grow in one-inch tufts at the top of the stems and branchlets. Wild marjoram flowers from June to October. The leaves have a light minty fragrance.

The flavor is somewhat reminiscent of thyme with an Italian overtone. Although this plant is called oregano, it should not be confused with Greek oregano (see page 130). Nor should it be confused with sweet marjoram (see page 155).

CULTURE

Because all the species of *Origanum* have basically the same requirements, I shall discuss them in this space. To keep confusion at bay, I will refer to them as *Origanum*, rather than using any common names. Most *Origanum* prefer dry, well-drained, alkaline, soil that is not too rich. Imagine the soil of their native Mediterranean hillsides.

The seeds of *Origanum* are slow to germinate. Start them indoors at least six weeks before the last frost date. Sow them on fine soil. Cover with shredded sphagnum moss and keep lightly moist. When the seedlings get to two to three inches tall, transplant them outdoors. Keep them well shaded and protected from wind until they are established. Space plants twelve inches apart.

Origanum can be grown from cuttings. Cut a piece of the woody stem from an established plant. Make sure to cut down to the base of the stem. Insert it one-inch deep in moist sand and cover with plastic wrap. Place in a cool, shady area until roots form. Then plant out, following the directions as above for a seedling.

Sweet Marjoram Majorana Hortensis (Origanum Majorana) Lamiaceae (Labiatae)

It was once believed that this herb could keep milk from spoiling, that is, keep it sweet, hence the first part of its name.

Sweet marjoram is native to the Mediterranean region. This culinary herb grows from twelve to fifteen inches tall. It is a tender perennial, often grown as an annual as it winter-kills easily. In northern areas it is grown as an annual, while in warmer climates it thrives as a perennial.

The oval, gray green, downy leaves are borne on slightly reddish, delicate woody stems. The flowers are tiny and white, seeming to come out of the green bracts. Sweet marjoram blooms in late summer. Sweet marjoram's flavor is warm yet spicy.

PURPLE OREGANO FLOWER VINEGAR

from Carole Saville, Los Angeles, California

rice wine vinegar
purple oregano flowers

Fill a clean, 1-pint glass container with rice vinegar. Begin collecting the purple oregano flowers as they blossom. Wash and pat them dry, then pack the container with the flowers and one 4-inch sprig of oregano leaves. The vinegar will turn pink in about 24 hours. Seal the container with a noncorrosive cap.

Make sure the flowers are covered with vinegar—if not, add more vinegar. Keep in a dark, cool cupboard for 1 week or so, then transfer to a decorative bottle if desired. The pink color of the vinegar is lovely but will disappear if stored on a sunny windowsill.

PORTUGUESE TOMATO SALAD

3 *large green tomatoes, cut into wedges*
3 *large ripe red tomatoes, cut into wedges*
8 *chive flowers, broken into florets*
3 *sprigs of sweet marjoram flowers*
3 *tablespoons vinaigrette dressing of your choice*

Toss all ingredients together in a large bowl. Let sit several hours before serving. Garnish with additional florets.

Serves 4.

ROAST CHICKEN WITH MARJORAM

from Pat Lanza, Shandelee Herb Garden, Livingston Manor, New York

1 *frying chicken, cut into 8 pieces*
salt and pepper
1-1/4 *cup wild marjoram flowers, coarsely chopped, divided*
1/4 *cup all-purpose flour*
1 *cup white wine*

Preheat oven to 375°F. Season chicken with salt and pepper and 3/4 cup marjoram flowers. Place in a shallow roasting pan. Bake for 45 minutes. Remove chicken to a warm platter.

Place roasting pan on stove top over a medium-low heat. Add 1/4 cup marjoram flowers. Slowly add flour to pan drippings, stirring continually. Cook for 5 minutes, stirring occasionally. Slowly add white wine, stirring until glazed. Pour sauce over chicken pieces. Garnish with remaining marjoram flowers.

Serves 4.

NAVAJO CORN CHOWDER

from Robert Werst, chef/owner, y.e. coyote, Hicksville, New York

2/3 cup oil
1-1/3 cups all-purpose flour
6 slices bacon, chopped
1/4 cup onion, minced
2 quarts chicken stock
4 dashes Tabasco
2 tablespoons oregano flowers, chopped
2 1-pound cans creamed-style corn
1 pint heavy cream
salt and pepper to taste

Heat olive oil in a nonaluminum pan. Slowly add flour, stirring constantly with a wooden spoon. The mixture should be the consistency of peanut butter. Reduce the heat and gently simmer for 18 minutes, stirring often. This is the roux.

While the roux is cooking, in a separate saucepan, sauté bacon over a medium heat until it begins to brown. Add onions and continue to cook until the onions turn translucent. Pour off all fat. Add chicken stock, Tabasco and oregano flowers. Bring to a boil. Whisking constantly, slowly add the hot roux a little at a time while the stock is boiling on high. When the soup reaches the consistency of heavy cream, stop adding roux. Turn down heat to medium and let boil for 20 minutes, skimming occasionally.

Strain the soup into a new pot. Add creamed corn and heavy cream. Heat over a low flame. Do not bring to a boil. Add salt and pepper to taste. Garnish with oregano flowers.

Serves 8 to 12 .

CHICKEN WITH PURPLE OREGANO FLOWER VINEGAR

from Carole Saville, Los Angeles, California

4 chicken breast cutlets

2 tablespoons all-purpose flour

3 tablespoons extra virgin olive oil

6 to 8 ounces shiitake mushrooms, sliced

1 clove garlic, chopped

1/2 cup Purple Oregano Flower Vinegar (see page 155)

1-1/2 cups chicken stock

1 bay leaf

1 sprig of purple oregano flowers for garnish

Dredge chicken cutlets in flour. Heat olive oil in skillet and brown cutlets over medium heat until golden brown, turning once. Add mushrooms and garlic. Cook 3 or 4 minutes, then add Purple Oregano Flower Vinegar, chicken stock and bay leaf. Cover skillet and cook over a medium heat for about 10 minutes.

Remove chicken and keep warm. Discard bay leaf. Reduce sauce in skillet for 3 to 4 minutes. Pour sauce over chicken and garnish with purple oregano flowers.

Serves 4.

MUSTARD

The name is derived from the Latin *mustum*, which was the unfermented wine that was mixed with mustard seeds to form the condiment, and from *ardens* meaning burning. The Greeks favored mustard as a vegetable more than two thousand years ago. They also discovered that the powdered seeds made a flavorful condiment. For centuries mustard was a treasured herb, grown by kings and poets from Charlemagne to Shakespeare.

White mustard (*Brassica sinapsis alba*) is a yellow flowered annual native to Europe. It is the cultivated variety often found in gardens. It grows to about eighteen inches tall, with slightly bristly, lobed leaves. The young greens have a piquancy that is a welcome addition to spring salad. They can also be cooked as a vegetable.

Black mustard (*Brassica nigra*) can grow up to six feet tall, but usually is three to four feet in height. The leaves are toothed—those lower on the plant are smaller and narrower than those higher on the plant. The yellow flowers appear from May through July, followed by seed pods from June through October. Each long, pointed seed pod holds about a dozen small brownish-black seeds used to make the condiment mustard. Black mustard can be seen growing wild in waste areas throughout America.

Field or wild mustard (*Brassica rapa*) is an annual herb growing two to two and one-half feet tall. It is

MUSTARD
Brassica spp.
Mustard family
Brassicaceae
(Cruciferae)
Spicy flavor
Annual/self-seeds
Well-drained soil
Full sun

distinguished from other mustards by the upper leaves that clasp the stem, with earlike lobes. The leaves are gray green and slightly succulent. The pale yellow flowers appear from June to October. It grows wild in fields throughout the country.

All mustards have small, yellow, four-petaled flowers with a characteristic spicy bite.

CULTURE

Mustard grows best in well-drained soil in full sun.

White mustard seeds itself freely and can easily become a garden pest. It germinates quickly and can be directly seeded in the garden in early spring.

Black mustard can grow in almost any kind of soil, but if growing it for seed, it needs moisture.

Plant seeds in spring as early as the soil can be worked. Allow six to ten inches between plants.

SCALLOPS WITH MUSTARD BEURRE BLANC

1 tablespoon olive oil

1 clove garlic, minced

1 cup dry white wine

3 tablespoons mustard flowers

1 pound scallops

3 tablespoons butter at room temperature

In a skillet, sauté the garlic in olive oil. Add white wine and mustard flowers. Poach the scallops for about 5 to 8 minutes. Do not overcook or they will be rubbery. Remove the scallops to a dish and keep warm.

Reduce the liquid in the pan to 1/3 of the original volume. While stirring, add the butter, a tablespoon at a time. Cook for 1 minute. Pour sauce over the scallops and serve immediately. Garnish with additional mustard flowers.

Serves 4.

NODDING ONION

Nodding onion is a wild onion that grows from British Columbia south into Oregon and east to Minnesota, in Michigan and from New York south to upland Texas, Mississippi, Alabama and Georgia. It is usually found along slopes, in rocky soil or in open woods.

All onions are herbs arising from bulbs. This is a perennial that will come back year after year with no care. It grows from four to twenty inches tall. The flower stem has a bend near the top causing the pink or white flower cluster to droop. The leaves are soft and flat.

It blooms in midsummer. The individual florets have an oniony flavor. Use them in any of the chive flower recipes.

CULTURE

Nodding onion is not widely cultivated. Collect the flowers (never take all flowers and do not dig up the plant) from the wild (be sure to make a positive identification) for use in the kitchen.

NODDING ONION
(Nodding wild onion)
Allium cernuum
Amaryllis family
Amaryllidaceae
Onion flavor
Bulb
Well-drained soil
Full sun

After identifying plants in the wild, you might want to mark the area. Go back later in the season and collect seeds. Plant the seeds in your garden in spring as early as the ground can be worked.

WARNING

As with all of the *Alliums*, the flavor can be quite strong. Always break up the flower into florets. Even as a garnish, do not present the entire flower.

EDIBLE FLOWERS

CREAM OF ONION SOUP

4 tablespoons butter

1/2 teaspoon cumin

1-1/2 cups nodding onion florets

2 tablespoons all-purpose flour

4 cups milk

3 egg yolks, beaten

salt and white pepper

sprigs of mint (optional)

In a saucepan, melt butter. Add cumin and cook over a low heat until fragrant. Add onion florets and sauté for several minutes. Stir in flour. Continue to cook for several minutes, stirring frequently. Slowly pour in milk, stirring mixture constantly. Cover and cook for 5 to 10 minutes. Add 1/4 cup of soup slowly to egg yolk. Beat well. Add an additional 1/2 cup of soup and beat. Pour beaten egg into soup and stir. Cook for several minutes, but do not allow to come to a boil. Season with salt and white pepper to taste. Serve garnished with a sprig of mint.

Serves 4 to 6.

NODDING ONION OMELET

3 eggs

1 teaspoon water

1 teaspoon parsley, finely chopped

2 teaspoons butter

2 tablespoons nodding onion flowers, finely chopped

2 tablespoons Swiss cheese, grated

additional nodding onion flowers for garnish

In a small bowl, beat together eggs, water and parsley until eggs are light and frothy. Melt butter in an omelet pan or 8-inch skillet. When butter is sizzling, pour in eggs, swirling the pan as you pour. Gently stir eggs, swirling pan until eggs begin to set. Sprinkle flowers and cheese on half of omelet. When cheese begins to melt, fold omelet in half and cook until eggs reach desired doneness. Serve immediately garnished with additional nodding onion flowers.

Serves 1.

AQUARIUM SOUP

from Peter Zambri, co-chef, Sooke Harbour House, Sooke, British Columbia, Canada

1/2 cup nodding onion flowers

1 carrot, peeled

1 stalk celery

1 leek, white part only

1 medium red bell pepper

2 bay leaves

2 cups mixed savory garden herbs (flat-leaf parsley, tarragon, rosemary, lemon thyme, chives, for example)

2 juniper berries

1 red rock or Dungeness crab, approximately 1-1/2 pounds

1 tablespoon tomato paste

2 egg whites

8 ounces dry vermouth

1 quart strong, clear fish stock

1 quart strong, clear chicken stock

low sodium tamari to taste

In a food processor, coarsely chop onion flowers, carrot, celery, leek, red pepper, bay leaves, herbs and juniper berries. Set in refrigerator to cool.

Break the live crab into two pieces with a cleaver or by hand and remove the entrails. With a mallet, crush shells and meat to a coarse pulp. Combine the vegetables and crab. Stir in tomato paste and egg whites, making sure to mix evenly. Set in refrigerator to cool for 15 minutes.

In a thick-bottomed, high-sided 8-quart pot, pour in vermouth, and then add fish and chicken stocks. Stir in the crab-vegetable mixture. Place pot over medium heat and carefully stir to ensure that nothing sticks to the bottom. When a raft (coagulated vegetable and crab mixture) starts to form, stop stirring. Be patient, the process is fairly time-consuming and will take about 15 minutes. Turn the heat down to a slow simmer. Cook for approximately 1 hour after the raft has formed. Be sure not to boil rapidly, or the raft will separate and a complete mess will fol-low. The raft should feel firm to the touch, not soft and mushy.

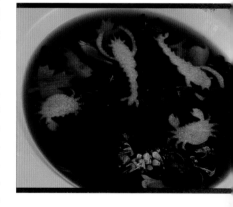

Remove from the heat and, with a large ladle, strain liquid through a cheese-cloth and strainer into an-other pot. Adjust for sea-soning with tamari, if de-sired, and serve at once, or cool, chill and reheat when desired. If desired, serve with thin slices of carrot and parsnip that have been cut into marine shapes (fish, crab, lobster, etc.) floating in the broth. A sprig of nodding onion flowers completes the dish.

Serves 6.

KRA

OKRA (Gumbo, Gombo)
Abelmoschus aesculentus
Mallow family
Malvaceae
Mild, sweet flavor
Annual
Clay or clay loam
Full sun, hot weather

Okra is a hot-climate vegetable. Depending on the variety, the plants grow from three to eight feet tall.

The plant has a woody central stem that is branched only by the leaves. The leaves are large, lobed and somewhat spiny. Red okra has red-tinged leaves and red flowers. The smaller okras are suitable for growing in a container. Larger varieties are handsome at the back of a flower border.

The flowers grow from the leaf axils. They are yellow blotched in the center with purplish black. The flowers have a slightly mucilaginous quality, but are rather sweet and vegetal in flavor.

CULTURE

Okra needs full sun and hot weather to grow well. It prefers clay or clay loam soil.

Plant okra after any danger of frost is past.

Before planting, wash seeds in dishwashing liquid. Rinse thoroughly then soak overnight in tepid water. In the morning, drain the seeds and dry them. Plant in groups of three, allowing twelve inches between plants.

SOUTHERN FRIED OKRA

———

from Patrick Quillec, chef, The Chattahoochee River Club, Columbus, Georgia

oil for deep frying
1 cup all-purpose flour
1 cup cornmeal
1/2 teaspoon cayenne pepper
salt and pepper
12 okra flowers
2 egg whites, beaten to a froth

Heat oil for deep frying. Mix flour, cornmeal, cayenne pepper, salt and pepper together in a bowl. Dip the okra flowers, one at a time, in the egg white. Roll in the flour-cornmeal mix and quickly deep fry until golden. Drain on absorbent paper and serve immediately.

Serves 3 to 6.

SPICY OKRA APPETIZERS

———

1 cup all-purpose flour
1 egg, beaten
1/2 cup milk
2 tablespoons granulated sugar
20 1/3-inch pieces of jalapeño pepper cheese
20 okra flowers
oil for frying

Beat together flour, egg, milk and sugar in a bowl. Place a piece of cheese in the center of an okra flower. Run a toothpick through the ends of the petals to close the flower. Dip flower in batter and fry in hot oil until lightly browned.

An interesting contrast of flavors and textures—spicy cheese with a sweetish flower and crunchy outside with melted cheese inside.

Serves 6 to 8 for hors d'oeuvres.

EDIBLE FLOWERS

SOUTHERN OKRA IN PARADISE

from Patrick Quillec, chef, The Chattahoochee River Club, Columbus, Georgia

10 to 15 okra flowers
2 pounds lobster, cooked—meat and caviar reserved
3/4 pound scallops
salt and freshly ground pepper
1/2 cup cream
1/2 teaspoon tarragon, finely chopped
1/2 cup peas
1/3 cup vegetable stock
1/2 cup cream
1 tablespoon butter
8 baby okra, sautéed until tender-crisp
2 slices bacon, cooked and crumbled

Put flowers in ice water for about 10 minutes. Remove the seed pods that form the backs of the flowers. Remove the pistils. Allow the flowers to dry. Cut the flowers lengthwise. Gently flatten the flowers. Place the flowers, overlapping, across the width of a 12-inch piece of plastic wrap. Overlap flowers to run the width of the wrap. Cover with a moist towel and set aside.

In a food processor, blend the lobster meat with the scallops. Add salt and pepper to taste. Add cream and continue to blend for about 1 minute. Do not over mix. Remove to a bowl. With a wooden spatula, stir in tarragon and 1/2 teaspoon lobster caviar. Check for taste and texture by taking a soup spoon of the mousseline and cook it in simmering water for 5 minutes.

Taste. Add more salt to the mixture if needed or cream if it is too rubbery. Refrigerate the mousseline for 2 hours.

Spoon the mousseline, 1-1/2 to 2 inches in diameter, on top of the flowers. Add a layer of flowers on top, wrapping around sides. Roll the plastic film around the flower sausage to seal it. Twist both ends of the wrap to seal the mousseline securely inside. Prick a few holes with a pin. Refrigerate for 30 minutes.

Steam the flower sausage in a covered steamer for 10 minutes. Remove and set aside.

Make the sauce by blending together peas, vegetable stock and cream. Blend until smooth. Strain through a fine sieve. Add salt and pepper to taste. Heat the sauce over a low heat until warm. Add butter and stir to blend. Pour sauce onto the plates.

Warm the flower sausage in a steamer for about 5 minutes. Remove from steam and carefully unwrap. Cut it into 1/2-inch slices and arrange on the plates with sautéed okra. Sprinkle with bacon bits. Serve immediately.

Serves 6.

ORANGE

The name comes from the Latin *sinensis* meaning of China. Oranges are native to China and Indo-China. They were introduced into Europe before 400 A.D. Columbus and other explorers brought them to the New World. In the language of flowers, orange blossoms denote purity.

Oranges are large, round, formal-looking trees ranging in height from twenty to thirty-five feet. The trunk and branches are occasionally spined. The leaves are fragrant when crushed. The leaves are dark green above with yellow spots, and light green below with dark green spots, with short-winged petioles.

Oranges make handsome landscape trees in zones 9 and 10. There is the added benefit of the delicious fruits that are borne from October through June. Nothing beats going outside and picking a fresh orange from your own tree for breakfast. Dwarf varieties, which can be grown in containers, are suited for indoor or cool greenhouse cultivation.

ORANGE (*Sweet orange*)
Citrus sinensis
Rue family
Rutaceae
Citrus flavor
Tender tree—zones 9 to 10
Well-drained, fertile sandy loam
Full sun

The small (one inch) white flowers appear singly or in small clusters from February to April. They are star-shaped and intoxicatingly fragrant with a sweet citrusy flavor.

CULTURE

Sweet oranges need full sun. They prefer well-drained, fertile, sandy loam. See Lemon (page 148) for complete culture instructions.

ORANGE BLOSSOM SPECIAL SALAD

1/4 cup lemon juice
1/2 cup orange juice
3 tablespoons honey
2 tablespoons lemon rind, finely grated
2 tablespoons ginger, finely grated
1/8 teaspoon cayenne pepper
4 cups carrots, finely grated
1/2 cup almonds, thinly sliced
1 cup golden raisins

1/2 cup calendula petals
1/4 cup orange petals
15 to 20 nasturtium leaves

Whisk together juices and honey. Mix in lemon rind, ginger and cayenne. Add carrots, almonds and raisins. Just before serving, toss in calendula petals and orange petals. Serve on a bed of nasturtium leaves.

Serves 4.

EDIBLE FLOWERS

DRUNKEN SHRIMP WITH ORANGE VINAIGRETTE

from Hugo Molina, executive chef, Parkway Grill, Pasadena California

1 pound large shrimp, unpeeled
8 ounces orange liqueur
2 heads mizuna, torn into bite-sized pieces
1 head spotted red radicchio
4 ounces baby garden greens
1 ripe papaya, peeled and cut in diagonals
edible flowers for garnish, including orange blossoms

Place shrimp and orange liqueur in a nonmetallic bowl. Toss shrimp to cover with liqueur. Refrigerate for about 30 minutes.

Remove shrimp from liqueur. Pour liqueur into saucepan and bring to a boil. Peel shrimp. Add to boiling liqueur and cook for 30 seconds. Remove from liqueur and set aside.

Place mizuna around plate. Spread radicchio and baby garden greens in center of plate. Arrange papaya around greens. Cut shrimp in half lengthwise and place over greens. Streak Orange Vinaigrette over top. Decorate with flowers and serve.

Serves 4.

Orange Vinaigrette
3 tablespoons lime juice
1 cup orange juice
3 tablespoons brown sugar
2 tablespoons fresh ginger, minced
2 tablespoons scallions, julienned, white part only
2 tablespoons red pepper, julienned
3 tablespoons orange liqueur
10 orange blossoms (if available)
1/2 cup peanut oil
salt and pepper to taste

Blend all ingredients together well.

Makes about 2 cups dressing.

EA

Peas are cool weather annual vegetables. There is a wide range of varieties from snow peas and sugar snap to traditional garden peas. Peas are fast growing, from fifty-five to seventy days from planting to harvest. When the objective is the flowers, the time is even quicker.

Peas are attractive plants with blue-green, oval leaves one to two inches long. They are true vines with tendrils that curl around objects for support. Indeed, if you look at the plant from a different perspective than just an entity that produces podded legumes, you find that much of it is edible. The young shoots are often used in the Far East and have a nice pealike flavor when stir-fried or steamed. The tendrils themselves are a little-known delicacy, excellent raw in salads or lightly cooked. The flavor is distinctly pealike. Of course the flowers must be edible as well.

Remember that picking the flowers will cut down on pea production. I advise just putting in a few more plants to keep you in flowers, shoots, tendrils and peas.

The flowers are usually white, sometimes with black or purple markings, or occasionally mauve. The flowers have a floral pealike flavor with a bit of a crunch.

CULTURE

Peas need full sun and sandy, well-drained soil. Plant seeds directly in the garden as soon as the soil can be worked in the spring in cold areas (two to four weeks before the last frost date). In warm areas of the Deep

PEA (*Green pea, Garden pea, English pea*)
Pisum sativum
Pea family
Fabaceae (Leguminosae)
Floral flavor
Annual
Sandy, well-drained soil
Full sun

South and West, plant peas in the fall or winter.

For best results, soak the peas overnight in luke-warm water and roll them in a legume innoculant powder before planting.

Space low-growing varieties of peas one to two inches apart in rows two feet apart, and tall varieties three feet apart. Peas need support. A trellis or support must be at least as tall as the variety planted.

Water peas at ground level to discourage mildew and fungus disease. Do not pick peas or flowers when wet or damp.

WARNING

Eat only true garden peas, *Pisum* spp. Flowering ornamental sweet peas are poisonous. Know what you are eating!

EDIBLE FLOWERS

CANDIED PEA BLOSSOMS ON SALMON TOAST POINTS

20 pea flowers

1 egg white, lightly beaten with 2 drops of 80-proof vodka

1/2 cup superfine granulated sugar

1/2 cup cream cheese

5 slices white bread, crusts removed, toasted and cut into 4 pieces on the diagonal

1/4 pound smoked salmon, thinly sliced

To candy pea flowers, lightly paint all surfaces of each flower with egg white. Sprinkle with sugar to coat.

Allow to dry at least 24 hours in a cool, dry area. Flowers will be stiff and brittle when dried. Once candied, the flowers can be stored for several months, double packaged, in the freezer.

To assemble, spread cream cheese on each toast point. Top with a small piece of salmon and a candied pea blossom. An easy-to-prepare (once the flowers are candied) hors d'oeuvres that is both elegant and delicious.

Makes 20 hors d'oeuvres

MACARONI SALAD WITH PEA FLOWERS AND THYME

from Pat Lanza, Shandelee Herb Garden, Livingston Manor, New York

2 cups elbow macaroni

1/4 cup sweet red pepper, diced

1/4 cup sweet yellow pepper, diced

1/4 cup green bell pepper, diced

1/4 cup Bermuda onion, diced

1/4 cup celery, diced

1/4 cup carrot, grated

1/4 cup snow peas, sliced

1/2 cup pea blossoms

1/4 cup thyme flowers, coarsely chopped

1/3 cup mayonnaise

1/4 cup society garlic vinegar

salt and pepper to taste

Cook macaroni al dente. Drain and put into a large bowl.

Toss in peppers, onion, celery, carrot, snow peas, pea blossoms and thyme flowers. In a separate bowl, whisk together mayonnaise and society garlic vinegar. Pour onto cooked macaroni and toss to mix. Season with salt and pepper to taste.

Serves 6 to 8.

STEAMED VERMILLION ROCKFISH WITH FRESH PEA BLOSSOM AND PEA SAUCE

from Peter Costello, co-chef, Sooke Harbour House, Sooke, British Columbia, Canada

Sauce:

3 tablespoons shallots, peeled and finely chopped

1-1/2 tablespoons sweet (unsalted) butter

1 cup Chenin Blanc wine (or Sauvignon Blanc)

2 cups white fish stock, preferably rockfish stock made without wine

1 cup fresh peas, hulled

1 tablespoon winter savory, finely chopped

1 tablespoon chives, finely chopped

1/2 cup pea blossoms with shoots attached

2 tablespoons nasturtium leaves, finely chopped

1 tablespoon white wine vinegar

4 ounces sweet (unsalted) butter, cut into 1/2-inch cubes

1 pinch nutmeg, finely grated

In a medium saucepan over medium heat, sauté the shallots in 1-1/2 tablespoons butter until they are translucent. Do not burn. This should take about 4 minutes. Add the wine and fish stock and bring to a boil over high heat. Cook until the liquid is reduced by half.

Lower the heat to a simmer, add peas and chopped herbs. Cook until peas are tender, but still retaining their vibrant color. This should take about 3 minutes. Add the pea blossoms and nasturtium leaves, and continue to cook for an additional 30 seconds. Remove from the heat.

Pour sauce into a blender or food processor. Add the vinegar and blend at a low speed. While blending, add the remaining butter bit by bit. Blend until the mixture is very smooth. Add nutmeg.

Strain the sauce through a coarse strainer. Set sauce aside without returning it to the stove. The steaming of the fish is very quick, and if you reheat the sauce, it will dull the vibrant color of the sauce and diminish the attractiveness of this dish for presentation.

Fish:

4 6-ounce vermillion rockfish fillets

4 4-by-6-inch rectangles of parchment paper or buttered aluminum foil

Place one portion of fish on each piece of parchment paper. Bring the water in a steamer to a light boil. Lay each portion of fish, paper side down, into the steamer. Cover the steamer. Steam the fish until the flesh is opaque and firm, but not flaky. This should take approximately 4 minutes. Remove the cooked fish from the steamer.

To serve, spoon the warm sauce onto each plate. Transfer the fish from the paper and place the fillet over the sauce. Garnish with additional pea blossoms, if desired.

Serves 4.

PINEAPPLE GUAVA

PINEAPPLE GUAVA
Feijoa sellowiana
Myrtle family
Myrtaceae
Floral flavor
*Evergreen shrub—zones 8
through 10*
Rich, well-drained soil
Full sun to light shade

I had never heard of pineapple guava before I started researching this book. Fortunately friends of mine on the West Coast told me about it—actually raved about it, saying it was one of the best-tasting flowers.

Although the common name indicates that it may be a type of guava, it is not. The flavor of the fruit is reminiscent of guava, but guava is a different species (*Psidium*) within the myrtle family. Botanically it was named in honor of Don de Silva Feijo, a nineteenth-century botanist, and Friedrich Sellow, a German botanist and plant collector who discovered it in South America. Pineapple guava is native to southern Brazil, Paraguay, Uruguay and northern Argentina. Early in this century it was brought to California, where it is cultivated today. It is hardy in zones 8 through 10.

The flowers appear in late spring or early summer, and are exquisite in look as well as flavor, measuring up to one and one-half inches across. The outside of the petals is white to pale pink, while the inside is deep fuchsia pink. Prominent, dark-colored stamens add to the effect of fireworks from the flowers. The petals are somewhat fleshy, and the flavor is incredible—sweet and tropical. To me it was somewhat like a freshly picked, perfectly ripe papaya or exotic melon, still warm from the sun. If you can resist picking all the flowers, the dark green fruit ripens in late autumn, with the flavor, I am told, of its name. Another bonus to this plant is its resistance to pests and to disease.

CULTURE

Pineapple guava is an evergreen shrub growing eight to ten feet tall. It responds well to pruning and can easily be maintained at a lesser height. Prune it back in the spring to keep it within bounds. The leaves are handsome—glossy dark green on top and woolly silver underneath. Use the foliage from pruned branches in flower arrangements.

In zones 8 through 10 grow it in rich, well-drained soil in a warm, sunny location. In very southern areas plant it in light shade. Mulch and protect it in late autumn as protection against fluctuating low temperatures. From zone 8 north, grow pineapple guava as a container plant outdoors in summer and bring it into a cool greenhouse for the winter.

EXPANDING YOUR PLEASURES

AVOCADO, PAPAYA AND PINEAPPLE GUAVA

———

1 avocado, sliced lengthwise
1 papaya, sliced lengthwise
petals of 10 pineapple guava flowers

Alternate slices of avocado and papaya on a colorful plate. Decorate with pineapple guava petals and one whole flower. If not eating immediately, sprinkle with lemon juice to keep the avocado from turning color.

Simple, beautiful and delicious—great for a light lunch in hot weather.

Serves 4.

FEIJOA SALSA

———

1 mango, cut into 1/4-inch cubes
1 tart Granny Smith apple, cut into 1/4-inch cubes
1 papaya, cut into 1/4-inch cubes
1/2 cup Vidalia onion, chopped fine
2 red plums, cut into 1/4-inch cubes
10 cherries, pitted and cut into 4 pieces
juice of 1 lemon
petals from 15 to 20 pineapple guava flowers

Stir all ingredients together in a nonmetallic bowl. Cover and refrigerate at least 8 hours. A superb accompaniment to grilled swordfish.

Makes 1 to 2 cups.

FEIJOA FRUIT SALAD

20 seedless green grapes, cut in half
20 seedless red grapes, cut in half
2 apricots, pitted and sliced
1 peach, pitted and sliced
1 red plum, pitted and sliced
10 cherries, pitted and cut in half
2 oranges, peeled, sectioned and cut into thirds
1 kiwi, peeled and sliced
petals of 15 pineapple guava blossoms

Gently mix all ingredients together. Refrigerate in a nonmetallic bowl for several hours to allow flavors to meld. Garnish with pineapple guava petals. Refreshing served alone; elegant topped with Pinapple Guava Sorbet (see below); delectable with a large dollop of Sweet Woodruff Yogurt Custard (see page 208).

Serves 4 as a luncheon course; 6 to 8 for dessert.

PINEAPPLE GUAVA SORBET

Bring water and sugar to a boil in a small, nonaluminum saucepan. Add petals and remove saucepan from the heat. Allow to slowly cool to room temperature. Transfer to an ice cube tray and freeze to a slush. Remove from freezer, turn into a bowl. Fold in beaten egg whites and lime juice. Return to freezer and allow to freeze.

1-1/2 cups water
4 tablespoons granulated sugar
2/3 cup pineapple guava petals
2 egg whites, beaten to form soft peaks
1 tablespoon lime juice

Keeps several weeks in the freezer, but it is unlikely that any will be left over.

Serves 4.

PINEAPPLE SAGE

Pineapple sage gets its name from the fruity fragrance of the leaves, reminiscent of the tropical pineapple.

It is a tender perennial, hardy only to zone 9. In cooler areas of the country it is usually grown as an annual. The plant, when grown as a perennial, can get up to five feet tall; when grown as an annual, it only reaches three feet in height.

The leaves are opposite on the stems, dark green and rough textured. The vibrant red, one-inch tubular flowers appear in late summer and fall. The flowers are on terminal spikes a foot or more above the foliage.

Pineapple sage is attractive in an annual or perennial border for the great display of color late in the season. The flowers are exquisite with the late afternoon sun shining on them, highlighting their bright red color.

The flavor of the flowers is wonderful—sweet and fruity with a hint of spice and mint.

CULTURE

Pineapple sage needs full sun. It prefers light, sandy, well-drained soil.

PINEAPPLE SAGE
(Pineapple-scented sage)
Salvia elegans
Mint family
Lamiaceae (Labiatae)
Sweet flavor
Perennial (tender)
Light, well-drained soil
Full sun

Plant it in the garden in the spring after all danger of frost is past. Space plants at least eighteen to twenty-four inches apart. Fertilize with an all-purpose organic fertilizer after planting.

If growing pineapple sage as a perennial, cut it back and fertilize every spring. The plant can also be divided in the spring.

CUCUMBER TOMATO SALAD

2 medium tomatoes, peeled, seeded and diced
2 medium cucumbers, peeled, seeded and diced
1/3 cup mint florets
1/3 cup pineapple sage florets, coarsely chopped
1 cup plain yogurt

Gently toss all ingredients together. Allow to stand for 1 hour before serving to let flavors meld.

Serves 4.

CORN FRITTERS WITH PINEAPPLE SAGE CHILI SALSA

from Bob Werst, chef/owner, y.e. coyote, Hicksville, New York

Pineapple sage chili salsa:

1 20-ounce can crushed pineapple in its own juice, drained

1/2 cup sweet red pepper, diced

1 tablespoon sweetened lime juice

1/2 teaspoon chipotle pepper, crushed (hot chili powder can be substituted)

1/4 cup pineapple sage flowers, coarsely chopped

Combine all ingredients in a nonmetallic bowl. Refrigerate at least 12 hours before using to allow flavors to meld.

The salsa is also good as a dip with chips or served on seafood.

Corn fritters:

24 ounces frozen corn, divided

1 teaspoon ground coriander

1 tablespoon medium chili powder

1/8 teaspoon salt

1 tablespoon granulated sugar

1/2 cup sweet red pepper

1/4 cup onion

1 tablespoon baking powder

3/4 cup all-purpose flour

2 eggs, beaten

vegetable oil for deep frying

Add half of the corn to the coriander, chili powder, salt, sugar, red pepper and onion in the bowl of a food processor fitted with a steel blade. Pulse until it reaches the consistency of oatmeal. Transfer mixture to a bowl. Sift together baking powder and flour. Add flour, eggs and remaining corn to first mixture. Stir to mix.

Heat oil to 350°F for deep frying.* Drop batter by rounded tablespoonful into the oil. Turn to brown evenly on all sides. Remove from oil and drain on absorbent paper. Serve immediately with salsa. If you have any left, they are pretty tasty cold the next day.

Serves 6 to 8.

* Although the fritters are crunchier this way, you can also cook them in a nonstick frying pan.

SAUCE GRIBICHE A LA HOLMES (ON GRILLED FISH)

from Barry Yates, corporate chef, House of Winston, Louisville, Kentucky

1 tablespoon red wine vinegar

1 tablespoon sherry wine vinegar

1/4 cup extra virgin olive oil

1/4 cup Walla Walla onion, minced

2 tablespoons cornichons, diced

1 tablespoon small capers

1/2 teaspoon Dijon mustard

3 tablespoons pineapple sage flowers, minced

salt and freshly ground black pepper

2 hard-boiled eggs, yolks and whites minced separately

4 striped bass fillets, grilled

In a small bowl, whisk vinegars together. Slowly add oil whisking continually. Continue to whisk until you get a nice emulsion. Add onion, cornichons, capers, mustard and 2 tablespoons of pineapple sage flowers. Mix well. Adjust seasoning with salt and pepper to taste.

Just before serving, stir in minced egg yolk and white. Pour over grilled fish. Garnish dish with remaining blossoms. This is zesty, bright French vinaigrette that is a perfect accompaniment over grilled fish.

Sauce can be stored at room temperature.

Serves 4.

TANGY ROASTED CHICKEN

2 sprigs anise hyssop

2 sprigs pineapple sage

2 sprigs sweet marjoram

roasting chicken

salt and freshly ground black pepper

1/3 cup pineapple sage flowers, coarsely chopped

1/3 cup anise hyssop flowers, coarsely chopped

1/4 cup sweet marjoram flowers, coarsely chopped

8 small red potatoes, halved

4 medium carrots, cut in thirds

6 small onions, peeled

Preheat oven to 350°F. Stuff anise hyssop sprigs, pineapple sage sprigs and sweet marjoram sprigs into the cavity of the chicken. Place chicken in shallow roasting pan. Season chicken, inside and out, with salt and pepper to taste.

Mix chopped flowers together and sprinkle over and around chicken. Put potatoes, carrots and onions around chicken. Roast for 1-1/2 hours or until juices around thigh run clear when cut.

Serves 6 to 8, depending on the size of the chicken.

LACE COOKIES

——

1-1/2 cups granulated sugar
1 cup almonds, finely chopped
3/4 cup all-purpose flour
juice of 1 orange
1/4 pound sweet (unsalted) butter, melted
1/4 cup pineapple sage flowers, coarsely chopped

Preheat oven to 400°F. In a large bowl, mix sugar, almonds and flour. Pour orange juice and melted butter into the center of the bowl. Add flowers. Stir well, mixing with a wooden spoon.

Grease a cookie sheet. Spoon a teaspoonful of batter into circles 2 inches apart. Gently flatten the cookie with a fork dipped in cold water. Bake for 5 to 7 minutes, until the cookies are lightly browned at the edge. Remove from oven and let sit 1 minute until the cookies start to firm up. Using a metal spatula, remove the cookies from the sheet before they become brittle.

Cookies can be placed over a rolling pin to form a curved shape.

Makes about 3 dozen cookies.

ADISH

The radish has its origins in China. The ancient Egyptians cultivated it. Wild radish grows extensively in the Mediterranean area.

Radish, a cool weather annual, is entirely edible. The swollen root is the part customarily eaten. When cooked, the young leaves are reminiscent of turnip or mustard greens.

There are two distinct types of radishes. The spring radish is commonly used in salads. It is usually eaten raw at an immature stage before it becomes pithy or too pungent.

Spring radishes come in a variety of shapes and colors including round, oval, cylindrical or icicle, and white, red, pink or any combination of these colors.

The winter radish, or Oriental radish (*Raphanus sativus var. longipinnatus*), has not been as commonly grown. As its name implies, the roots are harvested in winter. They are much larger than spring radishes, often with a long cylindrical shape.

Radish flowers may be white, pink or yellow, often with contrasting veination. Like other members of the mustard family, the four petals are in a cross formation. The flavor is spicy, with a distinct bite.

RADISH
Raphanus sativus
Mustard family
Brassicaceae (Cruciferae)
Spicy flavor
Annual
Well-drained, sandy soil
Full sun

CULTURE

Radishes like full sun. They grow best in sandy, rich, well-drained soil.

Seed spring radishes directly in the garden as early as the soil can be worked in spring. The earliest radishes will be ready to pick within a month; you have to be more patient for the flowers. Keep picking the flowers and they will rebloom.

Normally winter radishes are planted late in summer or in early fall to keep them from going to seed in warmer weather. Needless to say, for flower production, plant them earlier in the year and take advantage of the warm season bloom.

SALAD OF CARROT AND DAIKON

from James O'Shea, chef, West Street Grill, Litchfield, Connecticut

1/2 pound carrots, peeled
1/2 pound daikon radish, peeled
1/4 cup fresh orange juice
1/4 cup rice wine vinegar
1/2 cup olive oil
1 tablespoon sesame oil
4 scallions, thinly cut on the bias
salt and pepper
4 medium beets
1 tablespoon olive oil
1/2 cup daikon or other radish flowers

Cut carrots and daikon into long julienne strips. Blanch quickly (1 minute) in boiling salted water. Immerse immediately into an ice bath.

In a medium bowl, mix orange juice, vinegar, olive oil, sesame oil and scallions. Add salt and pepper to taste. Toss in the carrots and daikon. Refrigerate for at least 1 hour to let flavors marry.

After refrigerating carrots and daikon, preheat oven to 425°F. Toss beets in olive oil to coat. Season with salt and pepper. Roast beets in a shallow baking dish for 25 minutes or until tender. Remove from oven and let cool. Remove peels—they should slip right off. Julienne beets.

To assemble, arrange the carrots and daikon on 4 plates. Pile it high like a haystack. Garnish the top with the roasted beets. Sprinkle the daikon flowers around the entire plate.

Serves 4.

RED CLOVER

In Victorian times, red clover signified industry. Although it grows wild like a native plant, red clover was an introduction from Europe. Clover cordial was a popular drink in the early days of San Francisco.

Clover was used as a food by Native Americans from coast to coast. According to Sturtevant, "Where clover is found growing wild, the Indians practice a sort of semicultivation by irrigating it and harvesting." In Ireland and Scotland, clover was also a food source. The dried flowers and seeds of white clover were ground and made into a nutritious bread.

Red clover grows from six to sixteen inches tall, flowering from April to September. Upon close examination, what appears to be the one-inch pink flower reveals itself to be a densely packed head of small pealike flowers. The leaves are grouped in threes, but are narrower than most clovers, marked with a pale chevron.

Raw clover flowers are not easily digestible, especially when eaten in any quantity, but their sweet crunch is a nice addition to salad. The flowers can be dried and then brewed into a delicately flavored tea.

CULTURE

Red clover grows wild in fields and along road-sides throughout America. To some it may be consid-

RED CLOVER
Trifolium pratense
Pea family
Fabaceae (Leguminosae)
Sweet flavor
Annual, self-seeding
Any garden soil

ered a weed, but how lovely it is in a mass planting, gently swaying in the breeze, the honey scent of the flowers drifting toward you. You can grow it from seed—direct seed it in early to mid-spring or in late summer.

Clover is an added bonus in the garden—like most legumes, it fixes nitrogen from the air into the soil, so it helps fertilize the garden.

WARNING
Clover can cause a skin rash in some sensitive people.

CLOVER TEA

1/2 cup clover blossoms, fresh or dried
4 cups boiling water

Pour boiling water over clover blossoms in a teapot. Allow to steep for 5 minutes. Strain and serve.

Serves 4.

CRUNCHY CLOVER DRESSING

6 tablespoons olive oil
3 tablespoons balsamic vinegar
1 chive flower, broken into florets
salt and freshly ground pepper to taste
30 red clover flowers

Whisk together oil, vinegar, chive florets, salt and pepper. Pour over clover flowers. Cover and set aside for at least a half hour.

Serve over a bed of mixed greens.

Use the dressing within 2 hours of making it or the clover flowers will get soggy.

CLOVER SOUP

2 cups clover blossoms
2 tablespoons chive flower butter
3 medium potatoes, cut into 1-inch cubes (Yukon gold potatoes give a great color)
1/4 cup tahini
1 quart water
1/4 cup sesame seeds, toasted

In a heavy saucepan, sauté the clover blossoms in the chive flower butter. Do not let the blossoms brown. Add the potatoes and tahini and sauté for several minutes more. Add the water, cover and simmer for 20 to 30 minutes.

For a thicker soup, puree half of the soup in a food processor or blender, then return to the pot. Garnish with clover florets and toasted sesame seeds.

Serves 6.

CONFETTI BISCUITS

1 tablespoon mint flowers, chopped
1 tablespoon clover blossoms, chopped
1 tablespoon chive blossoms, chopped
1 tablespoon dandelion flowers, chopped
1/4 cup cottage cheese
1/3 cup milk
3 tablespoons vegetable oil
1/2 cup whole wheat flour
1/2 cup unbleached white flour
1/4 teaspoon baking soda
1/4 teaspoon salt

Preheat oven to 450°F. Sift dry ingredients together. Mix cottage cheese, milk, and oil together in a large bowl. Stir in chopped flowers. Add sifted dry ingredients. Mix well.

Turn out onto a floured surface and knead for several minutes. With a rolling pin, roll the dough out to a thickness of 1/2-inch. Cut with a biscuit cutter and place on an ungreased cookie sheet. Bake for 12 to 15 minutes, until lightly browned.

Makes 10 to 12 biscuits.

PICKLED CLOVER

red and white clover blossoms
white vinegar
honey

Alternate red and white clover in layers in a wide-mouthed jar. Pour in enough vinegar to cover the blossoms. Pour the vinegar out of the jar and into a measuring cup. For each 1/2 cup of vinegar, stir in 1 tablespoon honey. Pour the honey-vinegar mixture back over the clover. Cover with a cloth and let sit for a week before using.

Pickled clover makes a nice garnish with cooked vegetables, fish or assorted cheeses as hors d'oeuvres.

rEDBUD

REDBUD
(Judas Tree)
Cercis canadensis,
Cercis siliquastrum
Pea family
Fabaceae (Leguminosae)
Beanlike flavor
Tree
Sandy loam
Full sun to partial shade

Redbud is a lovely, early spring-blooming tree. The bright, cerise-pink, one-half-inch pealike flowers bloom in clusters on the branches, so it is often easiest to do selective pruning rather than trying to pick off individual flowers.

The large heart-shaped leaves appear after the flowers have faded. Redbuds are classified as small trees or large **shrubs**, as they may have single or multiple trunks. **They range from** fifteen to thirty-five feet in height, with a slightly flattened, round shape overall. Nothing is quite so lovely as a well-placed redbud in bloom. Against the background of a vibrant blue spring sky, the branches appear to be bright pink slashes with their multitude of flower.

Redbud can be picked in bud or in full flowers. It has a nice crunch, making it suitable for use in salads or as garnish to hot vegetables. The buds are often pickled. The flavor is like a cross between a green bean and a tart apple.

CULTURE

The native redbud, *Cercis canadensis*, grows from Connecticut south to Texas and northern Florida, also from southeastern Nebraska to southern Wisconsin. It is usually found in moist woods and thickets, and will thrive in the understory of a cultivated woodland garden. I have seen them planted on lawns under large pines or oaks, giving their great burst of color in early spring, from March to May depending on the location.

Redbuds are tolerant of soil pH, growing in acid or alkaline soil. They can be planted in full sun or partial shade. They like woodland conditions, with sandy loam, and they cannot tolerate heavy, moist soil. Although they are not large trees, relatively speaking, they do not transplant well once they reach maturity.

BLACK BEAN AND REDBUD SOUP

1/4 cup olive oil

1 tablespoon cumin

1 tablespoon curry powder

3 cloves of garlic, finely minced

2 cups Vidalia or Bermuda onion, finely chopped

2 cups carrot, finely grated

4 stalks celery, finely chopped

8 cups water

1 meaty ham bone or ham hock (optional)

5 sprigs parsley, finely chopped

5 sprigs cilantro, finely chopped

2 cups dried black beans

1/4 cup dry sherry (optional)

30 redbud flowers

sour cream or plain yogurt

In a large stock pot, heat oil with cumin and curry powder. Add garlic and onions. Sauté until just glistening. Add carrots and celery, sauté for an additional 5 minutes. Add water, ham, herbs and beans. Bring to a boil. Stir well, reduce heat, cover and simmer for 3 hours, stirring frequently. If soup becomes too thick, add water. Remove ham from bone, and return meat to soup. Add sherry and simmer an additional 30 minutes. Season to taste with salt and pepper. Add flowers (reserve some for garnish) to each bowl just before pouring in soup. Garnish with a dollop of sour cream or yogurt and top with a flower.

Serves 8.

SAUTEED REDBUD

1 tablespoon butter

1 cup redbud flower buds and flowers

Melt butter in a heavy frying pan over low heat. Add flowers and flower buds. Sauté for 5 to 10 minutes, stirring frequently. Serve immediately.

This dish can be served alone as a vegetable. An attractive and delicious variation is to toss the hot sautéed redbud with loose-leaf red lettuce. The lettuce will wilt slightly and you get a lovely combination of textures and colors.

Serves 2 to 4.

PEAS WITH MUSHROOMS AND REDBUD

1 teaspoon butter
1 tablespoon olive oil
1 tablespoon Madras curry powder
1 teaspoon cinnamon
1 pound mushrooms, sliced
1 pound peas (frozen or fresh)
50 redbud flowers

In a heavy frying pan, heat the butter and olive oil over a medium-high heat. Add curry and cinnamon, stir well. Lower to medium heat and cook the spices for several minutes, stirring frequently. Add the mushrooms and sauté for 5 minutes or until they are just cooked. If using fresh peas, steam them until they turn bright green, then add them to the mushrooms. If using frozen peas, they can be added directly to the mushrooms without cooking. Continue to cook for 5 minutes. Just before serving, add the redbud flowers and stir to distribute them evenly among the peas and mushrooms.

For a variation, stir in 1/4 cup of sour cream or plain yogurt for a tangy richness.

Serves 4 to 6.

REDBUD AND ASPARAGUS LINGUINE

1 pound asparagus, cut into 1-1/2-inch pieces on the diagonal
 (reserve two whole spears)
8 ounces beet linguine
8 ounces spinach linguine
1 cup cream
1/2 cup freshly grated Parmesan cheese
2 tablespoons freshly ground nutmeg
1 tablespoon dill
25 redbud flowers

Steam asparagus lightly until it turns deep green and is tender-crisp. Cook linguine according to package directions until al dente. Drain linguine and return to the pot. Toss in asparagus. Add cream and cheese, tossing well. Put on a very low heat. When sauce is hot, add remaining ingredients, reserving several flowers for garnish. Garnish with whole asparagus spears and flowers. Serve immediately. For a slightly different taste, substitute lilac flowers for the redbuds.

Serves 4.

ROSE OF SHARON

Rose of Sharon is the hardiest member of the mallow family, hardy to zone 5. A large shrub, it can grow from five to fifteen tall.

One of the main reasons for putting it in the garden is that it blooms in late summer. While annuals and perennials may be going strong, there is not much in the way of large shrubs or trees that can provide so much color at that time of year.

Not only does this shrub bloom late in summer, the leaves come out quite late in the spring. Do not despair at the sight of a leafless shrub in May.

The flowers are short-stalked, flaring out from three to five inches wide. Flowers may be single or double, in red, white, purple or violet. Before they open flowers have a nutty flavor; after, they are mildly sweet.

CULTURE

Rose of Sharon grows in any well-drained soil. Plant in full sun or partial shade. Fertilize with an organic fertilizer in spring.

To promote flower production, pinch the stem tips in spring and summer. Rose of Sharon benefits from hard pruning to promote a fuller shrub. Prune the plant before June or risk cutting off the summer's flowers.

ROSE OF SHARON
(Shrub Althea)
Hibiscus syriacus
Mallow family
Malvaceae
Mild flavor
Shrub
Well-drained soil
Full sun to partial shade

Deadhead after after they fade, or the shrub will look messy. Although it is a bit of a chore, it encourages new flower formation.

Although many varieties are available commercially, it is not too difficult to propagate the shrub yourself. Take a six- to ten-inch cutting in the spring. Dip the cut end into rooting hormone and plant it in moist sand or perlite. Once rooted, plant in a sheltered area in the garden or in a container. Within five years the cutting will grow to five feet tall.

STUFFED ROSE OF SHARON

20 rose of Sharon flowers
Flower Dip
1 tablespoon rose of Sharon petals, chopped

Remove pistils and stamens from flowers. Pipe or spoon the dip into the center of the flower. Garnish with chopped petals.

Serves 6 to-8 for hors d'oeuvres.

rOSELLE

ROSELLE (Jamaican sorrel)
Hibiscus sabdariffa
Mallow family
Malvaceae
Mild flavor
Hardy in zone 10
Well-drained, rich soil
Full sun

Roselle is native to the Old World tropics. Roselle is cultivated in Florida, the Caribbean and India for its yellow flowers and fleshy calyxes. These are made into delicious jellies, sauces and a fermented beverage called roselle. Its flavor is mild with a hint of citrus.

CULTURE

Roselle is hardy to zone 10. It grows best in full sun and rich, well-drained soil. Set plants twenty-four inches apart. See Hibiscus (page 132) for detailed culture information.

ROSELLE ICE CREAM

2 cups milk
1/2 vanilla bean, split
1/2 cup roselle flowers, shredded
4 egg yolks
1/3 cup granulated sugar

Pour milk into a heavy saucepan. Add vanilla and roselle flowers. Over a medium heat, bring milk to a scald. In a large bowl, beat egg yolks with sugar until yolks become pale yellow and form a ribbonlike consistency. Gradually whisk hot milk into eggs, adding milk slowly. Continue to whisk until completely blended. Return mixture to the saucepan. Over a medium heat, cook the liquid, stirring continuously until it coats the spoon. Do not allow it to boil or it will curdle. Remove from heat. Cool at room temperature about 15 minutes, then refrigerate until it is well chilled. Pour into an ice cream maker and process according to manufacturer's directions.

Serves 4 to 6.

ROSEMARY

Pliny named this pungent herb *Rosmarinus*, derived from the Latin *ros maris* meaning sea dew. Rosemary is attributed to restoring the memory. Over the centuries, it has had diverse uses. Rosemary is supposed to bring good luck, fend off witches and disinfect the air. In the Victorian language of flowers, rosemary means "you ever revive."

Rosemary is native to the rocky coasts of France and Spain, but is now cultivated as a culinary herb throughout the world. It is an excellent plant to include in seaside gardens.

Rosemary is a tender perennial shrub that can grow three to six feet tall. Hardy only to zone 8, it is grown as an annual in many areas of the country. It is evergreen with needlelike leaves. With the different varieties of rosemary, leaf color varies from gray green to dark green, usually lighter on the reverse side. In warm climates it makes a very attractive low hedge.

The pale blue flowers (occasionally white-rose, pale lavender or dark blue) appear in mid to late spring, and sometimes again in summer. The flowers have a flavor reminiscent of the leaves, but much less pungent.

CULTURE

Grow rosemary in full sun or partial shade in alkaline, well-drained, evenly moist soil.

ROSEMARY
Rosmarinus officinalis
Mint family
Lamiaceae (Labiatae)
Herbal flavor
Tender perennial shrub
Well-drained, evenly moist soil
Full sun to partial shade

Rosemary can be grown from seed, but it is slow to germinate. Often it can take three years from seed to flower. Propagate it from four to six-inch cuttings taken from the tips of growing stems. Root the stems in moistened sand or vermiculite. Once rooted, plant transplant to a small pot.

Set plants out in the garden two to four weeks before the last frost. Space plants twelve to eighteen inches apart. Fertilize with an organic fertilizer when planting. When it is kept as a perennial, outdoors or in a container, fertilize each spring when new growth appears.

Rosemary is happily cultivated as a container plant. It can easily be trained as topiary, commonly in a tree form, a rounded form or a circular wreath form.

EDIBLE FLOWERS

ROASTED ITALIAN PEPPER TOMATOES

from James O'Shea, chef, West Street Grill, Litchfield, Connecticut

2 tablespoons fresh basil, finely chopped
2 tablespoons Italian parsley, finely chopped
1 tablespoon oregano flowers, chopped
1 tablespoon rosemary flowers, chopped
2 shallots, finely minced
2 cloves garlic, minced
1/3 cup extra virgin olive oil
6 Italian pepper tomatoes
salt and pepper
2 tablespoons olive oil

Preheat oven to 350°F. Mix together basil, parsley, oregano flowers, rosemary flowers, shallots, garlic and 1/3 cup olive oil. Set aside for 1 hour to allow the flavors to meld.

Meanwhile, slice tomatoes in half. Toss tomatoes with 2 tablespoons olive oil to coat. Sprinkle with salt and pepper. Place tomatoes, cut side down, in a shallow baking pan. Roast for 30 minutes. Flip tomatoes over carefully. Spoon herb mixture evenly over tomatoes and roast 30 minutes more. Serve tomatoes garnished with oregano and rosemary flowers.

MEDITERRANEAN SOUP

8 cups chicken stock
2 carrots, coarsely chopped
1 onion, coarsely chopped
3 stalks celery, coarsely chopped
1/4 cup parsley
1 bay leaf

3 cloves
1/2 cup rosemary flowers, coarsely chopped
salt and freshly ground pepper to taste
2 tablespoons instant tapioca
2 hard-boiled eggs, chopped
plain yogurt
rosemary flowers for garnish

Pour chicken stock into a stock pot. Add carrots, onion, celery, parsley, bay leaf, cloves, and rosemary flowers. Bring to a boil, lower heat, cover and simmer gently for 45 minutes.

Strain soup. Return liquid to pot. Adjust seasoning with salt and pepper. Add tapioca and bring to a boil. Serve garnished with chopped eggs, a dollop of yogurt and rosemary flowers.

Serves 8.

ROSEMARY CHICKEN

from Eileen Mendyka, Good Thyme Farm, Bethlehem, Connecticut

1 pound skinless, boneless chicken breasts
3 tablespoons sweet (unsalted) butter
2 tablespoons rosemary flowers, coarsely chopped
juice of 1 lemon

Pound chicken breasts to 1/4-inch thickness. Melt butter in a skillet and add chicken. Add rosemary flowers. Quickly sauté each side until golden brown. Sprinkle with lemon juice. Serve chicken drizzled with pan juices.

Serves 4.

ROSEMARY VEAL CHOPS

from Carole Saville, Los Angeles, California

4 veal chops
salt and pepper to taste
2 tablespoons extra virgin olive oil
1 clove garlic, chopped
1 bay leaf
1 tablespoon rosemary flowers
2 tablespoons rosemary flower vinegar
1/2 cup chicken stock

Sprinkle salt and pepper onto both sides of the veal chops. Pour olive oil into a skillet over a medium-high heat. Add veal chops and brown about 5 minutes per side. Lower heat to medium. Add garlic, bay and rosemary flowers. Cook 3 to 4 minutes, then pour in rosemary vinegar and stock. Turn heat to low, cover and cook until tender, about 15 minutes. Remove chops and keep them in a warm place. Remove bay leaf from skillet.

Reduce sauce for 2 to 3 minutes. Place chops on a serving plate and pour sauce over them. Garnish each plate with a sprig of rosemary blossoms.

Serves 4.

EDIBLE FLOWERS

LAMB SHANKS A LA GRECQUE

1 teaspoon lavender flowers, coarsely chopped

2 tablespoons rosemary flowers, coarsely chopped

1 tablespoon thyme flowers, coarsely chopped

1 tablespoon oregano flowers, coarsely chopped

1 teaspoon brown sugar

1 cup rosemary vinegar

1 bay leaf

freshly ground black pepper

4 lamb shanks

4 potatoes, peeled and quartered

Mix together flowers, sugar, rosemary vinegar, bay leaf and freshly ground pepper to taste. Place lamb shanks and potatoes in a glass or plastic dish. Pour marinade over them. Turn to coat completely. Cover and refrigerate for 24 hours, turning occasionally.

Preheat oven to 350°F. Remove lamb shanks and potatoes from marinade and place in a shallow roasting pan. Bake for about 1 hour or until lamb reaches desired doneness. Turn shanks and potatoes once during baking to allow all-over browning.

Serve garnished with rosemary flowers. A flavorful alternative to more expensive cuts of lamb.

Serves 4.

ROSEMARY ICE

from James O'Shea, chef, West Street Grill, Litchfield, Connecticut

1-1/2 cups water

3/4 cup dry white wine

2 tablespoons granulated sugar

2 tablespoons freshly squeezed lemon juice

1/4 cup anise aquavit

1 tablespoon rosemary flowers, minced

1 tablespoon lemon thyme flowers, minced

salt to taste

In a small stainless steel saucepan combine all ingredients. Bring to a boil and simmer for 3 minutes. Transfer to a stainless steel bowl, cover and place in the freezer. Every half hour, remove the bowl from the freezer and quickly whisk the mixture. It will take several hours for the mixture to become slushy. When it has reached that consistency, allow it to freeze hard—at least overnight.

Serves 4 to 6.

rUNNER BEAN

Runner beans are perennial vegetables. In areas with very mild winters the deep taproots may overwinter successfully; however, runner beans are usually grown as annuals.

The plants are attractive, often grown ornamentally, trained to grow up a trellis or on an arbor. In fact the beans, when picked young, are as flavorful as any snap bean. The plants bear a resemblance to pole snap beans, but with darker green, denser leaves.

The young bean pods are dark green and straight. When cut into a cross-section, they appear oval. For best eating, pick the pods when they are no more than four inches long. As they get bigger, they become stringy. As the pods age, the surface becomes striated. Allow the pods to wither, and harvest the beans to use as a dried bean.

Different varieties have different beans and flowers. Scarlet runner beans have vibrant red-orange flowers. The immature beans are fluorescent pink; they mature to a mottled pink and black. 'Dutch White' runner beans have white flowers and white beans. 'Painted Lady' is an heirloom British bean with showy coral and white flowers.

Remember that if you are growing these plants for the flowers, the more you pick the more the plant will keep producing. Beans will not form, however, if the flowers are picked. Several plants usually supply more than enough flowers for picking and allowing some to mature into beans.

Runner beans have a delicate beany flavor with a nice crunch that holds up even with a bit of cooking.

RUNNER BEAN
Phaseolus coccineus
Pea family
Fabaceae (Leguminosae)
Beanlike flavor
Annual
Ordinary garden soil
Full sun

The recipes call for scarlet runner beans, but any type will do.

CULTURE

Runner beans need full sun and good air circulation around them.

Sow the beans directly into the garden after danger of frost has past and the soil has warmed up. In cool areas, plant them in a sheltered location, facing south and west so they can best benefit from the sun. Plant three or four seeds in a cluster one inch apart. Plant the next cluster at a distance of two to three feet from the first.

Runner beans grow eight to ten feet tall, but need support of some kind. Even a simple teepee made of long poles works well. Of course an arbor or a trellis gives a more formal look.

EDIBLE FLOWERS

SCARLET RUNNER BEAN SOUP

adapted from Rosalind Creasy, Cooking from the Garden

2 tablespoons chive oil (or use olive oil and florets from 6 chive
flowers)

1 tablespoon butter

1 medium sweet red onion, coarsely chopped

2 pounds scarlet runner beans, stringed and cut into 1-inch
lengths

2 cups scarlet runner bean flowers (reserve some for garnish)

8 cups chicken broth

1/4 cup barley

salt and pepper

Melt oil and butter in a large stock pot. Sauté onions over a medium heat until they are translucent. Add beans and flowers and sauté for several more minutes. Add broth and barley. Cover and simmer for 30 to 45 minutes. Remove from heat. Puree the soup in a blender or food processor. Adjust seasoning with salt and pepper to taste. If soup is still a bit stringy (you can use large pods even those with developed beans inside), strain it through a sieve. Serve garnished with flowers.

Serves 12 to 18.

SCARLET RUNNER BEANS AND THYME

4 tablespoons olive oil

1 Spanish onion, finely
chopped

2 cloves garlic, crushed

1 pound scarlet runner
beans, stringed and
cut into 2-inch pieces

1/4 cup thyme flowers

6 tablespoons water

30 scarlet runner bean flowers

Heat oil in a heavy frying pan over a low heat. Sauté onion and garlic until softened and translucent, not browned. Add beans and thyme flowers. Raise heat to medium high. Add water and bring to a boil. Lower the heat, cover and simmer for 10 to 15 minutes, until the beans are bright green and slightly crunchy. Toss in flowers and serve.

Serves 4.

POTATOES 'N' BEANS

1 tablespoon butter

1 tablespoon extra virgin olive oil

1 medium Walla Walla or Vidalia onion, finely chopped

4 red potatoes, boiled to fork tender, cooled and sliced
1/4-inch thick

1 cup scarlet runner bean flowers, divided

Heat butter and oil in a large skillet. When butter has melted, add onions and sauté until they turn translucent. Add slices of potatoes and 1/2 cup flowers. Continue to cook until potatoes are lightly browned on each side. Remove to a platter and garnish with remaining flowers. Serve immediately.

Serves 4 to 6.

$\mathcal{J}$AFFLOWER

SAFFLOWER

(American saffron, Azafran,
Bastard saffron, Dyer's
saffron, False saffron)
Carthamus tinctorius
Composite family
Asteraceae (Compositae)
Bitter flavor, yellow color
Annual
Light, dry, well-drained soil
Full sun

Today safflower is best known as a source for polyunsaturated oil produced from the seeds. For many centuries it was grown for the flowers that yielded dyes. The Portuguese are credited with first using the flower petals as a saffron substitute in the 1700s. Safflower is used as a dye plant and as a dried plant.

Safflower is originally native to the Middle East. It has been cultivated throughout North American and Europe. It is much cultivated in India.

Safflower is an annual herb growing two to three feet tall. It has a single stem with shiny, oval, spiny-edged leaves. Safflower blooms in midsummer with a profusion of one- to one-and-one-half-inch solitary, thistlelike flower heads that turn from deep yellow to deep red as they mature. By late summer, if not picked, the seeds are hidden under a downy mass.

Its flavor is slightly bitter, and the petals impart a lovely yellow color into cooked foods. Substitute safflower for calendula petals in other recipes.

CULTURE

Safflower needs full sun. It prefers light, dry, well-drained soil.

It is a tender annual. Grow safflower from seed planted directly in the garden after all danger of frost is past. It can be started indoors six weeks before the last frost date in spring. Allow six inches between plants.

WARNING

Safflower can act as a laxative. It also is used to induced perspiration. Moderation is advised.

GOLDEN RICE

2 tablespoons butter
1 cup rice
2-1/2 cups stock or water, boiling
2 tablespoons safflower petals

Melt butter in a heavy saucepan. Add rice and slowly sauté over a low heat for several minutes. Do not let rice brown. Chop petals and stir in with rice. Add liquid and stir well. Cover saucepan, reduce heat and cook until all liquid is absorbed (about 20 minutes).

Serves 4.

SCENTED GERANIUM

Scented geraniums come in a range of odors and flavors, with rose geranium still the most popular and consistent. Scented geraniums are native to the Cape of Good Hope. They were first introduced into Europe in the early 1600s. It took more than a century before they made their way to the America, yet by the late 1800s there were over 150 varieties described in catalogs.

In the Victorian language of flowers, lemon geranium expresses unexpected meeting while nutmeg geranium is expected meeting.

In their native habitat and in southern California, the scented geraniums are perennial. In most of the rest of the country, they are treated as annuals or tender perennials. The leaf form is highly variable and the leaf texture can be smooth, velvety or even sticky. It is the back of the leaf that releases the scent for which each geranium is known and named. Even when they are not in bloom, it is a joy to brush your hand against the plant and smell the aroma.

There are over fifty different geraniums with a rose odor. Some can reach a height of four feet in mild areas. They bloom in June and July in indescribable hues of lavender and pink. *Pelargonium graveolens* is a large plant with lavender flowers and deeply cut, gray green leaves. It is traditionally used in rose geranium jelly and tea. *Pelargonium graveolens*, 'Lady Plymouth' grows very large, yet is slow-growing. The leaf is deeply cut light green with a strong aroma. *Pelargonium graveolens*, Gray Lady Plymouth, is one of the best variegated plants. It

SCENTED GERANIUM
Pelargonium spp.
Geranium family
Geraniaceae
Floral flavor
Annual to tender perennial
Evenly moist soil
Full sun

is a vigorous plant with deeply cut gray green leaves bordered with white. *Pelargonium graveolens*, 'Rober's Lemon Rose', has one of the sweetest rose scents and flavors. The leaf is long and thick, resembling a tomato leaf. *Pelargonium capitatum* 'Attar of Roses' is considered by many the best of the rose-scented geraniums. Its three-lobed, crenated leaves are light green, soft and hairy and the flowers are lavender. *Pelargonium denticulatum* has finely cut leaves growing densely on a compact plant.

Lemon geranium leaves are usually flatter, with edges more toothed than rose geraniums. They also bloom in June and July, often with pink flowers. *Pelargonium crispum* is one of the finest lemon-scented geraniums. The leaves are small, fluted and ruffled, growing on upright stems. The flowers are orchid pink. With its treelike shape, it makes an excellent container plant. *Pelargonium crispum* 'Prince Rupert' with its strong lemon scent, can easily grow into a small shrub in a good growing season. *Pelargonium crispum* 'Prince Rupert Variegated' has ruffled green leaves variegated with a creamy white. The scent is milder than 'Prince Rupert', and it is not nearly so vigorous. *Pelargonium limoneum* 'Lady Mary' has fan-shaped toothed leaves and bears magenta flowers in summer.

Pelargonium fragrans 'Nutmeg' has a strong scent. It creeps, making it excellent at the edge of a border or in a planter allowed to trail down the sides. The leaves are small and grayish green.

The flowers of the scented geraniums are mild-flavored versions of the scent of the leaf. The recipes that follow call for rose geranium, but you can substitute any flavor you like.

CULTURE

Scented geraniums are well suited for growing in containers, but can also be planted in the ground. They thrive in sunny locations in evenly moist soil. They are not grown from seed, rather from rooted cuttings. They are available commercially, or you can share cuttings with friends. The popularity of scented geraniums is rapidly growing. Even the smallest nurseries can be relied on to carry several different varieties.

Plant scented geraniums in containers at least five inches deep—double that is preferable. Use a mixture of one part Perlite, one part well-rotted compost or garden loam and one part peat moss for potting them. Feed every two to three weeks.

Scented geraniums are frost tender. Remove any leaves as they yellow. Bring the plants indoors before frost to winter over in pots, or simply treat them as annuals and allow them to die in the garden. The entire plant can be brought in, or if space does not allow, take cuttings and root them. When you bring them indoors, place them in the sunniest location possible.

WARNING

Do not eat the 'Citronella' scented geranium, which is being touted as a mosquito and bug repellent, although it has yet to prove itself to me. In general, if the leaf does not have an appetizing aroma, do not eat the flowers.

ROSE GERANIUM JELLY

1 pint apple jelly

1/2 cup rose geranium petals

Heat the apple jelly over a low heat until it turns liquid. Add the rose geranium petals and stir. Remove from heat and pour jelly into a jelly glass. Allow to cool. Cover and refrigerate. Use within 2 weeks.

ROSE ANGEL CAKE

1 angel food cake, cut into 3 equal layers
orange juice
Rose Geranium Jelly (see page 198)
vanilla ice cream, softened

Place the first layer of the angel food cake in an angel food cake (tube) pan. Lightly sprinkle the layer with orange juice. Spread a thin layer of rose geranium jelly over the cake. Place the next layer atop the first. Sprinkle lightly with orange juice and spread thickly with ice cream. Add the last layer of cake. Sprinkle lightly with orange juice and spread with Rose Geranium Jelly. Spread with ice cream. Put cake in freezer until ice cream hardens.

Remove from freezer and gently unmold onto a serving plate. Spread ice cream over the entire cake and return to freezer until ice cream hardens.

Serve garnished with rose geranium petals.

Serves 10 to 16.

SCENTED GERANIUM ICE CREAM

from James O'Shea, chef, West Street Grill, Litchfield, Connecticut

5 to 7 scented geranium leaves (rose, lime or nutmeg), roughly chopped
2 teaspoons scented geranium petals (same scent as leaves)
1-1/4 cups half-and-half
1/2 cup granulated sugar
4 egg yolks
1 cup heavy cream

Combine leaves, petals and half-and-half in a small saucepan. Bring to a boil. Remove from heat and allow to cool for 20 minutes.

In a small stainless steel saucepan whisk together sugar and egg yolks. Continue to whisk until mixture is light and frothy. Slowly whisk in half-and-half. Cook over a low heat, stirring continually, until custard coats the back of a wooden spoon. Strain custard into a bowl and set into an ice bath to cool.

Beat heavy cream until it forms peaks. Gently fold cream into the cooled custard. Freeze in an ice cream maker according to manufacturer's instructions. Remove from ice cream maker and place in freezer overnight to set.

Serve in small glasses garnished with additional scented geranium leaves and petals.

Serves 4 to 6.

ROSE GERANIUM CAKE

2-2/3 cup cake flour
1 tablespoon baking powder
1 teaspoon salt
2/3 cup shortening
1-1/4 cups granulated sugar
1 cup milk
1 teaspoon vanilla
5 egg whites
1/2 cup granulated sugar
2/3 cup rose geranium petals, coarsely chopped
1 cup pecans, chopped
confectioners' sugar for decoration
rose geranium petals for garnish

Preheat oven to 375°F. Sift flour once, then measure. Sift together with the baking powder and salt three times.

In a separate bowl, cream shortening. Add 1-1/4 cups of sugar gradually, creaming until mixture is light and fluffy. Add flour and milk alternately to creamed sugar, beating with each addition until smooth. Add vanilla and blend.

In a separate bowl, beat egg whites until they are foamy. Gradually add in 1/2 cup sugar, beating until mixture forms soft peaks.

Beat egg white mixture into batter. Add rose geranium petals and pecans and mix well. Pour batter into a buttered and floured 13-by-9-inch baking pan (or use a Bundt pan). Bake for about 35 to 45 minutes or until a toothpick inserted in the center comes out clean.

Take cake out of the oven and cool it on a wire rack for 10 minutes. Remove the cake from the pan and leave on the rack until completely cooled. Decorate with sifted confectioners' sugar and additional rose geranium petals.

Serves 18 to 24.

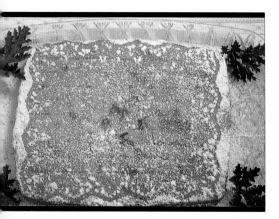

$\mathcal{S}$HUNGIKU

Originally native to the Mediterranean, shungiku was much cultivated in the Orient where the young leaves are eaten as greens. In Japan, especially, the flowers are eaten.

This hardy annual grows four to five feet tall, with numerous one-and-one-half-inch flower heads in summer. The ray petals are pale yellow, golden yellow or a combination of the two colors, surrounding a golden-yellow disk flower. Like chrysanthemums, shungiko have a mildly bitter flavor.

CULTURE

Shungiku grows in ordinary garden soil in full sun.

Since this is a species, not a hybrid, it can be grown from seed. Sow directly in the garden after all danger of frost is past.

SHUNGIKU (Garland chrysanthemum, chop suey greens)
Chrysanthemum coronarium
Composite family
Asteraceae (Compositae)
Bitter flavor
Annual
Ordinary garden soil
Full sun

Allow at least four to eight inches between plants. Sow in spring and in late summer for a fall harvest. Like many chrysanthemums it can take some frost before it succumbs.

SHUNGIKU HOT POT

---

8 cups chicken stock
1/4 pound bean thread noodles
2 chicken breasts, cut into thin pieces 2-inches long
1/2 pound pork tenderloin, cut into thin pieces 2 inches long
1/2 pound halibut or cod, cut into thin pieces 2 inches long
1 pound small shrimp, cleaned, peeled, cut in half
1 Chinese cabbage, finely shredded
1 pound fresh spinach, washed, finely shredded
2 tablespoons sherry
1 tablespoon cornstarch
1 tablespoon tamari
1 tablespoon rice wine vinegar

1 tablespoon water
1 cup shungiku petals

Bring chicken stock to a boil in a large stock pot. Add chicken and pork. Simmer for 5 minutes. Add halibut and simmer for 1 minute. Add shrimp, cabbage and spinach. Bring back to a simmer. In a small bowl mix sherry, cornstarch, tamari, rice wine vinegar and water. Pour into soup. Simmer for 2 minutes. Float shungiku petals on top of each bowl of soup when serving.

Serves 8 to 12.

SOCIETY GARLIC

SOCIETY GARLIC
Tulbaghia violacea (T.
cepacea)
Amaryllis family
Amaryllidaceae
Oniony flavor
Annual/ tender perennial
Rich, well-drained soil
Full sun to partial shade

Society garlic is native to South Africa. It is gaining popularity in the garden, not as an edible but as an ornamental.

It is hardy to zones 9 and 10, where the leaves are evergreen. In other areas it is treated as an annual. The gray green basal leaves form broad clumps. The fleshy leaves average three-quarter-inch wide and twelve inches long. The leaves smell strongly of onions or garlic when bruised. *Tulbaghia violacea tricolor* has gray green leaves that are variegated with cream and a touch of violet. 'Silver Lace' has white margined leaves.

The small, star-shaped, lilac flowers grow in clusters of eight to twenty in two-and-one-half–inch umbels atop a twelve- to twenty-four–inch stalk. Society garlic flowers over a long period of time from spring into summer. The sweet smell of the flowers belies their mild onion-garlic flavor.

CULTURE

Society garlic grows best in full sun, although it will tolerate partial shade. It prefers rich, moist, well-drained soil.

Plants are available commercially at nurseries and garden centers. Allow twenty-four to thirty inches between plants. Keep them well watered during the growing season; allow them to dry out between waterings when dormant.

In colder areas, try digging the plant out before the first autumn frost, planting it in a pot and moving it indoors to a sunny location.

GATEAU DE POMMES DE TERRE (POTATO CAKE)

from Barry Yates, corporate chef, House of Winston, Louisville, Kentucky

3 tablespoons butter (or duck fat)
2 pounds baking potatoes (russets), peeled and sliced very thinly
salt and freshly ground pepper
3 tablespoons garlic chive florets
3 tablespoons society garlic florets

Preheat oven to 400°F. In a large skillet, melt butter over a medium heat. Add potatoes and season with salt and pepper. Sauté, partially covered, until potatoes are lightly browned.

Transfer potatoes to a 9-inch round nonstick cake pan. Press the potatoes firmly and evenly into the pan. Bake uncovered until potatoes are crisp and golden, about 20 minutes. Remove from oven and invert pan onto 12-inch serving plate. Scatter garlic chive and society garlic florets on top of crisp potato cake and serve immediately.

Serves 4 to 6.

SOCIETY PASTA WITH PEANUT SAUCE

3/4 cup unprocessed peanut butter
1-1/4 cup hot water
3 tablespoons apple cider vinegar
2 tablespoons tamari
4 tablespoons sesame oil
3 drops Chinese hot oil (optional)
3 tablespoons society garlic florets, divided
12 ounces Oriental noodles, cooked al dente and tossed with 1 tablespoon peanut oil to keep it from sticking
1/2 cup chopped peanuts

In a saucepan, mix peanut butter and water. Cook over a low heat, stirring until smooth. Add vinegar, tamari, sesame oil, hot oil and 1 tablespoon society garlic florets, finely minced. Mix well and cook for 3 minutes. In a large bowl, toss pasta with the sauce and 1 tablespoon society garlic florets. Garnish with remaining florets and peanuts. Serve with sliced cucumber to cool the heat of this spicy dish.

Serves 4 as a main dish, or 6 to 8 as an appetizer.

Sunflower

SUNFLOWER

Helianthus annuus

Composite family

Asteraceae (Compositae)

Bittersweet flavor

Annual

Well-drained soil

Full sun

The Aztecs worshipped this giant of flowers as a symbol of the sun. Indeed, the shape and brilliance of this annual is like the sun. It can grow a prodigious ten feet tall, with flowers measuring twelve inches or more across in cultivation. In the wild, the flower becomes more diminutive in size, but still impressive.

The sunflower was one of the flowers chosen as an almost perfect model of design for modern art by the Aesthetic Movement. In the Victorian language of flowers, the sunflower stands for false riches.

Wild sunflowers, the diminutive parent of the domesticated giant, grow in the prairies and roadsides from Minnesota to Texas. In other areas sunflowers simply escaped from cultivation. Native Americans cultivated the sunflower for several thousand years. In Arizona the Hopi and Havasupai Indians developed hybrid strains several hundred years ago. In fact, the sunflower is the only major crop that originated in the lower forty-eight states. The sunflower was introduced from America to Europe in the late 1500s. Today the Russians are the largest producer of sunflower seeds, having developed most of the cultivars we now grow in America.

The broad, heart-shaped leaves are rough and somewhat hairy. Large flower heads consist of twenty to twenty-five showy yellow-orange ray flowers surrounding a yellow, brown or purple-brown central disk. The flowers bloom in midsummer and continue into early fall. The flat seeds develop from the disk flowers and are a delicacy to birds, animals and humans. It is often a challenge to harvest seeds in your own garden for your enjoyment. Sometimes it is best to get your enjoyment from watching the creatures that come to feed from this magnificent plant.

The flower is best eaten in the bud stage when it tastes similar to artichokes. Once the flower opens, the petals may be used like chrysanthemums, the flavor is distinctly bittersweet.

CULTURE

Sunflowers grow best in full sun. They prefer well-drained, friable soil of almost any type. The looser the soil, the deeper the roots can establish themselves.

Sunflowers can get unwieldy in the garden, often toppling after heavy winds or rains. Staking will help only if the stakes are deep enough in the ground. Protect tall varieties by planting in a sheltered location. Sunflowers make a lovely screen to hide an ugly wall or fence. 'Sunspot' is a dwarf variety growing only two feet tall, yet bearing full-sized flowers that are perfect for the front of a flower border.

Sunflowers grow quickly from seed. Plant seeds one inch deep or more in the ground two weeks after the last spring frost date. Allow ten to fifteen inches between plants.

WARNING

The pollen can cause allergic reactions in sensitive individuals.

SUNBUDS

8 sunflower buds
2 tablespoons butter
3 tablespoons bread crumbs
juice of 2 medium lemons

Bring a pot of water to a boil. Add sunflower buds. Boil for 2 minutes. While water is boiling, bring a second pot of water to a boil. After the sunflower buds have cooked for 3 minutes, transfer them to the second pot of water. Discard the first pot of water. This gets rid of any bitterness. Continue to cook buds until fork tender. Drain and set aside.

In a skillet, melt the butter. Add bread crumbs and stir, sautéing lightly. When bread crumbs turn golden, toss in sunflower buds. Pour on lemon juice to taste, toss to coat. Serve immediately. Garnish, if desired, with sunflower petals.

Serves 4.

SWEET WOODRUFF

SWEET WOODRUFF

Galium odoratum

Madder Family

Rubiaceae

Sweet flavor

Perennial

Well-drained, rich soil

Partial to full shade

Sweet woodruff is sometimes seen listed as *Asperula odorata*. It is a fragrant, low-growing perennial herb. More often than not, it is grown for its ornamental properties—as a shade-tolerant ground cover—than for any herbal properties.

"Wood" in the common name refers to the fact that sweet woodruff grows wild deep in the dark woods. "Ruff" comes from the French *rovelle*, meaning wheel, relating to the arrangement of the leaves around the stem.

Traditionally sweet woodruff has been used as an aromatic ingredient in May wine. Often a sprig of sweet woodruff is placed in a glass of wine in spring. Germans drink May wine as a spring tonic as well as to greet the season.

Native to Europe and Eurasia, sweet woodruff has become naturalized in some areas of America. Growing up to twelve inches high, it makes an ideal groundcover.

The leaves are deep green in whorls of six to eight around the square stem. In mid-spring small, white, funnel-shaped flowers appear in loose clusters.

The flowers are sweet smelling and tasting with a nutty, vanilla flavor. The foliage has no scent when freshly picked, but soon the sweet aroma of newly mown hay appears. The smell intensifies as the plant dries. For this reason, it was often strewn in homes and churches to freshen rooms.

CULTURE

Sweet woodruff can grow in almost any type of soil, but prefers well-drained, rich soil. It is a perfect choice for shade, performing equally well in partial to full shade.

You can grow sweet woodruff from seed, but it is slow to germinate. It is much easier to divide existing clumps to create new plants. Once established, it will self-seed. Since it also spreads by underground runners, sweet woodruff can become somewhat invasive. If you find it is, dig some up and share it with friends.

WARNING

Sweet woodruff can have a blood-thinning effect in large amounts. Anyone taking coumarin should avoid eating the flowers.

MAY WINE

1 gallon dry white wine

10 sprigs sweet woodruff with leaves, coarsely chopped

4 tablespoons granulated sugar

1 bottle (32 ounces) ginger ale

12 fresh strawberries

12 sprigs sweet woodruff with flowers

In a large bowl, mix 4 cups of wine with the chopped sweet woodruff. Stir occasionally and let sit for at least 12 hours. Strain and remove the woodruff. Add sugar and mix well. Pour in remaining wine and ginger ale. Stir to blend liquids. Serve with a sprig of sweet woodruff and a strawberry in a tall wineglass.

For a more festive drink, substitute champagne for the ginger ale. Cheers.

Serves 12.

SWEET WOODRUFF ICE CREAM

2 cups half-and-half (for a very rich dessert, use heavy cream, less rich use milk)

6 sprigs of sweet woodruff (leaves and flowers)

2 egg yolks

2 teaspoons honey

Put the sweet woodruff and half-and-half in a heavy saucepan over a low heat. Cover and heat until it almost comes to a boil (10 to 15 minutes). Remove from the heat and strain the liquid. Beat the egg yolks and honey until frothy. Add the half-and-half in a steady stream, beating continuously. Continue to beat the mixture into a light froth. Pour the mixture into an ice cream machine and process according to manufacturer's instructions. Serve before it freezes completely hard. It will keep several months in the freezer.

Serves 6.

SWEET WOODRUFF YOGURT CUSTARD

———

1 cup plain yogurt

1 tablespoon honey

2 egg yolks

6 sprigs sweet woodruff (with flowers)

Whisk the yogurt, honey and egg yolks until frothy. Pour into the top of a double boiler over a low heat. Add the sweet woodruff. Cover and let cook slowly for 10 minutes, stirring occasionally. Remove the sweet woodruff and discard. Continue to cook over a low heat, stirring constantly as custard thickens. This can take up to 20 minutes. When thickened, remove from heat. Serve hot, at room temperature or chilled.

Serves 4.

HYME

The name is derived from the Greek *thymon* meaning sacrifice. Thyme was used as incense in ancient Greek temples. The Romans brought thyme into the kitchen as a culinary herb and cultivated it in the garden for their bees. During the Middle Ages thyme symbolized courage; ladies embroidered thyme on scarves for their knights on the Crusades. In the Victorian language of flowers, thyme symbolizes activity.

Thyme is native to southern Europe. It is widely cultivated in northern Europe and throughout North America, where in some cases it has escaped into the wild. It can be found in warm, sunny fields. Thyme is a perennial, evergreen herb that grows to fifteen inches tall. The stems are stiff and woody, with velvety, white twigs. The aromatic, one-quarter-inch, gray green leaves are opposite on the stems.

The bloom time varies with the type of thyme. Flowering can begin as early as April and go well into the summer. The flowers are lavender-pink to white, occurring in small whorls along the upper parts of the stems. The flavor of the flowers is similar to yet milder than the flavor of the leaves.

Wild Thyme (Creeping Thyme, Lemon Thyme, Mother-of-Thyme),
Thymus Serpyllum Vulgaris

This plant's common names are easily explained. It has creeping woody stems that grow to twelve inches

THYME
(Common thyme)
Thymus vulgaris
Mint family
Lamiaceae (Labiatae)
Herbal flavor
Perennial
Well-drained soil
Full sun

long, easily rooting along their length. The narrow, oblong leaves give off a lemony scent.

Wild thyme, native to Europe, has naturalized from Quebec west to Ontario, south to North Carolina and west to Indiana. Occasionally it is found in the Pacific Northwest, west of the Cascades. The rosy-pink to purplish flowers that appear on erect branches in small head from June to September have a milder flavor than cultivated thyme but with a lemon overtone.

The many varieties of wild thyme add color and interest into the garden. *Thymus serpyllum albus* is a tiny plant with bright green leaves and a lemon scent. The white flowers appear in June. *Thymus serpyllum argenteus* 'Silver Lemon' grows six inches tall with a shrubby form. Its green leaves are variegated silver. Unfortunately it is not as hardy as the other thymes and needs to be sheltered in the winter. *Thymus serpyllum aureus*

'Golden Lemon' has gold-edged leaves. It is one of the later-blooming thymes with light purple flowers. It also is not winter hardy. *Thymus serpyllum* 'Gold-leafed' has, as its name implies, golden leaves. It thrives in a drought, blooming in mid- to late summer with pale lavender flowers. Unlike the other *Thymus serpyllum* varieties mentioned, which are all lemon-scented, it has a pungent scent and flavor. *Thymus serpyllum coccineus* has close-set, dark green leaves that turn crimson in autumn. The flowers are lovely magenta-pink in June and July. *Thymus serpyllum languinosus* 'Woolly Thyme' is handsome with its low-growing gray foliage. It is not evergreen in cold areas, and new leaves appear every spring with sparse pink flowers in early summer. There are more than sixty varieties of thyme, enough choice for anyone.

CULTURE

Thyme thrives in poor, rocky, alkaline soil. Although it can grow in a range of soils, it is ironic that the richer the soil, the less flavorful the thyme. Thyme must have, above all, full sun and good drainage.

Start thyme seed outdoors in spring. Sow the seed in a semi-shaded moist location. Once the seedlings are several inches tall, transplant them into a sunny location. Thyme can also be started indoors six to eight weeks before the last frost date. Transplant outdoors when the plants are two to three inches tall. Allow ten to fifteen inches between plants (eighteen inches for spreading varieties).

Because of its low, creeping habit, thyme is perfect planted between flagstones in a pathway, at the edge of a garden or in a rock garden.

THYME FOR GUACAMOLE

3 ripe avocados, peeled and mashed—
  reserve pits·
1/4 cup freshly squeezed grapefruit juice
juice of 2 limes
1 tablespoon thyme flowers, coarsely
  chopped
2 tablespoons parsley, coarsely chopped
6 tomatillos (optional), chopped
2 ripe tomatoes, finely chopped
1/3 cup salsa (or substitute 1 teaspoon chili powder with an
  additional small tomato, finely chopped)
1 tablespoon coriander flowers

Put mashed avocados in a nonmetallic bowl. Stir in fruit juices, thyme flowers, parsley and tomatillos. Add tomatoes, salsa and coriander flowers and mix well. Put avocado pits on guacamole, cover with plastic wrap and refrigerate several hours before serving. The avocado pit helps keep the guacamole from turning brown.

Spoon guacamole into a hollowed out round loaf of bread, surrounded by melba toast rounds. When watching calories, I put the guacamole in a hollowed out red cabbage and use it as a dip for crudités. Of course, it can be served in the traditional manner with a bowl of tortilla chips.

Sreves 12 to 16 for hors d'oeuvres.

EXPANDING YOUR PLEASURES

STUFFED SHELLS

———

8 ounces ricotta cheese

1 clove garlic, minced

1 tablespoon thyme flowers, coarsely chopped

1 tablespoon oregano flowers, coarsely chopped

8 ounces large pasta shells, cooked al dente

In a bowl combine ricotta cheese, garlic and flowers. Cover and let sit at room temperature for 1 hour to allow flavors to meld.

Preheat oven to 350°F. Stuff shells with cheese and place in a greased, shallow baking pan. Cover with aluminum foil and bake for 35 minutes.

The stuffed shells can be served plain or with your favorite pasta sauce drizzled on them.

Serves 4.

THYMED FLOUNDER

———

2 medium tomatoes

1 tablespoon olive oil

1/2 cup onion, coarsely chopped

8 ounces fresh mushrooms, sliced

2 tablespoons thyme flowers

4 flounder fillets

2 tablespoons thyme butter, softened

Preheat broiler. Core tomatoes. Slice one into 4 slices, set aside. Dice remaining tomatoes.

In a heavy skillet, heat oil. Add onion and mushrooms. Sauté over a medium heat until onions turn translucent.

Add diced tomatoes and thyme flowers (reserving a small amount for garnish). Sauté over a low heat until mushrooms are tender.

While sauce is cooking, place fish on a flat pan and brush lightly with thyme butter. Top each fillet with a slice of tomato brushed with thyme butter. Put under the broiler for about 3 minutes, until the fish appears opaque. (When fish has reach the stage of being flaky, it is actually overcooked.) Remove fish to serving plates, surround each fillet with the sauce. Garnish with reserved flowers.

Serves 4.

MUSSELS WITH THYME FLOWERS AND FENNEL IN SAFFRON CREAM SAUCE

from Jim Bain, executive chef, East Hill Woods, Southbury, Connecticut

9 tablespoons olive oil, divided

4-1/2 pounds mussels, scrubbed

18 cloves

3 tablespoons thyme flowers, coarsely chopped

3 small carrots, julienned

1 sweet red pepper, julienned

1 bulb fresh fennel, julienned

6 tablespoons water

6 egg yolks

1-1/4 cup heavy cream

pinch of saffron threads

salt and freshly ground black pepper

3 tablespoons parsley, coarsely chopped

thyme flowers for garnish

In a stock pot, heat 6 tablespoons olive oil. Add mussels, cloves and thyme flowers. Cover and simmer on high until mussels are cooked. Shells open when they are cooked. Remove mussels from pot and arrange on a serving plate. Save cooking broth.

Pour remaining 3 tablespoons olive oil and water into a skillet. Add julienned vegetables. Season with salt and pepper to taste. Simmer until water has evaporated. Spread vegetables around mussels.

In a bowl, whisk together egg yolks, heavy cream and saffron. Carefully strain mussel cooking broth to remove any grit or sand. Pour broth into a saucepan. Bring to a boil. Lower heat. Slowly add egg mixture, whisking constantly. Bring the sauce to a simmer, but do not boil. Pour sauce over the mussels and vegetables. Sprinkle with parsley and thyme flowers. Serve immediately.

Serves 6 to 8.

tUBEROUS BEGONIA

Begonias are named for Michel Begon, a French patron of botany. Hybrid tuberous begonias, as their name implies, are a manmade hybrid, created from crosses between seven different species of begonia. The first hybrids appeared in the early 1870s. The British were trying to achieve great numbers of flowers on the plants coupled with variations of colors. At the same time the French were creating double-flowered varieties. In 1875, John Laing, a well-known British hybridizer, got the best of the British and Continental hybrids and started his own breeding program, which ultimately surpassed both of his sources. Even though they were new on the scene, tuberous begonias found their way into the Victorian language of flowers, signifying deformity.

As their name also implies, these begonias are bulblike, growing from tubers. They are hardy only in zone 10. Tuberous begonias grow up to eighteen inches tall, with upright or spreading habits. The stems are fleshy (and edible). Leaves vary in color and shape, and are often somewhat wrinkled in appearance. Tuberous begonias are often grown as container plants. Some with pendulous flowers, especially lend themselves to growing in hanging baskets.

This plant is grown for its large (up to four inches), showy, waxy flowers that bloom in summer. The colors range through white, yellow, orange, pink, red and combinations. The flowers come in different shapes, leading to the classification as rose, carnation,

TUBEROUS BEGONIA
(Hybrid tuberous begonia)
Begonia x tuberhybrida
Begonia family
Begoniaceae
Citrus flavor
Tuber
Moist, fertile soil
Partial to full shade

camellia, ruffled or picotee. The flowers are usually in groups of three, with two smaller female flowers surrounding the larger, central male flower.

The flower has no scent to give any clue to its flavor. Surprisingly the flower has a tangy citrus taste. This is due in part to the oxalic acid in the petals.

CULTURE

In zone 10, tuberous begonias can be grown and kept outdoors year round. They prefer partial to full shade. In spring, plant them in moist, fertile, well-drained soil. Mulch them well to keep the soil cool and moist. In fall, dig up the bulbs after the foliage has been browned out by frost. Store the bulbs in a cool, dry place over the winter.

In all other areas, treat tuberous begonias as tender bulbs. In late winter, place the tubers on top of a shallow pan of soilless mix (moistened peat works well). They grow best at a temperature of sixty-five degrees Fahrenheit. I place the pan on a moist heating pad set to low. (Only use the type of heating pad that specifies moist and dry heat, or you can run into major electrical problems.) This gives excellent bottom heat. At the first signs of life, they are potted up, using a soilless potting medium. Keep them in bright light, but avoid direct sun. Once all danger of frost has passed, move them outside into a cool area in partial to full shade. Bring the plants indoors in the fall. Stop watering. Once the stems wither, pull them off. Store the tubers in a cool dry place in a mixture of peat and sand.

WARNING

The petals contain oxalic acid. Eat them in moderation. Do not eat petals from any other begonias. Only hybrid tuberous begonia flowers are edible.

KENTUCKY BIBB LETTUCE SALAD

from Anoosh Shariat, executive chef, Remington's, Louisville, Kentucky

2 golden delicious apples, thinly sliced
juice of 1 lemon
3 heads Bibb lettuce, washed and trimmed
1/2 cup toasted pecans
petals from 4 tuberous begonias
1 sweet red pepper, stemmed, seeded, and julienned
8 tuberous begonia flowers

Soak apples slices in lemon juice in a nonmetallic bowl for 15 minutes. Divide lettuce leaves among 4 plates. Arrange apple slices on lettuce. Sprinkle with pecans and tuberous begonia petals. Arrange julienned red pepper on lettuce. Place 2 tuberous begonia flowers in center of dish. Serve with Bourbon Tuberous Begonia Vinaigrette.

Serves 4.

Bourbon Tuberous Begonia Vinaigrette
1 teaspoon red wine vinegar
1 tablespoon whole-grain mustard
1 tablespoon maple syrup
1 cup salad oil
1/4 cup tuberous begonia vinegar
1 teaspoon Kentucky bourbon
salt and white pepper

In a mixing bowl, combine red wine vinegar, mustard and syrup. Mix well. While mixing, slowly add oil. Whisk in tuberous begonia vinegar and bourbon. Add salt and pepper to taste. Recipe may be adjusted to taste for tartness or sweetness.

Makes 1-1/2 cups dressing.

MAHIMAHI WITH TUBEROUS BEGONIAS

4 mahimahi steaks, about 3/4 inch thick
1 teaspoon butter
1 teaspoon olive oil
1 leek, finely sliced
juice of 1/2 lemon
petals from 4 tuberous begonia flowers

Grill the mahimahi steaks, about 3 to 4 minutes per side. Fish should still be firm when done.

While fish is grilling, prepare the sauce. In a small frying pan, melt butter in olive oil. Add leeks and sauté over a medium-low heat for 5 minutes, or until leeks are softened and glisten. Add lemon juice and tuberous begonia petals. Gently stir and cook for 1 minute. Serve immediately over mahimahi steaks.

Serves 4.

PEACHY KEEN BEGONIAS

1 pint plain yogurt
2 peaches, pureed *
tuberous begonia petals

Mix yogurt and peach puree together in a nonmetallic bowl. Refrigerate at least 2 hours. Serve as a dip, garnished with a whole begonia flower surrounded by begonia petals.

Serves 1 to 10, depending on how much yogurt they dip and eat.

*The easiest way to puree a ripe peach is to run it over a grater—instant puree without a lot of dishes to wash.

ULIP

TULIP
Tulipa spp.
Lily family
Liliaceae
Beanlike flavor
Bulb
Well-drained soil
Full sun to partial shade

Tulips are probably the most popular and widely planted of all the bulbs in cultivation. Today, tulips are considered native to central Asia, Asia Minor and southern Europe. There are more than one hundred species of tulips, and there have been thousands of cultivated varieties grown around the world. Tulips were introduced in western Europe in 1554 when the Belgian diplomat Ogier de Busbecq sent seeds and bulbs from Turkey to the royal gardens in Vienna. Fortunes were made and broken during the height of "Tulipomania" (1634 to 1637) when tulip growing and speculation was rampant.

In Victorian times, the intended message was varied with the color of the tulip. Red was a declaration of love, while yellow indicated hopeless love and a variegated tulip symbolized beautiful love. The name tulip comes from the Turkish *tülbend*.

Tulips are bulbs that produce a leafy stem with one (more in the "bouquet" hybrids) terminal flower. The pointed leaves are relatively long and broad. Some of the species are small and grow close to the ground, with petals no more than one inch long. Hybrid varieties can grow more than twenty-four inches tall, with flowers that open fully and measure more than eight inches across. The flower is usually cup-shaped, consisting of six petals (actually three petals and three sepals). Although you may see a tulip marketed as black or blue, the flowers only come close to those descriptions but miss the mark. Tulips are available in all other colors under the rainbow, from vibrant reds to stately ivories, pure colors and mottled, petals edged with contrasting colors or striped down the center. With so many tulips to choose from, you can have varieties that bloom from late winter all through the spring.

Flavor varies from tulip to tulip, but generally it can be described as a pea or bean flavor, occasionally with a green apple overtone. Flavor can also vary with the location. I tasted 'Court Lady', a viridiflora tulip—cream with a green streak in the center of the petals—in one garden near Philadelphia and it tasted just like a sugar snap pea. In my own Long Island garden the flavor was more reminiscent of French beans—a bit disappointing but still delicious. The area near the base of the tulip petal is somewhat fleshy, giving a slight crunch.

CULTURE

In all areas, except zones 8 through 10, tulips can be planted as soon as they are commercially available, usually in September. Planting can be delayed, but cannot be done after the ground freezes. It is recommended that tulips be planted four to six inches deep. However, I have found that planting them deeper, down to eight or ten inches, results in hardier plants that will come back year after year without lifting them in spring after the foliage dies back. Tulips should be planted four to six inches apart, but do not plant them in a regimented style or they will come up looking like rows of little soldiers. Instead, dig up the area in which you want to plant the bulbs, add some Bulb Booster or bonemeal to the soil, and place the bulbs, pointed end up, in groups of ten or more. Cover with soil and water well. Once the ground has frozen, mulch over the planting. In spring the leaves will appear, followed by the flowers.

In the warmer climatic zones, tulips need to be precooled. They can be purchased from suppliers, or they can be put in the refrigerator for at least ten weeks. Be sure not to have apples or pineapples in the refrigerator, as both emit ethylene gas which inhibits flower growth. After chilling, usually in January or February, plant the bulbs in a cool, semi-shady location.

After the bulbs bloom, remove the spent flowers, but leave the foliage to ripen and rejuvenate the bulb.

Once the foliage starts to turn yellow, the bulbs can be lifted, dried for several days in the sun and stored in a cool, dry, well-ventilated area until they are replanted in the fall.

Tulips can also be forced in pots indoors for winter bloom. Plant five to seven bulbs in a six-inch bulb pan, with the flat side of the bulb facing the outside of the pot. Cover the bulbs with soil. The tip of the bulb should be barely visible and even with the rim of the pot. Water well and place in a cool (thirty-five to forty degrees Fahrenheit), dark area (a refrigerator, unheated basement or cold frame will do well) for twelve to fifteen weeks, or until there is about one inch of growth. Over a period of a week, bring the pot to a sunny windowsill, and you should have flowers within three weeks.

WARNING

Some people have an allergic reaction to tulips. The reaction varies considerably from species to species and cultivar to cultivar. Toxicity to tulips takes two forms. The first is an allergic reaction, often called tulip fingers, that produces a rash on the fingers, eyelids or nail beds. This is most often seen as an occupational illness of gardeners and bulb handlers, caused by the allergen tulipalin A. The second is an acute reaction to the ingestion of the bulb or flower parts, which may cause nausea, vomiting, palpitations, sweating and salivation. Unless a person is highly allergic, this type of reaction is unlikely to occur from eating a petal or two. (Moderate symptoms were seen in a family that ate goulash made from five tulip bulbs.)

EDIBLE FLOWERS

TULIP PETAL SALAD DRESSING

from Edward Tuson, co-chef, Sooke Harbour House, Sooke, British Columbia, Canada

1 cup tulip petals (Emperor series have good flavor)
1 cup pear cider (or apple cider)
1/3 cup apple cider vinegar
1 egg yolk
2 tablespoons maple syrup
2 cups safflower oil

Place all ingredients, except safflower oil, into a blender. Blend at low speed until a smooth texture is obtained. Turn the blender to high speed and slowly pour the oil into the mixture. This should take approximately 1 minute. Refrigerate until needed.

Makes approximately 3-1/2 cups dressing.

COYOTE BEANS WITH TULIP

from Robert Werst, owner/chef, y.e. coyote, Hicksville, New York

5 quarts warm water
1 cup dried red kidney beans
1 cup dried great northern or
* other white beans*
1 cup dried pinto beans
1 cup medium chili powder
2 tablespoons salt
1/4 cup ground cumin
1/2 cup coriander flowers, snipped
2 cups corn
tulips
cilantro for garnish

Pour water into a large stock pot. Add all beans, chili powder, salt, cumin and coriander flowers. Bring to a boil, reduce heat to a gentle simmer and cook, covered, for about 1-1/2 hours. If you like beans softer, cook longer, or if you prefer them al dente, cook less time. Add corn and stir well.

For an elegant presentation, arrange tulip petals and cilantro leaves in a circle on a plate or shallow bowl. Place cooked beans in the center.

This is a perfect dish for a chilly spring day. The spices will warm your insides and the presentation will cheer your soul. This recipe makes enough for a party, and it freezes well.

Serves 12 or more.

TULIP DANDELION PANCAKES

———

1 cup all-purpose flour

2 teaspoons baking powder

1/8 teaspoon salt

1/2 cup milk

2 eggs

30 dandelion flowers

15 tulips (use a mixture of brightly colored petals—yellow, red, orange and lavender)

Sift together the dry ingredients. In a small bowl, beat the eggs and milk. Cut the petals from the dandelions—save the petals and discard the rest of the flower. Slice the tulip petals into 1/4-inch strips. Add the dry ingredients and the flower petals to the wet ingredients. Stir until moistened.

Pour batter (make 2-inch rounds or whatever size you wish) into a hot, nonstick frying pan. Turn pancakes when the bubbles on the top have broken. Cook for about 1 minute or until other side browns. Serve immediately.

The batter can be made up to 6 hours ahead of time.

Serves 4 to 6.

TULIP TUNA

———

12 brightly colored tulips (reds, yellows, oranges or multicolored are preferable)

2 cans albacore tuna packed in water, drained

4 stalks of celery, coarsely chopped

1 teaspoon curry powder

1/3 cup mayonnaise

lettuce

Remove the petals from 8 of the tulips, cutting off 1/4 inch where petal was attached (this can be bitter). Julienne the petals. In a large bowl, mix the tuna, celery, curry and mayonnaise. Add the julienned petals and gently toss. Cut off the stems and remove the pistils and stamens from the 4 reserved tulips. Lay each tulip on a bed of lettuce. Gently spoon the tuna mixture into the tulips.

Although most people won't eat the whole tulip, this makes a dynamite presentation.

EDIBLE FLOWERS

POTATO SEAFOOD SALAD STUFFED TULIPS

1 pound unpeeled white potatoes

4 sprigs lemon thyme flowers

1 teaspoon lemon juice

4 tablespoons mayonnaise

3 tablespoons olive oil

1/2 cup spinach or sorrel leaves, finely chopped

1/4 cup parsley, minced

3 chive flowers, broken into florets

1 cup cooked shrimp or crab, diced

2 tomatoes, finely chopped

lemon wedges

6 red ('Red Emperor' is good) tulip flowers with anthers and
   stamens removed, reserve petals from 2 for garnish

lettuce

Steam potatoes until tender in water with lemon juice and lemon thyme. Cool, peel, dice potatoes and set aside. Combine mayonnaise, olive oil, spinach, parsley, chive flowers, seafood and tomatoes. Add cubed potatoes. Toss well. Season to taste. Stuff flowers with seafood mixture. Garnish with chopped petals and chive florets. Serve with lemon wedges on a bed of lettuce.

Serves 4.

SAUTEED BEANS

1 pound string beans, stringed and ends cut off

1 tablespoon sesame oil

petals of 5 tulips, cut into small pieces *

Steam string beans until they turn bright green and are crispy-tender. Heat oil in a large frying pan or wok over a medium-high heat. Add beans and toss to coat with oil. Let cook for several minutes, stirring often. Add tulip petals and serve immediately. The flavor of the tulips complements the green beans, while the color of the petals brightens an otherwise plain-looking vegetable.

Serves 4.

* It is faster to do this with a scissors than with a knife. Simply place 5 or 6 petals on top of each other and cut away.

VIOLET

The ancient Greeks and Romans looked to violets to help cure some of their ills, from insomnia and gout to headaches and even to calm anger. Violets mean different things in the Victorian language of flowers depending on the color of the flower. Blue for faithfulness, purple for ever in my mind, white means modesty and yellow denotes rural happiness.

Although violets are native to North Africa, Europe and Asia, they have now become naturalized throughout most of North America. Violets are hardy from zones 6 to 9. Violets have been cultivated for more than two thousand years. They are related to pansies and Johnny-jump-ups, two other edible flowers.

Sweet violets are creeping perennials that bloom in early spring. The dark green, heart-shaped leaves grow low to the ground in rosettes. The plant is only about six inches tall. Flowers are sweetly scented, appearing singly on long stalks. Flowers range in color from deep violet to rose, white and mottled white.

The flavor of the sweet violet is sweet and perfumed. The slightly tart leaves are a delicious salad accompaniment. Violets go well with fruit, desserts and salads. The flowers can be steeped to make a delightfully fragrant tea. Candied violets are an old-fashioned decoration for wedding cakes.

CULTURE

Violets grow best in partial shade. They will grow happily in poor soil, yet will thrive in a well-fertilized lawn. For best results, plant them in fertile, moist, well-drained soil rich in organic matter.
To some, violets are second only to dandelions as a spring lawn weed.

VIOLET (English violet, sweet violet, sweet-scented violet, blue violet)
Viola odorata
Violet family
Violaceae
Perfumed flavor
Perennial
Moist well-drained soil
Sun to shade

Violets spread by rooting runners called stolons. The easiest way to cultivate violets is to dig up one or more clumps from an existing area and transplant wherever you want them. If you do not have violets in your garden, you can probably find some growing at friends, neighbors or relatives. They will probably be more than happy to share some with you. You can transplant violets in spring or fall.

Violets can be grown from seed. Place the seeds in the refrigerator for several days. This is called stratifying. Then sow the seeds outdoors in the spring or start them indoors eight to ten weeks before the last frost date in spring. Violet seeds need darkness to germinate, so cover outdoor seeds with enough soil to eliminate light. Indoor seeds can be placed in a closet until germination takes place. Seeds take from one to three weeks to germinate. Transplant seedlings outdoors around the last frost date. Allow five to eight inches between plants.

VIOLET SALAD

1 8-ounce package of mushrooms, cleaned and sliced

1 teaspoon lemon juice

1 teaspoon extra virgin olive oil

1/8 teaspoon cayenne pepper

1/2 teaspoon oregano, minced

1 pound fresh spinach, washed and dried

6 tablespoons extra virgin olive oil

3 tablespoons tamari

3 tablespoons lemon juice

2 hard-boiled eggs, sliced

3/4 cup crispy croutons

1 cup violet flowers

Toss first 5 ingredients together and refrigerate for several hours. Just before serving toss mushrooms into spinach. (Violet leaves can be used for up to 1/3 of the spinach.) Add olive oil, tamari and lemon juice, mixing well. Serve topped with croutons, egg slices and violet flowers.

Serves 4.

VIOLET LAVENDER SORBET

1-1/2 cups water, divided

3/4 cup granulated sugar, divided

1/4 cup lavender flowers

1/2 cup violets

2 tablespoons lime juice

Pour 1 cup water into a saucepan. Add 1/2 cup sugar. Bring to a boil and continue to cook for 4 minutes. Remove from heat and allow the syrup to cool to room temperature.

Fit a food processor with the metal chopping blade. Add lavender flowers and 1/4 cup sugar to the bowl. Process for 3 minutes, or until the flowers and sugar are completely blended and in tiny pieces. Add the pro-cessed mixture to the cooled syrup and stir well. Allow to stand for 1 hour at room temperature. Strain to remove any particles. Set strained syrup aside.

Bring 1/2 cup water to a boil in a nonmetallic saucepan. Remove from heat and add violets. Allow to steep for 15 minutes, stirring occasionally. Strain through a piece of cheesecloth. Squeeze cheesecloth tightly to release the blue color.

Blend the lavender syrup with the violet infusion. Add lime juice. Freeze in an ice cream maker according to manufacturer's instructions.

Serves 4 to 6.

CHOCOLATE VIOLET CAKE

2 cups cake flour

1/2 cup unsweetened cocoa

2-1/2 teaspoons baking powder

1 teaspoon salt

1-1/3 cups violet sugar

3/4 cup butter

3 eggs

1 teaspoon vanilla extract

1/2 cup milk

Preheat oven to 350°F. Sift together flour, cocoa, baking powder and salt in a bowl. Set aside. Cream together violet sugar and butter in a large bowl. Add 1 egg, continue to beat until light and fluffy. Add remaining eggs, beating after each addition. Add vanilla. Alternate adding flour mixture and milk into creamed butter mixture, gently folding to mix ingredients.

Lightly grease and flour two 9-inch cake pans. Divide batter between the two pans. Bake about 20 to 25 minutes. When done, top will spring back when gently pressed and toothpick inserted into center of cake comes out clean. Remove from oven and cool pans on a wire rack for 10 minutes. Gently remove cakes from pans, and cool completely on wire rack.

Decorate with your favorite icing (either chocolate or vanilla is good on this cake), or simply dust with confectioners' sugar. Candied violets add the finishing touch to this sinful dessert.

Serves 10 to 12.

ORANGES WITH VIOLET SYRUP

Syrup:

1 cup water

3 cups granulated sugar

1-1/2 cup violets

In a nonaluminum saucepan, boil all ingredients for 10 minutes or until thickened into a syrup. Strain through cheesecloth into a clean glass jar. Seal and store in the refrigerator for up to 2 weeks.

Darker colored flowers yield a darker syrup.

Slice 3 oranges and cut in half. Arrange the slices on plates and drizzle with violet syrup. Garnish, if desired, with candied violets.

WINTER SAVORY

WINTER SAVORY

Satureja montana

Mint family

Lamiaceae (Labiatae)

Spicy flavor

Perennial

Light, sandy soil

Full sun

Pliny named the genus *Satureia* as it was believed that these herbs belonged to the half man-half beast, Greco-Roman mythical satyrs. Perhaps it was this association that led to its use as an aphrodisiac.

Medicinally winter savory was believed to relieve the pain of a bee sting. The poet Virgil mentioned savory for its fragrance. Winter savory was a popular strewing herb in the seventeenth and eighteenth centuries.

Winter savory, a highly aromatic herb, is native to the mountains of southern Europe. Like so many other herbs, savory was brought to England by the Romans. It was among the first herbs the colonists planted in America.

A perennial herb, winter savory has a stiff, spreading habit. It grows from six to twelve inches tall. The leaves are gray green, thick and needlelike. White or pink flowers appear on spikes in summer. *Satureja montana pygmaea* is a four-inch dwarf winter savory, ideal for rock gardens.

The flavor of the flowers is somewhat hot and peppery.

CULTURE

Winter savory needs full sun. It thrives in light, sandy, well-drained soil with a minimum or organic matter.

Set plants out in the garden a month before the last frost date in spring. Allow six to eight inches between plants. Keep the soil evenly moist; do not let the soil dry out. Winter savory can winter kill if the soil is too rich or too moist.

Fertilize with an organic fertilizer in early spring. Plants can be divided in spring.

Winter savory is propagated by layering. In the summer, gently anchor a small section of stem in the soil. You want to have several inches of stem above ground on either side of the area you are trying to root. By the next spring, the area under the soil should have rooted. Cut between the main plant and the rooted section. Transplant the rooted section. Another method of propagation is mounding soil up around the base of the plant in fall. In spring, the plant can be easily divided.

Summer Savory
Satureja Hortensis,
Lamiaceae (Labiatae)

The flavor of this tender annual is best when the herb is picked in early summer, thus the common name of summer savory.

Summer savory is native to the Mediterranean area. It is a fragrant annual with slender woody stems. It grows to eighteen inches tall, but has a tendency to sprawl, giving it a bushy look. The dark green leaves are one-half inch long, narrow and blunt-tipped. When it blooms in summer the plant is covered with tiny pink flowers.

The leaves are traditionally used to flavor string beans. Summer savory's leaves and flowers are somewhat less piquant than those of winter savory.

CULTURE

Summer savory needs full sun. Plant it in the garden after all danger of frost is past. Space plants six to eight inches apart.

Sow seeds directly in the garden in a dry, sandy, moderately rich soil. after danger of frost is past. Allow four weeks for the seeds to germinate. Mulch with salt hay to keep weeds down and to keep the leaves and flowers clean for harvesting.

SWORDFISH WITH WINTER SAVORY

from Carole Saville, Los Angeles, California

4 swordfish steaks, 1 inch thick
1/3 cup milk
1/4 cup all-purpose flour
4 tablespoons extra virgin olive oil, divided
2 tablespoons butter
1/3 cup capers
2 tablespoons winter savory flowers

Dip swordfish in milk, dredge in flour. Brush with 2 tablespoons olive oil. Sauté in a preheated skillet until golden, turning once. Remove swordfish from pan and keep warm. Add remaining 2 tablespoons olive oil and butter to skillet over a low heat. When butter is melted add capers and winter savory flowers. Cover skillet for 3 to 4 minutes to allow flavors to meld. Remove lid and whisk sauce briefly. Pour over fish and serve immediately.

Serves 4.

TURKEY TAMALE PIE

1 tablespoon olive oil
1 Vidalia or Walla Walla onion, chopped
2 pounds ground turkey
1 pound can pitted olives, drained and sliced
16 ounces mushrooms, cleaned and sliced
1-1/2 cups tomato puree
6 cups water, divided
1/4 cup dried hot peppers, seeded and chopped
1 tablespoon summer savory flowers, coarsely chopped
3 cups cornmeal
butter

Preheat oven to 375°F. Heat olive oil in a large skillet. Add onion and sauté until translucent. Add turkey a bit at a time, stirring to keep it from sticking together in chunks. When turkey is cooked, drain any excess fat from pan.

In a large saucepan, heat tomato puree, adding enough water to make it the consistency of a thick sauce. Add meat, olives, mushrooms, pepper and savory flowers.

Cover and gently simmer for 15 minutes. Mixture should be thick and chunky, yet moist. If too dry, add more water. If too moist, cook uncovered.

While the mixture is simmering, bring 5 cups of water to a boil in a large saucepan. Slowly add cornmeal, stirring continually to keep it from forming clumps. Lower heat and simmer until it reaches the consistency of thick paste.

Generously butter the sides and bottom of a large, deep baking pan. Spoon in cornmeal mush to a depth of about 1 inch. Spread the tomato turkey mixture over the cornmeal mush. Top with the remaining cornmeal. Dot the top with butter.

Bake for 20 to 25 minutes, or until the top begins to turn golden brown.

Serves 6 to 8.

YUCCA

Yuccas are considered to have been one of the most important plants to the Indians of the Southwest. The flowers and fruits of the yucca provided food and the leaves provided fibers from which the Indians made baskets. The roots, called *amole*, form suds when soaked in water and pounded. The suds were used for general washing of the body and clothes and also ritualistically in many ceremonies. Not only were the yuccas useful, they were also readily available to the Indians.

Datil (Spanish Bayonet, Wide-Leaf Yucca)
Yucca Baccata and *Yucca Arizonica*

Yucca baccata is native to southwestern Colorado, southern Utah and Nevada, and from southwestern Texas to southeastern California. It grows on mesas and foothills at elevations from three thousand to eight thousand feet. *Yucca arizonica* is native to southern Arizona and northern Mexico, growing at elevations below four thousand feet. Both of these yuccas are distinguished by having no leafy stem and the crown at ground level. The flower stems are relatively short.

Palmilla (Soap Tree, Narrow Leaf Yucca)
Yucca Elata

The word *palmilla* is Spanish for small palm, describing the resemblance of this plant to a small palm tree. *Yucca elata* is native to the grasslands and deserts from western Texas to central and southern Arizona at elevations ranging from fifteen hundred to six thou-

YUCCA
Yucca spp.
Agave family (Lily family)
Agavaceae (Liliaceae)
Sweet flavor
Perennial
Well-drained, sandy soil
Full sun

sand feet. The stem is prominent, covered with dried, straw-colored leaves, bearing two or more crowns of spine-tipped bright green leaves. The clusters of white flowers appear in spring in panicles at the ends of long stalks.

Indians not only ate the flowers of the palmilla and other yuccas, but also the stem. The large (two inches or more) waxy white flowers bloom in the spring. They often simply boiled the flowers and lightly seasoned them. Navajo Indians dried and roasted the flowers and considered them a great delicacy. Yucca flowers were also used for thickening soups.

Yucca petals are delicately sweet with a nice crunch.

CULTURE
All yuccas grow well in well-drained, sandy loam. They all require full sun.

The yuccas described above are grown in the Southwest and West. *Yucca filamentosa* (Adam's needle) is the most commonly grown yucca for Eastern landscapes, as it is hardy to zone 5. It is almost stemless with the stiff pointed leaves for which yuccas are noted. This plant is distinguished by the long, curly, white threads on the leaf margins. The leaves grow to three feet tall with a flower spike to six feet tall in mid- to late summer.

Yuccas are most commonly purchased in nurseries or garden centers. With patience a yucca can be grown from seed. Yuccas are slow growing; even a small plant may take five years or more before it begins to bloom.

WARNING
Eat only the petals of the flowers, the centers are very bitter.

YUCCA FLOWER SOUP

3 cups yucca flower petals
water
2 tablespoons butter
2 tablespoons all-purpose flour
3 cups milk
1 cup cream
1/8 teaspoon freshly ground nutmeg
salt and pepper to taste

Place the yucca petals in a saucepan and cover with water. Bring to a boil over medium heat and continue to cook for 15 minutes. Drain petals, discarding cooking water. In a bowl, mash petals with a potato masher or put through a ricer. In a saucepan, melt the butter. Add flour and cook over a low heat for several minutes, stirring frequently. While stirring, slowly add milk and cream. Add yucca petals and cook until soup thickens. Add nutmeg. Salt and pepper to taste.

Serves 6.

HOT YUCCA SALAD

2 bunches arugula, carefully cleaned, washed and dried

1 tablespoon extra virgin olive oil

1/2 cup pecans

20 to 30 yucca flowers, bitter centers removed

3 tablespoons red wine vinegar

Arrange arugula leaves on plates. Heat olive oil in a small skillet. Add pecans and cook quickly over a medium-high heat, stirring frequently. As pecans begin to darken, toss in yucca flowers. Keep them moving in the pan, cooking for no more than 2 minutes. Spoon the pecans and yucca over the arugula.

Add the vinegar to the hot pan. Keep it away from your face as it will sizzle. Deglaze any brownings that may have stuck to the pan. Spoon vinegar over salads. Serve immediately.

Serves 4.

YUCCA HASH

2 cups yucca petals

2 cups water

1 tomato, diced

1 medium yellow onion, coarsely chopped

3 cloves garlic, finely minced

1/4 cup sweet red pepper, coarsely chopped

1/4 cup green pepper, coarsely chopped

1 tablespoon granulated sugar

1 cup peas

salt and pepper

8 tortillas, corn or flour, fried

Boil the yucca petals in water for 15 minutes. Drain and reserve petals. In a saucepan, gently simmer tomato, onion, garlic and red and green pepper until tender. Add sugar, peas and yucca petals. Salt and pepper to taste. Serve on fried tortillas.

Serves 4.

*E*DIBLE FLOWERS IN THE GARDEN

THE TEN RULES OF EDIBLE FLOWERS

1. Eat flowers only when you are positive they are edible.

2. Just because it is served with food does not mean a flower is edible (see Rule 1).

3. Eat only flowers that have been grown organically.

4. Do not eat flowers from florists, nurseries or garden centers (see Rule 3).

5. If you have hay fever, asthma or allergies, do not eat flowers.

6. Do not eat flowers picked from the side of the road. They are contaminated from car emissions (see Rule 3).

7. Remove pistils and stamens from flowers before eating. Eat only the petals.

8. Not all flowers are edible. Some are poisonous.

9. There are many varieties of any one flower. Flowers taste different when grown in different locations.

10. Introduce flowers into your diet the way you would new foods to a baby—one at a time in small quantities.

WHAT IS SAFE, WHAT IS NOT— TOXIC FLOWERS

The history of edible flowers dates back thousands of years to the Chinese as well as Greek and Roman cultures. Yet all flowers are not edible; some are poisonous. While the main thrust of this book is promoting the edibility of flowers, it is equally important to know which flowers should not be eaten under any circumstances.

EDIBLE FLOWERS IN THE GARDEN

In a way, flowers can be compared to wild mushrooms. Many are truly culinary delights, some have little flavor, others taste bad and a few are poisonous. I certainly do not want to frighten anyone. Only a few flowers are as deadly as poisonous mushrooms, yet the point needs to be made that some flowers can cause unpleasant side effects and should not be eaten.

Certain chemicals are more concentrated in the flower—those responsible for scent and, in some cases, those responsible for flavor. In some cases the toxicity of the plant is concentrated in the flower.

As the popularity of edible flowers has grown, so has the inappropriate use of flowers. I tend to see things in black and white. Anything that is on a plate of food, whether it is an individual plate or a serving platter, should be edible. That is not always the case. Over the years I have seen several incidences of toxic flowers used to decorate wedding cakes and put on plates as garnishes. In each case I make a point of speaking to whomever is responsible for the food.

Often the people respond that the flowers are from their own gardens and were grown organically. I suppose we should be grateful that at least the idea of using only organically grown flowers on food has managed to sink into people's consciousness. Unfortunately, usually the next words out of their mouths are, "Well, we didn't expect anyone to eat it. It's just to look pretty."

To my way of thinking, if you want the table or presentation to look pretty, arrange flowers in a vase. If they are on a plate, they should be edible. Not enough studies have been done on the toxicity of plants to know how much is toxic. Is the plant so toxic that several drops of sap from a cut stem on a wedding cake

could cause stomach distress or worse? Toxicity not only varies from plant to plant, but what affects one person might not affect another. Perhaps I, as a healthy, active adult who is on no medication, could tolerate eating a potentially toxic petal with no untoward side effects. Give that same petal to a two-year-old child who only weighs thirty pounds, and the results might be very different. Or give the same petal to an eighty-five-year-old woman with high blood pressure and heart problems who is on a variety of medications. Once again, the result could be quite different.

In an attempt to help you discern what is safe to eat and what is not, I include an extensive list of toxic plants at the end of this chapter. You may have noticed that this chapter has no photographs. This was a purposeful decision on my part. Every flower that is shown in this book is edible. The individual identification photographs for each plant are large enough so that, coupled with the written description, you can positively identify a flower as edible before it passes your lips. If you are at all uncertain of a flower's identity, play it safe and do not eat it. There is no way to tell just by looking at a plant whether it is edible, nontoxic or toxic; that is, unless you are looking at it with a keen eye and a good reference book that not only gives clear photographs (or color illustrations) of the plant, but also a description of it.

IT'S ALL IN A NAME

The flowers that are included in this book as safe and edible have been extensively researched. Some of them have warnings about amounts that are safe to eat and possible allergic reactions. A number of flowers that have been listed in other books or articles as edible are not included in this book. That is because I could not find sufficient (or any) reliable documentation of their edibility.

I had to reject, out of hand, any source that used only common names. Common names vary too much from one locale to another, and certainly from one country to another. Botanic names had to check out. As I delved deeper, I sometimes discovered why a particular plant suddenly appeared on or disappeared from an edible flower list. Invariably it boiled down to common names—two or more totally disparate plants had the same (or similar) common name. Which one has the edible flowers? Only a check of botanic names can sort all this out.

IF IT'S NOT TOXIC IT MUST BE EDIBLE—WRONG

If a plant is not listed on the toxic list, is it edible? Definitely not. First of all, the list of toxic plants at the end of the chapter is by no means definitive. It includes some of the more commonly known and grown plants in the United States.

For a flower to be considered edible, there should be something more enticing than the fact that it is not toxic. Certainly appearances count when it comes to flowers, but the biggest consideration is flavor. All the edible flowers have flavors that are identifiable to the palate. Not everyone has the same tastes in food or flowers. Some people like sweets; they are likely to be drawn to the sweet flowers. Other people enjoy spicy or piquant food; the spicy and bitter flowers may be more to their liking. Yet despite the range and intensity of flavors, all the flowers included are palatable.

Not enough research has been done on the edibility and/or toxicity of plants in general, not to mention plant parts like flowers. It would be foolhardy to go into the garden and sample flowers that might be considered safe because they are not on the toxic list. Let me repeat, the list is by no means complete. Perhaps that flower is attractive, and the color is lovely, but what else is known about it? Perhaps there is a chemical in the petals that acts as an abortifactant (causes spontaneous abortion)—unless you were pregnant, who would know? Let's examine toxicity in a bit more detail.

PLANT TOXINS

There has been poor documentation of plant poisoning; even less exists specific to flower poisoning. To further muddle the issue there has been a lack of adequate research on the chemical makeup of plants. So many questions have yet to be answered concerning plant toxicity. The very nature of plants and their complexity only confounds the problem.

Within a single plant species the degree of toxicity may vary depending on where in the world the plant is grown. The variables are many and diverse: soil type, moisture content, amount of sunlight and the age of the plant, to name a few. One plant can have hundreds of chemical compounds in varying amounts. It is a monumental task for a well-funded researcher to determine which substances and at what levels of concentration cause toxic effects. That is without the variable mentioned earlier in the chapter—the person who is ingesting the plant. If the material is ingested on an empty stomach, logic tells us that the effect will be different than if it were eaten after a large meal. How do the chemicals in the plant interact with all the other food-stuffs? Or with the aspirin, cold pill, antibiotic or diuretic that was taken at the same time, one hour ago, two hours ago, etc.?

To confound the issue, a plant may contain toxic substances and not cause poisoning. The toxins must be present in high enough concentrations that are then assimilated to cause poisoning. So chemical analysis alone may not indicate whether or not a plant is toxic.

A great deal of what we know about toxicity and plants comes from reports of farmers on reactions that livestock have had to plants. Unfortunately our digestive system is much different from that of a cow or horse—cat or dog for that matter. Laboratory research with mice (which are strikingly similar to man in so many ways that they have become vital to medical research) has helped determine the potential toxicity of many plants.

There are many ways plants cause poisoning. Nontoxic and even edible plants accumulate substances from the soil, including pesticides. Some plants contain small amounts of toxic substances. Spinach and tuberous begonia flowers contain some oxalic acid. Only when they are eaten in abundance does this pose a threat.

Poisoning in humans is usually the result of eating plants that contain toxic substances that are a natural part of them. Little is known about why plants produced toxic substances. Some may simply be a waste product of plant metabolism. Others may have a function in plant maintenance. Some toxins act as natural insecticides, keeping potential predators at bay.

The types of plant toxins are widely varied. Science has only discovered the tip of the iceberg of the chemical nature of plants and animals. The most frequently found toxins in plants are alkaloids. They are complex organic compounds, like nicotine in tobacco and the many alkaloids in marijuana that cause a drug effect. Another group of toxins are glycosides, that are poisonous carbohydrates. Cyanogenetic glycosides, for example, give off cyanide (a very poisonous substance) as a by-product. Digitalis (foxglove) contains cardiac glycosides that affect the heartbeat. In therapeutic dosages it is a valuable medical tool. Many other plant substances, including resins, acids (let's not forget oxalic acid) and amines can cause toxicity.

TOXIC EFFECTS

The toxic effects, as demonstrated from all the information above, of ingesting a "poisonous" plant can be quite variable.

Effects may be slight—mild irritation of the mouth, sneezing, or a little heartburn. They can be moderate—burning feeling in the mouth and throat, nausea, upset stomach, diarrhea or cramping. Even more pronounced effects demand immediate medical attention (call your local poison control center)—sweating, rapid breathing or difficulty breathing, rapid or slow heartbeat, vomiting, unconsciousness, numbness or tingling in the extremities. If there is any toxic reaction to eating a flower, especially if it is immediate—get medical attention. Bring the plant along for more accurate diagnosis.

For the last time—IF YOU CANNOT POSITIVELY IDENTIFY A FLOWER AS EDIBLE, DO NOT EAT IT.

EDIBLE FLOWERS

POISONOUS PLANTS AND FLOWERS—A BRIEF LIST

COMMON NAME	BOTANIC NAME
Aconite (wolfsbane, monkhood)	*Aconitum* spp.
Anemone (windflower)	*Anemone* spp.
Anthurium	*Anthurium* spp.
Atamasco lily	*Zephyranthes* spp.
Autumn crocus	*Colchicum autumnale*
Azalea	*Azalea* spp. (*Rhododendron* spp.)
Baneberry	*Actaea* spp.
Black locust	*Robinia pseudo-acacia*
Bloodroot	*Sanguinaria canadensis*
Boxwood	*Buxus* spp.
Burning bush (strawberry bush, spindle tree, wahoo)	*Euonymus* spp..
Buttercup	*Ranunculus* spp.
Butterfly weed	*Asclepias* spp.
Caladium	*Caladium* spp.
Calla (calla lily)	*Calla palustris* (*Zantedeschia aethiopica*)
Carolina jasmine (yellow jessamine)	*Gelsemium sempervirens*
Castor bean	*Ricinus communis*
Cherry laurel	*Prunus caroliniana*
Chinaberry (bead tree)	*Melia azedarach*
Christmas rose	*Helleborus niger*
Clematis	*Clematis* spp.
Daffodil	*Narcissus* spp.
Deadly nightshade (belladonna)	*Atropoa belladona*
Death cammas (black snakeroot)	*Zigadenus* spp.
Delphinium (larkspur)	*Delphinium* spp.
Dogbane	*Apocynum androsaemifolium*
Dumbcane	*Dieffenbachia* spp.
Elephant ears	*Colocasia antiquorum*

POISONOUS PLANTS AND FLOWERS—A BRIEF LIST (continued)

COMMON NAME	BOTANIC NAME
False hellebore	*Veratrum viride*
Four o'clock	*Mirabilis jalapa*
Foxglove	*Digitalis purpurea*
Giant elephant ear	*Alocasia* spp.
Gloriosa lily	*Gloriosa superba*
Golden chain tree (laburnum)	*Laburnum anagryroides*
Goldenseal	*Hydrastis canadensis*
Heavenly bamboo (nandina)	*Nandina domestica*
Henbane (black henbane)	*Hyoscyamus niger*
Horse chestnut (Ohio buckeye)	*Aesculus* spp.
Horse nettle	*Solanum* spp.
Hyacinth	*Hyacinthus orientalis*
Hyacinth bean	*Dolichos lab lab*
Hydrangea	*Hydrangea* spp.
Iris	*Iris* spp.
Ivy (English ivy)	*Hedera helix*
Jack-in-the-pulpit	*Arisaemia triphyllum*
Jerusalem cherry	*Solanum pseudocapsicum*
Jessamine (jasmine)	*Cestrum* spp.
Jetbead (jetberry)	*Rhodotypos tetrapetala*
Jimson weed	*Datura* spp (*Brugmansia* spp.)
Jonquil	*Narcissus* spp.
Kentucky coffee tree	*Gymnocladus dioica*
Lantana	*Lantana camara*
Leopard's bane	*Arnica montana*
Lily of the valley	*Convallaria majalis*
Lobelia (cardinal flower, Indian tobacco)	*Lobelia* spp.
Marsh marigold	*Caltha palustris*
May apple (mandrake)	*Podophyllum peltatum*
Mescal bean (Texas mountain laurel, frijo lillo)	*Sophora secundiflora*

POISONOUS PLANTS AND FLOWERS—A BRIEF LIST (continued)

COMMON NAME	BOTANIC NAME
Mistletoe	*Phoradendron* spp.
Morning glory	*Ipomoea violacea*
Mountain laurel	*Kalmia latifolia*
Nightshade	*Solanum* spp.
Oleander	*Nerium oleander*
Periwinkle (myrtle, vinca)	*Vinca* spp.
Philodendron	*Philodendron* spp. (*Monstera* spp.)
Pittosporum	*Pittosporum* spp.
Poison hemlock	*Conium maculatum*
Potato	*Solanum tuberosum*
Privet	*Ligustrum* spp.
Rhododendron	*Rhododendron* spp.
Rock poppy (celandyne)	*Chelidonium majus*
Schefflera	*Schefflera* spp.
Spring adonis	*Adonis vernalis*
Spurge	*Euphorbia* spp.
Star of Bethlehem	*Ornithogalum umbellatum*
Sweet pea	*Lathyrus* spp.
Tobacco	*Nicotiana tabacum*
Trumpet flower (chalice vine)	*Solandra* spp.
Water hemlock	*Cicuta maculata*
Wild cherry (black cherry)	*Prunus serotina*
Wisteria	*Wisteria* spp.
Yellow allamanda	*Allamanda cathartica*
Yellow oleander (tiger apple, be still tree, lucky nut)	*Thevetia peruviana*
Yesterday-today-and-tomorrow	*Brunfelsia* spp.

THE ORGANIC EDIBLE FLOWER GARDEN

Toxicity has been discussed at length in the preceding chapter. However, one aspect of toxicity was saved for this section. Chemicals can become more concentrated in the flower than in the rest of the plant. This is especially true for those that are applied to the plant in the form of fertilizers, or taken in through the roots and leaves. The plant absorbs pesticides, and even herbicides, from the surrounding soil. For that reason, flowers should only be eaten from organic gardens.

Beware of plants purchased in nurseries and garden centers. Flush them well with water. If possible, remove all the soil and replant in the garden or in a container using no chemical additives. I prefer to wait at least a year before eating anything from a nursery-grown plant. However, in the case of annuals, such a wait is impossible. Give them as much time as possible to rid themselves of any toxic material that may have been applied.

Cut flowers are even more dangerous. Consider the fact that the cut-flower industry is thriving in countries where chemicals are not nearly as regulated as they are in the United States. Many of the chemicals that have been outlawed here are now shipped abroad and still used. Once the flowers are cut, they are put in various chemical solutions to keep them in a salable state as long as possible. As tempting as the flowers from a florist may look, use them to decorate the table only, not the plate.

Excellent books have been written on organic gardening practices. Read one or two if you want more information. This is merely an overview of some of the methods used in organic gardening.

FROM THE BOTTOM UP—THE SOIL

Big, strong, healthy (and delicious) plants grow from healthy soil. Soil is not just dirt. Soil is a living substance with myriad biological, chemical and physical forces constantly at work. It is staggering to think of all that is going on right in the garden, day and night, year after year. Soil is composed of five major elements: air (oxygen, nitrogen, etc.), living organisms (from those too small to see—microscopic bacteria, viruses and fungi—to larger ones—earthworms and insects), humus (organic matter in varying states of decay), water and inorganic matter (particles of minerals and rock).

The culture section in each flower profile gives the best conditions for growing the plant. It is important to learn about the different types of soil, and to know what the soil type is where you want to plant. In one backyard, soil can vary greatly, depending

on how it was used and treated in the past. An area that had been a path would have very compacted soil; an area that had been a garden would have a rich, loose loam.

Soil can be sent to a laboratory for a complete analysis, but that is not always necessary. You can determine the basic type of soil you have right in your own garden. Gently squeeze a small amount of moist soil in the palm of your hand. Then rub it between your fingers. Sandy soil feels gritty to the touch. It is made up of the largest particles, and will not hold together

when squeezed. Sandy soil is easy to dig in. It drains well—actually almost too well as water draining through it removes most of the nutrients. Silt has a smooth texture, and is made of smaller particles than sandy soil. It can be squeezed, but it does not stay compacted, especially when it is dry. Clay, or heavy soil, is made up of such small particles that it holds its shape when compressed. It feels slick when rubbed between your fingers. That does not allow for air and water movement. Uncompressed, clay can absorb and hold a large amount of water.

The best soil for general gardening is called loam, which is a mixture of the three types just described. When rubbed between the fingers it breaks up into smaller bits. It holds moisture well and encourages the biological activity necessary for happy, healthy soil.

Considering that the soil is the major source of food and water for a plant, it is well worth the effort to create the best possible soil. Good soil should have plenty of organic matter, good drainage and an abundance of nutrients available to the plant. Almost all soil can benefit from the addition of organic matter. Turn the soil with a pitchfork or spade, breaking up any large clods. Add at least ten to fifteen pounds of compost or well-rotted manure and two pounds of rock phosphate (ground up rocks) per hundred square feet. Or simply amend each hole as you plant individual flowers with a couple of handfuls of compost and one-half cup of rock phosphate.

No discussion of soil is complete without talking about pH. pH is a measurement of alkalinity and acidity, ranging from 0 (most acid) to 14 (most alkaline), with 7 as neutral. If the soil pH is not right for a particular plant, it cannot get the nutrients it needs from the soil. There are simple kits for home pH testing. The local Cooperative Extension Service often offers pH testing for a small fee, as do some nurseries and garden centers. Knowing the pH of the soil, and the requirement of the plant leads to the next step—changing the soil pH. Add elemental sulfur (apply according to package directions) to make the soil more acid, or limestone to make the soil more alkaline (sweet).

MULCH

Mulching with organic material benefits the garden in several ways. Several inches of mulch cuts down on weeds. It conserves water, by cutting down on moisture lost from the soil through evaporation. It keeps the soil temperature more constant. It eventually breaks down, adding humus to the soil, improving soil structure and providing nutrients. As the lower layer of mulch becomes part of the soil, new mulch has to be added, usually once a year. I mulch in the spring, before weeds have established a stronghold. In warmer areas of the country, winter would be the ideal time.

There is a large choice of organic mulching materials. Not all are available in every part of the country. The material used for mulch is a personal choice. Some have a more formal look while others are more natural. Some are free, while others may be pricey for a large area. The choices include grass clippings, straw, cocoa hulls, peanut hulls, pecan hulls, buckwheat hulls, pine needles, wood chips, wood shavings, sawdust, shredded bark, pine bark nuggets, chopped oak or other leaves, well-rotted manure or ground corn cobs. An addition of nitrogen when mulching helps maintain the carbon-nitrogen ratio of the soil.

COMPOSTING

So much is written about composting that it puts some people off. Composting can be as simple or as complex as you wish. The simplest way to compost is to have two bins. They don't have to be anything fancy, even turkey wire or fencing shaped into a box, thirty-six by thirty-six inches (or round if you prefer). Start out with a couple of inches of soil (the good stuff with all those worms and microorganism). Then add the small weeds you pull up, cuttings from the garden (material no more than one-half inch in diameter; larger items take too long to break down—make a brush pile for these), shredded leaves (run them over with the lawnmower), grass clippings (no more than one inch at a time as they compact) and all the kitchen garbage except animal products (vegetable peels, leftover cooked vegetables, coffee grounds, egg shells (the exception to the animal rule), the moldy lettuce left in the crisper—you get the idea. Lightly water the pile when first started. After that, if rain does not supply needed moisture, water the pile every week or two. Keep adding to the pile as you accumulate material. It's interesting how there is much less guilt about throwing food out when it's going to the compost pile. It is good to have two bins, because when one becomes filled, you just start material to the second. I have found that by the time the second bin is filled, the material in the first has broken down into black gold. No turning, no muss, no fuss.

FERTILIZERS: N-P-K REVEALED

Look at a package of fertilizer and there are three numbers on it, like 5-10-5 or 20-20-20. Those numbers are called the N-P-K ratio, representing the percentage of nitrogen (N), phosphorus (P) and potassium (K) in the fertilizer. What do these elements do for plants?

Nitrogen promotes leaf growth. Phosphorus promotes strong roots, speeds up maturity and is essential for seed and fruit development. Potassium, also called potash, is necessary for cell division in roots and buds.

If it is necessary to amend the soil further, what are the choices for an organic gardener? Nitrogen is readily available in blood meal, cottonseed meal, fish meal and fish emulsion. Activated sewage sludge is also a good source of nitrogen, but it may be high in heavy metals, so avoid it for edibles. Phosphorus is contained in bone meal and rock phosphate. The best sources for potassium are granite dust and ash from hardwoods.

WATERING

Life as we know it cannot exist without water. The most efficient way to water is drip irrigation. Water is released at ground level, right where the roots are. There is minimal water loss through evaporation. An added advantage is that by keeping the leaves dry, some fungal diseases can be avoided. Kits are available to create a customized system, complete with emitters, supply lines, and timers. Systems can be complicated or simple. They are worth the trouble for areas where the soil is not frequently turned and replanted. Another way is to use "leaky pipe" hoses. They are made of a material that water can slowly seep through, delivering water right at ground level, near the root zone.

PESTS AND DISEASES

Although no garden is pest-proof, planting a diversity of plants usually results in fewer problems. Try to include one or two plants that persist through the winter (a small tree or shrub, a dwarf evergreen), which may provide a safe haven for praying mantises to deposit their egg cases. Praying mantises eat a prodigious number of aphids, whiteflies and garden pests.

A clay pot turned on its side in a shady spot in the garden may attract a toad or frog. They, too, are good guys on the war against insect pests.

It is important, if you have a pest or disease problem, to identify the pest accurately. The local Cooperative Extension Service can be of help—many have telephone hotlines and places to bring plants and pests for identification. Hand pick insects, early in the morning when they are slow to react. If only a small section of a plant is diseased, cut it out and get rid of that portion. (Do not put diseased material on the compost pile.) Dip pruners in alcohol after every cut to avoid spreading disease.

Avoid using any chemical in the garden, even the "organic" ones—they still impact on all the creatures that live in the garden, good and bad. It is best to try and be in harmony with your garden. That is what organic is it all about.

GARDEN SCHEMES

Edible flowers are so versatile they can fit into any garden scheme. As you look out into your own garden, you are now able to recognize those flowers that can serve double duty by playing a role in your culinary life.

The following gardens are made up only of edible flowers. They show the duality of the flowers—the gardens are beautiful and can be appreciated even without knowing that all of the flowers are edible.

WINDOW BOX

Any of the smaller plants can be used in window boxes. Never plant anything that will grow more than two to two and one-half feet tall, as there is insufficient room for proper root development.

Grow a single variety (all geraniums, pansies, etc.) or mix flowers for more interest. As the flowers fade, replant the box with fresh plants to keep it going through the seasons.

Window boxes dry out quickly. Check the soil moisture regularly to keep plants from getting stressed.

CONTAINERS

If space is limited, containers are ideal for growing a few edible flowers. Even if you have a large garden, a container of an often-used edible flower can be handy to have by the kitchen door.

You can grow a whole crop of flowers in containers. Almost any plant can be grown in a container, as long as the container is large enough to support the plant and its root system.

A good rule of thumb is to choose a container that is about twice as large as the spread of the foliage on the plant (when it is fully grown). Do not use galvanized metal with edibles. Otherwise there is no limit on the size and shape of containers except for the space you have to put them. Containers can be small and simple, such as a plastic pot or decorative basket, or large and ornate, such as a terra cotta pot, whiskey barrel or even an old claw foot tub or an unused horse trough.

RAISED BED GARDEN

I was asked to design an edible flower garden in an existing raised bed at a nursery near my home. The semicircular garden is approximately fifteen feet across the back and five feet from front to back. The garden is about three feet high.

More than forty different plants fill the garden—from Rugosa roses providing the backdrop to thyme and oregano spilling down over the stones at the front of the garden. I designed it to change colorfully from spring to summer. By fall, any ragged plants are replaced with chrysanthemums.

I brought some plants from my own garden to put into the raised bed. It was amazing to see how much better they did in the raised bed. With three feet of great, loose, rich soil for the roots to burrow into, the plants needed much less watering than those in my home garden. An added benefit of working in a raised bed garden is no backache, even after a long day of planting, as there is no bending and back wrenching with a bed three feet off the ground.

THE AUTHOR'S GARDEN

Everything (with the exception of the dwarf Japanese cutleaf maple, the flowers of which may yet prove edible) that was not edible was mercilessly ripped out of my garden when I began this book project. I designed an edible flower garden for interest in all seasons.

With more than sixty different plants (and several varieties of many of them) within a wedge-shaped garden less than twelve feet in radius, there was, and continues to be, a constant battle for space. Before I knew it, the nasturtiums had grown over the dianthus, shading them out of existence. Likewise, scarlet runner beans on a trellis shaded out the thyme growing below between stepping stones. Greek oregano, planted in front of the first stepping stone, got sufficient light and grew to three feet tall. I had to take a running jump to vault over this plant to get into the rest of the garden. This garden continues to grow and evolve, with new plants introduced each season, while reserving enough space to keep old favorites.

Some of my garden gems may be considered weeds to others. A friend volunteered to help weed the garden and to my dismay promptly pulled out all the dandelions I had painstakingly grown from French seeds.

A CALIFORNIA HILLSIDE GARDEN

Carole Saville, garden designer and long-time edible flower enthusiast, designed her hillside backyard for this book. The garden, in poor soil on a steep terrace, includes more than fifteen different lavenders, as well as other favorites like borage, miniature roses, and Johnny jump-ups. The plants selected are particularly suited for the drought conditions so prevalent in the West and Southwest. The garden is exquisite from spring through winter, with the lavenders providing interesting form and muted color even when not in bloom.

BIBLIOGRAPHY

Aaron, Gregory C., ed. 1991. *The Language of Flowers.* Running Press, Philadelphia.

Bailey, L. H. 1933, 1963. *How Plants Get Their Names.* Dover Publications, New York.

Bailey, L. H., and staff of the L. H. Bailey Hortorium. 1976. *Hortus Third.* Cornell University, Macmillian Publishing Company, New York.

Barash, Cathy Wilkinson. 1991. *Roses.* Chartwell Books, Secaucus, New Jersey.

Bellis, Willis H., and F. Castetter. 1941. "Ethnobiological Studies in the American Southwest VII: The Utilization of Yucca, Sotol & Beargrass by the Aborigines in the American Southwest." University of New Mexico Bulletin, vol. 5, no. 5, Biological Series.

Bittman, Sam. 1992. *The Salad Lover's Garden.* Doubleday, New York.

Blackwell, Will H. 1990. *Poisonous and Medicinal Plants.* Prentice-Hall, Englewood Cliffs, New Jersey.

Bryan, John E., and Coralie Castle. 1974. *The Edible Ornamental Garden.* 101 Productions, San Francisco.

Carson, Jane. 1985. *Colonial Virginia Cookery.* The Colonial Williamsburg Foundation, Williamsburg, Virginia.

Clarke, Charlotte Bringle. 1977. *Edible and Useful Plants of California.* University of California Press, Berkeley.

Clifton, Claire. 1983, 1984. *Edible Flowers.* McGraw-Hill, New York.

Coombes, Allen J. 1985. *Dictionary of Plant Names.* Timber Press, Portland, Oregon.

Creasy, Rosalind. 1988. *Cooking from the Garden.* Sierra Club Books, San Francisco.

Creasy, Rosalind. 1986. *The Gardener's Handbook of Edible Plants.* Sierra Club Books, San Francisco.

Curtin, L.S.M. 1949. *By the Prophet of the Earth.* San Vincente Foundation, Inc., Santa Fe.

Elias, Thomas S., and Peter A. Dykeman. 1982. *Edible Wild Plants— A North American Field Guide.* Sterling Publishing Co., New York.

Foster, Steven, and James A. Duke. 1990. *A Field Guide to Medicinal Plants—Eastern & Central North America.* Houghton-Mifflin, Boston.

Furlong, Marjorie, and Virginia Pill. 1974. *Wild Edible Fruits & Berries.* Naturegraph Publishers, Happy Camp, California.

Gessert, Kate Rogers. 1983. *The Beautiful Food Garden.* Van Nostrand Reinhold, New York.

Ghanoonparvar, M. R. 1982. *Persian Cuisine.* Mazda Publishers, Costa Mesa, California.

Gibbons, Euell. 1962. *Stalking the Wild Asparagus.* Alan C. Hood & Company, Putney, Vermont.

Halpin, Anne. 1990. *The Naming of Flowers.* Harper & Row, New York.

Hamel, Paul B., and Mary U. Chiltoskey. 1975. *Cherokee Plants.* (LC# 75–2TT16)

Hedrick, U. P., ed. 1972. *Sturtevant's Edible Plants of the World.* Dover Publications, New York.

Heinerman, John. 1988. *Heinerman's Encyclopedia of Fruits, Vegetables and Herbs.* Parker Publishing Company, West Nyack, New York.

Hjorth, N., and D. S. Wilkinson. 1968. Contact dermatitis IV. Tulip fingers, hyacinth itch, lily rash. *Br. J. Deratol.* 1968; 80:696–698.

Kavasch, Barrie. 1979. *Native Harvests: Recipes and Botanicals of the American Indians.* Vintage Books (Division of Random House), New York.

Keeler, R. F., and A. Tu, eds. 1983. *Handbook of Natural Toxins, Volume 1: Plant and Fungal Toxins.* Marcel Dekker, New York.

Killingback, Stanley. 1990. *Tulips.* Chartwell Books, Secaucus, New Jersey.

Kingsbury, John M. 1985. *Deadly Harvest.* Holt, Rinehart and Winston, New York.

Kirk, Donald. 1970. *Wild Edible Plants of the Western United States.* Naturegraph Publishers, Heraldsburg, California.

Knochmal A., S. Paur, and P. Duisberg. 1954. "Useful Native Plants in the American Southwest Deserts." *Economic Botany*, vol. 8, no. 1, (January–March, 1954).

Kourik, Robert. 1986. *Designing and Maintaining Your Edible Landscape Naturally*. Metamorphic Press, Santa Rosa, California.

Lampe, Dr. Kenneth F., and Mary Ann McCann. 1985. *AMA Handbook of Poisonous and Injurious Plants*. American Medical Association, Chicago.

Leggatt, Jenny. 1987. *Cooking with Flowers*. Fawcett Columbine, New York.

Lust, John. 1974. *The Herb Book*. Bantam Books, New York.

Maretic, Z., Russel and J. Ladavac. 1978. Tulip bulb poisoning. *Period. Biol.* 1978;80:141–143.

Meuninck, Jim. 1988. *The Basic Essentials of Edible Wild Plants and Useful Herbs*. ICS Books, Inc., Merrillville, Indiana.

Miloradovich, Milo. 1952, 1980. *Growing and Using Herbs and Spices*. Dover Publications, New York.

Neal, Bill. 1992. *Gardener's Latin*. Algonquin Books, Chapel Hill, North Carolina.

Newcombe, Duane and Karen. 1980, 1989. *The Complete Vegetable Gardener's Sourcebook*. Prentice-Hall, New York.

Niethammer, Carolyn. 1974. *American Indian Food and Lore*. Collier Books, Macmillan Publishing, New York.

Oster, Maggie. 1991. *Flowering Herbs*. Longmeadow Press, Stanford, Connecticut.

Peterson, Lee Allen. 1977. *A Field Guide to Edible Wild Plants—Eastern and Central North America*. Houghton-Mifflin, Boston.

Pfefferkorn, Ignaqz (translated and annotated by Theodore E. Treutlein). 1949. *Sonora, A Description of the Province*. University of New Mexico Press, Albuquerque.

Phillips, Roger. 1986. *Wild Food*. Little, Brown, Boston.

Potterton, David, ed. 1983. *Culpepper's Color Herbal*. Sterling Publishing, New York.

Rappaport B. Z., and W. H. Welker. 1936. Tulip bulb dermatitis. *J. Allergy* 1936; 8:379–380.

Reilly, Ann, ed. 1990. *Taylor's Pocket Guide to Herbs and Edible Flowers*. Chanticleer Press Edition, Hougton-Mifflin, Boston.

Sargent, Claudia Karabaic and Peg Streep. 1991. *A Gift of Herbs*. Viking Penguin, New York.

Saunders, Charles Francis. 1934, 1948, 1976. *Edible and Useful Wild Plants of the United States and Canada*. Dover Publications, New York.

Schmutz, Ervin M., and Lucretia Breazeale Hamilton. 1979. *Plants that Poison*. Northland Publishing, Flagstaff, Arizona.

Schneider, Elizabeth. 1986. *Uncommon Fruits & Vegetables: A Commonsense Guide*. Harper & Row, New York.

Simmons, Adelma Grenier. 1964. *Herb Gardening in Five Seasons*. Plume, Penguin Books, New York.

Smith, Leona Woodring. 1973. *The Forgotten Art of Flower Cookery*. Pelican Publishing Company, Gretna, Louisiana.

Stevenson, Matilda Cox. 1909. "Ethnobotany of the Zuni." 30th Annual Report of the Bureau of American Ethnology, Government Printing Office, Washington, D.C.

Sweet, Muriel. 1976. *Common Edible & Useful Plants of the West*. Naturegraph Publishers, Happy Camp, California.

Tatum, Billy Joe. 1976. *Wild Foods Field Guide and Cookbook*. Workman , New York.

Taylor, Norman (De Wolfe, Gordon P., revised and edited). 1961, 1987. *Taylor's Guide to Vegetables & Herbs*. Houghton-Mifflin, Boston.

The Reader's Digest Association, Inc. 1986. *Magic & Medicine of Plants*. Pleasantville, NY.

Tillona, Francesca, and Cynthia Strowbridge. 1969. *A Feast of Flowers*. Funk & Wagnalls, New York.

Tull, Delena. 1987. *A Practical Guide to Edible and Useful Plants*. Texas Monthly Press, Austin, Texas.

Van der Werff, P. J. 1959. Occupational disease among workers in the bulb industries. *Acta. Allerg.*; 14:338.

Weiner, Michael A. 1980. *Earth Medicine Earth Food*. Fawcett Columbine, New York.

Whisler, Frances L. 1973. *Indian Cookin*. Nowega Press, United States.

The Wise Garden Encyclopedia. 1990. HarperCollins, New York.

INDEX

EDIBLE FLOWERS

INDEX

INDEX